BRIDE&
GROOM
COOKBOOK

BRIDE&
GROOM
COOKBOOK

AUTHORS
Gayle Pirie & John Clark

GENERAL EDITOR
Chuck Williams

PHOTOGRAPHER
David Matheson

Contents

Starters

Soups and salads

Meat, poultry, and seafood

continued >

Desserts

About this book

This cookery book aims to help you navigate an important part of your new married life: the business of cooking, and eating, together. A fine set of kitchen equipment is often given to a new couple by their family and friends, but it won't be much help if you're not sure what to do with it.

This is a book you'll be able to use for years to come. If you're new to cooking, you'll learn how to arrange your kitchen, what equipment you'll need, and how to stock the storecupboard. You'll gain a basic understanding of the different ways of cooking and which foods they apply to. And you'll gain a wonderful collection of recipes. The dishes in this book are classics that every family should be able to prepare, but they're not fussy or old-fashioned. Most of the recipes are quite simple, but you'll soon be able to work your way up to the more challenging ones. Some recipes are intended as weekday meals and serve two, but most serve more with an eye to entertaining and a growing family.

I wish you happiness in the coming years and hope the recipes and knowledge shared in this book will sustain you for the journey ahead.

-GENERAL EDITOR

Creating a meal

Cooking together in your own kitchen, then sitting down together to eat dinner, enjoy your food, and talk, is at the core of many strong marriages and happy family lives. But cooking can seem mysterious, even intimidating, if it's not something you've always seen done at home.

Knowing that many of our readers have not learned the art of cooking at their grandmother's knee, we've included in this book all the basics for getting started. We've tried to answer every common question: What equipment do I need? How do I know what's in season? What foods should I keep in the storecupboard? How do I skin a tomato? Which wine should I serve with this roast pork? When should I serve cheese?

Once you learn a few essentials, you'll find that cooking is not as hard as it sometimes looks. Dishes won't always turn out perfectly at first, but if you approach them methodically and keep practising, you can soon become a very good cook. It all boils down to determination and a sense of humour – two qualities that will serve you well in your marriage, too!

Before you attempt cooking for guests, get comfortable cooking for yourselves. True novices can start out by preparing one cooked dish at a time. You can round out any meal with some good bread and a simple green salad, which lets you focus your efforts on a main course. When you're ready to have some friends over, turn to page 236 for entertaining basics and page 240 for menu suggestions.

RECIPE KEY

preparation **30** minutes | cooking **50** minutes | **2** servings

The spoon icon at the top of each recipe lets you know how difficult the recipe is: one spoon indicates a simple recipe, two an intermediate one, and three a relatively complex dish.

The preparation and cooking times given with each recipe will help you estimate when you should start cooking if you want to eat at a particular hour. However, keep in mind that these and other time estimates are just that: approximate calculations. Allow yourself additional time if you are new to cooking.

Planning the dishes

When you're ready to cook up a multi-course meal, either for yourselves or for guests, the first thing you need to do is to figure out what you feel like eating. Always think seasonally. Is it hot midsummer, when lighter foods like salads and cold soups or grilled foods sound good? Is it spring, when the markets are overflowing with asparagus and artichokes? Is it chilly autumn or winter, when you want a satisfying stew or roast to warm you up?

You might start with one dish or even one ingredient you want to eat, and build a menu from there. When selecting dishes to make for a meal, scan the recipes to make sure they work together in terms of time and how they are cooked *(see right)*.

Once you've decided what to serve, the next step is a shopping list. Here's where a well-stocked storecupboard comes into play. On pages 24–29, we list commonly used ingredients that you can keep on hand all the time if you find them useful. It's less daunting to cook dinner when you don't need to shop for a lot of basics first.

On pages 24–29

COMBINING DISHES

Compare the ingredients lists of recipes you're considering for a meal, both to make sure the dishes mesh well together and to see whether you can combine the preparation of common ingredients.

Compare recipe methods to look for conflicts. For example, if you are planning to roast a chicken in the oven, it won't be free for baking a tart, especially if the tart cooks at a higher temperature (and you don't want your tart to taste like chicken). Choose another dessert that can be cooked on the hob.

Make it easy on yourself. If one of the dishes that you've chosen – such as a pan sauce or a soufflé – requires a bit of last-minute attention, make sure the other parts of the meal lend themselves to advance preparation, so that you can take care of them earlier.

GETTING ORGANISED

When you're ready to start cooking, pull out all the items on your ingredients lists, then check your tools lists and do the same.

Next, create a written timeline. This can be as general or as detailed as you like. Estimate when you'll need to start cooking each dish so that everything will be ready around the same time. As you grow more experienced as a cook, you'll be able to keep this schedule in your head, but even an old hand will make a time-line for a more complex dinner. Use a timer to keep track of various items as they cook.

A spouse who's not actively cooking can turn off the TV, lower the lights, put on some soft music, and set the table. Make sure there's a jug of fresh water, or a bottle of fizzy mineral water available, with some lemon slices and ice cubes, if you like.

Serving it forth

If you're new to cooking, just getting the food onto the plate will be enough. But once you start to feel comfortable in the kitchen, try to pay attention to the niceties of presentation, making the food and the setting visually appealing.

About ten minutes before you're ready to serve, place plates in a low oven to warm or in the refrigerator to chill, depending on whether the food is hot or cold. Food is more enjoyable when it stays at the correct temperature as you eat it.

Keep portion sizes moderate, and arrange the food on the plate in an attractive way. Place a chicken thigh on top of a bed of polenta instead of alongside, or swirl a spoonful of sauce over a fillet of fish. Use kitchen paper to wipe spatters from the rim of the plate. Garnish the food with a little herb or citrus used in the recipe, for both colour and a hint of freshness, or scatter over cheese shavings or coarsely milled pepper. Fill your wineglasses, don't forget to toast the chef, and appreciate your meal together.

Dinner for four

Here we take you through the steps of creating a simple meal for four. We began putting together our menu *(right)* by choosing an easy and quick pasta dish. This main dish will leave plenty of time to prepare a starter or pre-dinner nibble, a salad or vegetable, and a dessert. Since the pasta dish is Italian, we continue the Mediterranean theme with marinated olives to start and a summery tomato salad to follow. The salad is served at room temperature, so you can make it first and leave it to sit while you attend to the other dishes. Roast figs need only a few minutes in the oven, so you can pop them in after you serve the salad, and they'll be ready when you are.

2 5 . 2
M M

MENU

Warm Marinated Olives • 58

Pasta Carbonara • 136

Tomato, Mozzarella,
and Basil Salad • 84

Mascarpone-stuffed Figs • 196

TIMELINE

This sample timeline anticipates serving the olives to your guests just after they arrive and the pasta dish about 40 minutes later. This plan assumes two sets of hands in the kitchen; with one cook, allow a bit more time for advance preparation before your guests arrive.

40 MINUTES AHEAD
Prepare and weigh or measure all ingredients; arrange salad on plates.

20 MINUTES AHEAD
Chill wine; blend eggs and cheese for pasta; stuff figs; sauté olives.

GUESTS ARRIVE
Serve wine and olives.

20 MINUTES AFTER
Put pasta water on to boil.

30 MINUTES AFTER
Put pasta in boiling water; put plates in oven to warm; cook bacon for pasta.

JUST BEFORE SERVING
Blend pasta, eggs, and bacon.

AFTER SALAD COURSE
Pop figs into oven.

SHOPPING LIST

FROM THE STORECUPBOARD

– OLIVES
– LEMON
– GARLIC
– SPAGHETTINI (OR OTHER LONG NOODLES)
– BACON
– OLIVE OIL
– EGGS
– NUTMEG
– PECORINO OR PARMESAN
– ALMONDS
– HONEY

FROM THE SUPERMARKET

– ORANGES
– FRESH THYME
– TOMATOES
– FRESH MOZZARELLA
– FRESH BASIL
– FRESH FIGS
– MASCARPONE

Setting the scene

The same dishes can be presented in different ways depending on the mood you want to create. For this menu, choosing simple white dishes and classic wine glasses will let the different colours of the foods shine. For a more casual feel, you might pick up the green of the olives, red of the tomatoes, or purple of the figs in place mats, candles, or flowers. To invoke the dishes' rustic Mediterranean origins, choose sturdy earthenware dishes and tumblers for wine.

Use citrus wedges or zest left over from the olives and figs to flavour the water jug or glass at each place setting.

Choose a pretty dish for the olives, and provide an empty bowl to hold discarded stones. Use tongs to twist each serving of pasta into a neat coil, then top with a small pile of grated cheese and cracked black pepper. For the salad, overlap alternating slices of tomato and mozzarella cheese, and tuck varying sizes of basil leaves here and there. Arrange three figs per person on small dessert plates – odd numbers look better than even ones.

WINE PAIRINGS

Offer the olives with a chilled crisp white wine, such as Sauvignon Blanc or Pinot Grigio, or a festive glass of Champagne. Champagne is often overlooked as a wine choice, but goes well with many appetizers and also acts as an aperitif itself, whetting the appetite for the meal to come.

You can match the same wines with the pasta to cut the richness of the egg, bacon, and pecorino. Alternatively, select a light-bodied red, such as Pinot Noir or Beaujolais, to reinforce these savoury flavours with fuller body. Lighter reds can be served slightly chilled, especially Beaujolais.

Serve a late-harvest dessert wine, such as a Muscat, or tawny port with the figs. To appreciate the sweetness of a dessert wine, the wine should taste sweeter than the dessert.

Keep a flat, over-the-sink colander on one side of the sink for rinsing vegetables or draining clean dishes.

Store your most commonly used appliances on the worktop, but put others away to reduce clutter.

Keep everyday dishes on shelves near the sink or the dishwasher to simplify putting them away.

Keep serving bowls and platters on shelves near the cooker for ease in warming and serving.

Put specialised tools and gadgets into drawers near the sink, work space, or cooker, depending on use.

Keep cleaning supplies near the sink but away from foodstuffs, to avoid contact and contamination.

Use dividers to keep drawers orderly and tools easy to find. Group like items such as graters or sieves.

Keep a portion of commonly used items like salt, pepper, herbs, spices, and/or olive oil within reach of the cooker.

Hang commonly used tools or saucepans near the cooker, or knives on a magnetic strip near a work space.

Keep a crock of essential tools, like spoons and spatulas, near the hob.

Put heavy items like stockpots and appliances on lower, rather than upper, shelves for ease of handling.

Use vertical dividers in a cupboard for storing narrow items like pan lids, chopping boards, and baking trays.

Organising the kitchen

After the two of you have spent some time working together in your kitchen – or before you move into a new one – take the time to think about how best to organise it. An efficient use of space will help make cooking a pleasure, whether your kitchen is big or small (but especially if it's small). Think about your usual cooking routines and how you tend to work in the kitchen, and examine what has gone smoothly in the past and what hasn't.

Planning the space

If you have to hustle across the room to get an oven glove when a saucepan needs to come off the heat, or search madly through a drawer for tongs while your chicken fillets start to scorch, your kitchen organization is not working for you.

Think of your kitchen as made up of three zones: the prep area (refrigerator, sink, and work surfaces); the cooking area (cooker and work surfaces); and the cleanup area (sink, work surfaces, and refrigerator). For the best use of space, the paths between cooker, refrigerator, and sink should form a triangle, and a work surface should be only a step or two away from each. You may not be able to change the layout of your kitchen, but this basic concept can help you figure out how to arrange the items you can move. You may also be able to add a movable butcher's block to help create a work surface in an area that lacks one.

A basic rule is to store equipment and tools near the areas where they'll be used. Keep knives near the chopping board, pans and spatulas near the hob, food storage containers and wrappers between the sink and refrigerator. This is common sense, but it's surprising how often a tool can end up stored in an awkward place. Keeping work surfaces clear and uncluttered will make your kitchen more inviting to work in. Find spots in cupboards or a larder for appliances you don't use every day. And adopting the professional cook's habit of cleaning up after yourself as you cook – clearing worktops and washing tools – will reduce frustration and even accidents, and both of you will be grateful when it's time to do the washing up.

Outfitting the kitchen

You're likely to have received a selection of cooking equipment as wedding gifts, but it's rare that you'll get everything you need – or want. Even if you have a lot of gaps to fill in, don't worry. Experienced cooks know it's best to outfit a kitchen tool by tool.

You don't need a matched set of pans. In fact, different materials are often best for different equipment. The only rule is to buy the best that you can afford, because good-quality pieces will last longer and will make cooking easier, and your food will turn out better. This is especially true of pans: a good heavy-gauge, thick-bottomed pan will heat evenly and prevent food from burning.

The bare necessities

With the basic cooking and baking equipment, tools, and machines at right, you'll be able to create a wide range of dishes, from a batch of biscuits to a pot of stew, an omelette, or a roast chicken – nearly anything that comes to mind. As you develop your own style of cooking and signature dishes, turn to pages 22–23 to see which specialized tools will help you pursue your particular cooking interests.

When choosing pans and tins in particular, you'll be faced with choices of materials. Each type of metal conducts heat differently, and aluminium and cast iron react to acidic foods and eggs, resulting in off flavours or colour. For everyday pans, two very good choices are stainless steel and anodised aluminium. Steel heats up more slowly and less evenly than aluminium, but is more sturdy and long-lasting, and is nonreactive. Some steel pans have aluminium cores to help them heat quickly and evenly. Anodized aluminium has been treated to strengthen it and to prevent the aluminium from reacting with acidic foods or eggs.

Copper is the best conductor of heat and beautiful, but requires a lot of maintenance, and it can be costly. Cast iron is used for some pans, and although this metal has a mild reaction with acidic foods, it heats up evenly and holds heat well. Enamelled cast-iron casseroles are good for long-simmered dishes, and the enamel coating makes the casserole nonreactive.

STOVETOP PANS
- frying pans
  small non-stick
  large cast-iron
- saucepans
  small
  medium
  large
- sauté pans
  medium
  large
- stockpot

OVENWARE
- baking dishes
  square
  rectangular
- 2 baking sheets/trays
- loaf tin, 500 g (1 lb)
- pie dish
- pie tin, 23 cm (9 inch)
- roasting tin, medium, with rack
- 2 round cake tins, 23 cm (9 inch)

KNIVES
- chef's or cook's knife
- paring knife
- serrated bread knife
- serrated small knife
- sharpening steel
- slicing knife

ELECTRICS
- blender
- coffee machine (optional)
- food processor
- heavy-duty stand mixer
- kettle
- toaster

TOOLS

- bowls, stainless steel
  - medium
  - large
- box grater
- can opener
- chopping boards
- colander
- corkscrew
- juice reamer
- kitchen scales
- kitchen scissors
- ladle
- measuring jug
- measuring spoons
- mortar and pestle
- oven mitts or gloves
- palette knife
- pastry brush
- pepper mill
- potato masher
- poultry shears
- salad spinner
- sieve, fine-mesh
- spatulas
  - silicone rubber
  - wooden
- spoons
  - solid metal
  - slotted
  - wooden
- string
- thermometer, instant-read
- timer
- tongs
- vegetable peeler
- whisk, balloon
- wire racks

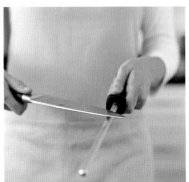

HONING A KNIFE

Before you put a knife away after each use, it's a good idea to hone it to keep it sharp. The best tool to use is a sharpening steel, available wherever good-quality knives are sold. Swipe each side of the blade's cutting edge across and along the length of the steel, holding the blade at a 15-degree angle to the long metal rod. Repeat to swipe each side three times.

Caring for your equipment

Good-quality kitchen equipment will last for many years – in some cases, a lifetime. It will serve you best when you follow the manufacturer's instructions for using and cleaning. Some pans and bakeware are better washed by hand than in a dishwasher, which may be an important consideration in your selection.

In the case of wooden tools and chopping boards, avoid washing in the dishwasher or soaking them in water as this causes the wood to swell and eventually split. Wooden boards should be rubbed occasionally with mineral oil to keep the wood from drying out.

Caring for knives

Knives are considered by many cooks to be the most important tools in the kitchen, and they require particular care. With a well-made, keenly sharpened kitchen blade of the right size and shape, you can easily and efficiently prepare any dish. Start with a good-quality chef's knife and paring knife that fit your budget and feel good in your hand. Add others from the list as dictated by the way you like to cook and the kinds of foods you like to prepare.

Like wooden tools, knives should not be soaked in water, which can cause the handles to swell and loosen. They should be kept in a wooden knife block or hung from a magnetic strip rather than loose in a drawer, where they will be nicked by collisions with other tools as well as present a danger to anyone reaching into the drawer.

Get yourself into the habit of honing your knives *(see left)* each time you use them, whether before slicing or after washing. The reason that knives should be kept honed is not only that they slice better when sharp, but because a dull knife is a dangerous one. Cutting with a dull knife requires more pressure, which can result in slippage and a threat of injury.

Even with regular honing, you will sense a knife's edge becoming dull over time. When this happens you should have it professionally sharpened. Check with the shop where you bought your knives, to see if they can recommend a professional knife sharpener, or ask your local butcher who might well be willing to bring your knives back to razor sharpness.

Follow your passion

It's not only handymen who live by the motto "The right tool for the job". Cooks, too, find that specialized equipment makes specialized dishes much easier to create. Once you've got your bearings in the kitchen and have discovered a type of cooking that appeals to you, it's time to develop your speciality. A few extra tools will help you become accomplished at whatever you choose.

For example, many cooks decide their speciality should be baking, which typically embraces breads, pastries, cakes, and biscuits, and is sometimes even stretched to include all desserts, whether baked or not. Baking usually requires precision – careful measuring, specific mixing techniques, attention to timing – and an array of specialized equipment. But you will be rewarded for that attention to detail and for using the proper tools when your mixture of eggs, butter, and flour emerges from the oven as a beautifully risen cake.

On pages 22–23 we list basic items you need to tackle a wide range of specialities, from baking to ethnic food to breakfast. Be warned: whatever speciality you choose, it can become an obsession.

Stocking a kitchen with a selection of tools that are useful for the way you like to cook is a life-long process. Specialized tools make particular tasks easier and cooking more pleasant.

Once you have acquired the basics, you may want to add a few extras. Base these choices on the things you enjoy preparing, rather than what you think you ought to have. If you find yourself doing a certain task repeatedly, that's your cue to pick up a tool that will help you with it. When selecting a tool, be sure to hold it and consider how it feels in your hand. Handles should be comfortable and the tool should feel sturdy, not flimsy.

Gadgets, as opposed to tools, will quickly lose their initial appeal, while poorly made tools will wear out or break. If you invest in good-quality tools, on the other hand, they will last for years. Well-made ones will never let you down.

FOR GENERAL COOKING

- asparagus steamer
- bain marie pan or double boiler
- citrus zester
- deep-fryer
- cooking thermometer (for deep-frying and sugar)
- fish lifter or slotted turner
- fondue pot
- lobster crackers
- mandolin
- meat mallet or cutlet bat
- milk pan with spout
- oyster knife and mesh glove
- paella pan
- potato ricer
- ridged grill pan
- small sauté pan

FOR BARBECUING

- barbecue
- chimney starter
- instant-read thermometer
- long-handled tongs, spatula, basting brush
- wire grill

FOR BREAKFAST

- citrus press or juicer
- coffee grinder
- crêpe pan
- egg poachers
- espresso machine
- griddle
- slotted metal turner
- waffle iron

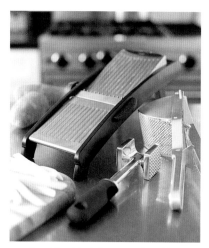

Specialised tools for general cooking

Specialised tools for soups and stews

Specialised tools for breakfast

FOR PIZZA AND PASTA

- lasagne dish
- pasta fork
- pasta machine
- pasta pan
- pizza cutter
- pizza peel
- pizza stone
- stand mixer with dough hook

FOR SOUPS, STEWS, SAUCES, AND STOCKS

- flameproof casserole
- flat coil whisk
- food mill (mouli-légumes)
- hand-held blender
- muslin
- perforated skimmer
- stockpot

FOR ORIENTAL FOOD

- boning knife
- Chinese cleaver
- skimmer/strainer
- long-handled spatula/scoop
- rice cooker
- Santoku knife
- steamer insert or stacking bamboo steamers
- wok

FOR CHRISTMAS

- carving board
- carving knife and fork
- gravy strainer
- roasting tin, large

FOR GENERAL BAKING

- baking parchment
- balloon whisk
- ceramic or glass mixing bowls
- citrus zester
- flour sifter
- graduated canisters
- hand-held electric mixer
- ice cream maker
- ice cream scoop
- juice reamer
- non-stick cooking liner
- oven thermometer
- pastry brush, reserved for sweet items
- pastry scraper
- ramekins, 150 ml (5 fl oz)
- rolling pin
- skewers, metal or wooden
- small prep bowls
- springform tin
- wooden spoon, for sweets only

FOR CAKES

- cake comb
- decorating turntable
- icing spatula
- oven thermometer
- piping bag and nozzles
- tube tin, smooth (angel cake) or fluted (kugelhopf)

Specialised tools for general baking

Specialised tools for pies and tarts

Specialised tools for yeast and quick breads

FOR BISCUITS

- baking sheets (rimless)
- biscuit cutters
- oven thermometer
- pastry board, wood or marble
- piping bag and nozzles
- rolling pin, wood or marble

FOR PIES AND TARTS

- cherry stoner
- individual tart tins
- pastry board, wood or marble
- rolling pin, wood or marble
- tart or flan tin, 23 cm (9 inch)

FOR CUSTARDS AND SOUFFLÉS

- bain marie pan or double boiler
- blowtorch
- cooking thermometer
- oven thermometer
- piping bag and nozzles
- ramekins
- soufflé dishes, large (19 cm/7½ inch diameter) and small (10 cm/4 inch diameter)

FOR YEAST AND QUICK BREADS

- American muffin sheet
- bun sheet
- ceramic mixing bowls
- stand mixer with dough hook
- wooden board for kneading

FOR THE SPICE RACK

SPICES

CAYENNE PEPPER

CHILLI FLAKES, DRIED

CHILLI POWDER (MILD)

CINNAMON, WHOLE & GROUND

CLOVES, WHOLE & GROUND

CREAM OF TARTAR

CUMIN, SEEDS & GROUND

FENNEL SEEDS

MACE, GROUND

NUTMEG, WHOLE

PAPRIKA, SWEET & HOT

VANILLA EXTRACT, PURE

DRIED WOODY HERBS

BAY LEAVES

MARJORAM

OREGANO

ROSEMARY

SAGE

THYME

SALT AND PEPPER

SALT, SEA

PEPPERCORNS, WHOLE BLACK

USING SPICES

• For the best flavour, buy spices whole and grind them yourself in a mortar and pestle, an electric spice grinder, or a coffee grinder reserved for spices only.

• Toast spices briefly in a dry frying pan over moderate heat to bring out their aromas and flavours before using.

The storecupboard

Having to stop at the shops on the way home from work to buy all you'll need for a meal can make cooking dinner a discouraging prospect. Keeping a number of the items you commonly use on hand – in the fridge and freezer as well as the cupboards – will simplify the planning and preparing of good home-cooked meals.

Get yourself into the habit of sitting down at the same time every week to plan the meals you want to cook — even if it's just two or three — and make a weekly shopping trip for the fresh items you'll need. If you can come home after a long day knowing that all the ingredients for supper are on hand, cooking becomes a pleasure, rather than a chore. What follows are lists of the common storecupboard items called for in the recipes in this book. As you cook meals, take note of the items you find yourself needing often, and use the checklists in this section to help jog your memory when you make a shopping list. Tailor your larder to suit your own taste, keeping on hand the ingredients you need for your favourite dishes. That way you'll always be able to fix a good meal without a lot of fuss.

Herbs and spices

Spices and herbs are aromatic flavourings derived from plants. In general, spices are the hard seeds, bark, roots, and dried buds of plants, while herbs are leaves and stalks. Spices have a more concentrated flavour than herbs, and both have their role in the kitchen.

The herbs and spices on the page opposite represent the basis of a spice rack. If you live near a shop that sells bulk items, you can buy spices in small quantities. This is ideal, because they start to lose flavour after 6 months and should be replaced every year.

Herbs can be divided into two main types: woody and tender. "Woody" describes the stalks, and these are the herbs that dry well and can be kept for up to 6 months before losing flavour. Tender herbs are practically flavourless when dried and are best used fresh. This category includes basil, chives, coriander, mint, parsley, and tarragon. Herbs are hardy and easy to grow, even on a sunny windowsill — and that way you always have a fresh handful on hand.

FRESH AND DRIED HERBS

- Dried herbs have a more concentrated flavour than fresh and should be used in smaller quantities when substituted.

- Put the stalks of bought fresh herbs in a glass of water, like a flower bouquet. Drape a plastic bag over the top and keep in the fridge for up to 1 week.

- Keep dried herbs in a dark cupboard or drawer; if you want to keep them in an open area, such as on the worktop, use opaque containers to prevent them from being exposed to the light.

SALT AND PEPPER

These most common spices deserve a special mention. Salt, indeed, is essential to all kinds of cooking. It brings out and balances the flavours of foods, making it useful in every type of dish, including sweet fruit desserts. Pepper, too, is ubiquitous and goes into many dishes both savoury and sweet, pleasing the palate with its subtle heat. Since these flavourings are used in practically every dish, it is well worth putting care into the types you use.

Sea salt is the best choice for everyday cooking, as well as for the table, because it has a clean, pure salt flavour. For convenience, keep salt in a bowl or salt cellar next to the cooker. Use the large crystals or flakes whole (they adhere well to food) or ground in a salt mill or mortar. Fine sea salt is the best for even seasoning. Reserve expensive, very high-quality sea salt, such as the pure white French *fleur de sel*, for sprinkling on food at the table.

Peppercorns should always be ground fresh just before use, because the flavour begins to dissipate soon after grinding. Keep a pepper mill by the cooker and another on the table, and replace the peppercorns frequently.

In the cupboard

The items in the list opposite constitute a well-stocked storecupboard, and they appear in many of the recipes in this book. Group similar items together in cupboards so you can find things quickly. For example, you might have one area for liquids like oils, vinegars, sauces, and honey; another area for dry ingredients for baking like flour, sugar, and baking powder; yet another area for canned foods; and finally an area for rice, pasta, and polenta.

All these items will keep longest when stored in a cool, dark cupboard rather than out in the kitchen exposed to light and heat. If you need to keep items like oil or flour on an exposed shelf, use opaque metal or ceramic containers. Beware of open packets and spills in the cupboard, which can attract insects and other vermin. Keep flour and other dry ingredients in canisters or sealed containers, and wipe spills from jars and bottles before returning them to storage.

OILS FOR THE KITCHEN

Different cooking tasks require different types of oil. For most savoury uses, olive oil is a good and healthful choice, high in monounsaturated fat. But there's more than one kind of olive oil. A good extra virgin olive oil, which is created without the use of heat, is best reserved for uncooked uses. Its wonderful flavour is destroyed by heat. An ordinary extra virgin or a "pure" olive oil is better used for cooking.

Another good all-purpose oil is canola. This oil, made from rapeseed, is also high in healthful monounsaturated fat, like olive oil. Unlike extra virgin, it is neutral in flavour, so ideal for baking.

For high-heat cooking, such as deep-frying, groundnut oil is a good choice.

CANNED FOODS

FISH
- ANCHOVY FILLETS
- SALMON
- TUNA
TOMATOES
- CHOPPED, IN RICH JUICE
- WHOLE PLUM

BOTTLES & JARS

ARTICHOKE HEARTS, PACKED IN
  OLIVE OIL OR MARINATED
CAPERS
HONEY
MOLASSES
SPIRITS
- BRANDY
- VERMOUTH (WHITE)
TABASCO SAUCE
TOMATOES, SUN-DRIED
VINEGAR
- BALSAMIC
- RED WINE
WINE
- DRY RED
- DRY WHITE
WORCESTERSHIRE SAUCE

OILS

CANOLA (RAPESEED) OIL
EXTRA VIRGIN OLIVE OIL
GROUNDNUT OIL
OLIVE OIL

DRY INGREDIENTS FOR BAKING

BAKING POWDER
BICARBONATE OF SODA
CHOCOLATE, BEST DARK
FLOUR, PLAIN
SUGAR
- BROWN SUGAR
- CASTER SUGAR
- GRANULATED SUGAR
- ICING SUGAR

OTHER DRY FOODS

BREADCRUMBS, FINE DRIED
BOUILLON POWDER
COUSCOUS
FRUIT, DRIED
GARLIC
ONIONS
- ORDINARY ONIONS
- SHALLOTS
PASTA, DRIED
POLENTA, "INSTANT"
POTATOES
- BAKING (FLOURY)
- BOILING (NEW, WAXY, SALAD)
PULSES, DRIED (OR CANNED)
- BLACK BEANS
- CANNELLINI BEANS
- LENTILS
RICE
- LONG-GRAIN BROWN
- LONG-GRAIN WHITE

Nota bene

• Oils are high in fat and therefore perishable. Some unrefined oils, notably nut oils and sesame oil, are best stored in the fridge. The oils will become cloudy, but this will not affect their flavour.

• Flours and meals are perishable as well. This is especially true of wholemeal flours and meals and nut meals. More perishable flours and even plain flour that is kept for more than a year should be stored in the refrigerator.

• Keep white vermouth on hand for cooking. When you need a little white wine for a dish but don't want to open a bottle solely for that purpose, vermouth can be used. Because it's fortified, it keeps for months.

• There are many brands of balsamic vinegar on the market, but most of them are not true balsamic. Look for the Consorzio label for true aged balsamic from Modena, Italy. Choose a younger one for cooking and for use in salad dressings, and save a long-aged one to use as a condiment. When choosing a red wine vinegar, look for an aged one.

• Light and dark brown sugars are often interchangeable. Dark contains more molasses and has more flavour.

• Canned items should be free of dents or bulges, which encourage bacterial growth and spoilage. Do not store food in an open can in the refrigerator; transfer it to a storage container.

In the refrigerator

The modern storecupboard includes items that are stored in the fridge or freezer, not just the cupboard. We find that keeping the items shown at left on hand in the fridge makes it easier to put together a meal at short notice. And here's another reason to keep the fridge stocked: a full refrigerator works more efficiently than an empty one. Cold foods help keep their neighbouring foods cold.

Note that the chilliest areas of the refrigerator are usually the rear and the lowest shelf. The warmest is the door. Keep dairy, eggs, and meats in the coldest spots, cheeses and oils in the warmest. A refrigerator thermometer will let you know whether you're keeping foods cold enough: 2–3°C (35–38°F) is ideal.

Although they may seem like cupboard items, nuts, whole grains, and wholemeal flours all contain oils that will eventually go rancid, so keep them in the fridge or freezer for longer storage.

In the freezer

One of the most useful items to keep on hand in the freezer is home-made stock (pages 216–17). You can make your own on a free after-noon, divide it into useful portions of 300 ml (10 fl oz) or 1 litre (2 pints), and freeze it for up to 6 months. Some supermarkets sell freshly made stock in cartons. It is also possible to find good-quality frozen stock in concentrate. Bouillon powder is excellent too. If you use stock cubes, which tend to be salty, take care when seasoning the dish in which the stock is used.

Butter, meat, and poultry freeze well for longer storage. Keep these foods in the freezer – they'll keep for 6–8 months – and you'll always be able to make a satisfying quick meal.

If bread goes stale, chop it into crumbs in the food processor and freeze it for later use. If your fresh herbs are in danger of wilting, make a herb butter (see page 67) and freeze to use for flavouring meat or vegetables.

Make sure to wrap food well for freezing. If exposed to air, the food will develop freezer burn and dry out. Use freezer wrap, re-sealable freezer bags, or self-sealing plastic containers. Label and date the items you freeze; they may not be clearly identifiable in a few weeks.

THE SCIENCE
OF REFRIGERATION

Storing foods in cold conditions slows down the process of spoilage, by slowing down the activity of the microbes or the food's own enzymes that cause it. Foods do continue to deteriorate in the refrigerator and even the freezer, but at a much slower rate than when kept at room temperature.

The reason food should be carefully wrapped before being put in cold storage is to prevent the dry air of the refrigerator or freezer from depleting its moisture and drying out the food.

FREEZING AND THAWING

• Wrap foods for freezing in freezer-weight film or in several layers of regular cling film, foil, or freezer paper. If the surface of the food is exposed to the cold air of the freezer, it will develop a condition called freezer burn, which leaves the food dry and unpalatable. This is especially true for meat and poultry. Liquids can be frozen in a freezerproof container.

• When a food is frozen, the water in its cells is converted to ice crystals, whose sharp edges pierce the cell walls and soften the food's texture. This is one reason that foods should not be thawed and re-frozen; the texture worsens with each freezing. Foods that are commercially flash-frozen suffer the least amount of damage, while foods frozen at home suffer the most because the process is slower and results in larger ice crystals.

• To minimize further damage to the texture and in the interest of food safety, frozen foods should be thawed slowly in the refrigerator, not at room temperature or in a bowl of warm water. Thawing may take several hours. You can also use the microwave for a quick thaw, but the quality of the food will suffer.

Following a recipe

The first step in following a recipe is to read it, start to finish, before you do anything else. This prevents unpleasant surprises – like discovering one hour before eating that the meat you planned to cook requires two hours of marinating before it can be grilled!

Read the ingredients list and method, then make a shopping list. If you follow our advice on pages 25–29 and stock your storecupboard with plenty of commonly used staples, your shopping list won't be too long. We've also created lists of required tools for each of the recipes in this book, so you will know at a glance whether you have the right equipment on hand. (If you don't, think creatively and you may be able to come up with a substitute.)

Once you have all your ingredients and tools, it's time to set up what chefs call *mise en place*. This French phrase, which translates as "putting in place", means preparing and measuring out all your ingredients according to the ingredients list and gathering and preparing your equipment according to the recipe method. Once all the ingredients are weighed and measured, chopped as described, and arranged in piles or in bowls, your oven is preheated, and your tins are greased, you're ready to start cooking.

Preparing ingredients

A recipe's ingredients list includes information about how each ingredient should be prepared before cooking: peeled, trimmed, diced, chopped. (We explain some of these techniques in detail on pages 232–35.) If you read the ingredients list carefully, you'll notice that the order of these words varies. The placement of the word "chopped" is as essential as the word itself. For example:

115 g (4 oz) walnuts, finely chopped

tells you to weigh out 115 g (4 oz) walnuts, then chop them finely afterwards. But:

2 tbsp finely chopped walnuts

tells you to measure out 2 tbsp finely chopped walnuts; they are chopped before measuring in the tablespoon.

When measuring dry ingredients in measuring spoons, note that a "scant" measure is shy of the full amount. "Heaping" means a little extra. A "pinch" is as much as you can pick up between thumb and index finger. A "good pinch" is a slightly more generous amount. With all these more inexact measures, a little more or less will not make a great difference to the recipe result.

Unless otherwise noted, ingredients should be at room temperature, because they combine better when they are not cold from the refrigerator. If an item should be cold, as in the case of butter for pastry, this is specified in the recipe. Otherwise, allow food that has been refrigerated to sit out for 20 minutes to take off the chill.

A word on measuring

Now that we're on to the finer points of preparing and measuring ingredients, we need to point out that there are different ways to measure larger quantities of liquid and dry ingredients – liquids

TWO COOKS
IN THE KITCHEN

If both of you are interested in cooking, it can be a fun activity for two – or the first test of your marriage vows. The question is how to divide up the work.

One of you can play the role of sous-chef and work on chopping and otherwise preparing the ingredients, and the other can act as the chef of the day; or, if a recipe has a component such as a sauce that is prepared separately, one of you could tackle that element while the other makes the main element.

If one of you is more organized and detail-oriented than the other, he or she may enjoy the role of family baker – careful measuring and orderly mixing are essential in baking.

by volume and dry ingredients by weight. A liquid measuring jug is made of clear glass or plastic and has graduated measures indicated on the side, both metric (ml, or millilitres, and litres) and imperial (fl oz, or fluid ounces, and pints). You'll need to hold the jug at eye level to take an accurate reading of the contents. Dry ingredients are weighed on kitchen scales, which are normally either battery-operated electronic scales or spring-balance. Scales will usually show the weights in metric (g, or grams, and kg, kilograms) or imperial (oz, or ounces, and lb, pounds).

Preparing equipment and preheating

The recipe method tells you whether the oven should be preheated and what needs to be done to pans and tins before cooking. Allow about 20 minutes for an oven to preheat (unless you have a fan oven, which takes much less time). Grills need preheating too. The food will brown better if the oven or grill is good and hot, and browning equals flavour. The same goes for pans on a hob: allow them to heat up for a minute or two before you add oil or butter, and then let the cooking fat heat up before you add the food.

Especially in baking, tins may need to be greased. This will help the cake or bread release from the pan after cooking. The recipe will suggest a fat that is used in the mixture, but butter and oil are basically interchangeable. Don't use a strongly flavoured oil such as olive; instead select one with a neutral flavour.

Testing for doneness

The time frames given in a recipe are not to be taken as gospel; they are guidelines only. With all the variables of different ingredients at different temperatures before cooking begins, different pans and tins, and different hobs and ovens, it's impossible to say to the minute how fast any item will cook. For determining doneness, always rely on your senses rather than the clock: look for a sensory clue in the recipe, such as "cook until golden brown" or "toast until fragrant". Get into the habit of looking at, listening to, smelling, touching, and tasting food as it cooks. This is how good cooks know when something is ready to come off the heat. For meat and poultry, you may want to use a thermometer to make sure the food is cooked through. For internal temperatures, see page 225. For egg safety, see page 226.

MEASUREMENT EQUIVALENTS

All of the weights, volumes, and dimensions in this book are given in both metric and imperial measurements. As the measurements are not exact equivalents, having been rounded up or down slightly to make measuring easier, they should not be used interchangeably. Instead, use metric only or imperial only, and never mix the two measuring systems.

Spoon measures – tbsp (tablespoon) and tsp (teaspoon), and fractions of these – should be measured using a set of accurate metric spoons. The equivalents are 1 tbsp = 15 ml and 1 tsp = 5 ml. Spoons are always level unless otherwise stated.

Oven temperatures are given in degrees Celsius and their Fahrenheit equivalents. If you have a fan-assisted oven, reduce the Celsius temperature by 10–20°C, or according to the manufacturer's handbook.

Seasoning

A recipe will tell you when to season food as you cook it, but you should also rely on your own judgement. Taste and season with salt, pepper, herbs, and spices at various points throughout the cooking for the deepest and most complex flavour. (Of course, exercise caution when you are working with raw egg or meat, or common sense when working with raw flour – until these items are cooked through, you may want to season without tasting.) And always give a dish a final taste and season it to your liking just before you serve it. If you watch professional cooks seasoning a dish, you may be amazed at their liberality with salt and pepper, not to mention lemon juice, vinegar, fresh herbs, and spices.

ADDITIONS
AND SUBSTITUTIONS

When you're a novice cook, following recipes exactly can help you develop your cooking skills. As you get more comfortable in the kitchen, try experimenting. You can add an ingredient you think might enhance a dish, or replace an ingredient with a similar one – lime for lemon, or shallot for onion. Some of our recipes include variations to help you bring out your creative side in the kitchen. If you come up with a change you like, make a note of it.

About wine

In our house, wine is regarded as food, as indispensable to a fine meal as a good loaf of bread or a leafy green salad. Wine balances the food, aids in digestion, and gives the occasion a convivial feel.

Wine is the happy result of yeast fermenting in grape juice, followed by ageing the juice in a wooden cask or bottle that brings on subtle or profound changes. The differences among wines begin with the grape variety or varieties from which each is made *(see below)*. Each grape bestows its unique characteristics of flavour, body, and colour on the finished wine. The geographical region in which the grapes are grown and made into wine also contributes to a wine's character. The ineffable effects created by a particular soil and climate are known as *terroir*. When a wine is made entirely or predominantly from one grape variety, it is called a varietal wine. While European

REGIONS AND THEIR GRAPES

When you see the following European regions on a wine label, here's the grape that's used:

Beaujolais: Gamay

Bordeaux: Cabernet Sauvignon and Merlot

Burgundy: Pinot Noir

White Burgundy, Chablis: Chardonnay

Côtes du Rhône: Grenache

Sancerre: Sauvignon Blanc

Vouvray: Chenin Blanc

Barolo: Nebbiolo

Chianti: Sangiovese

Rioja: Tempranillo

Ribera del Duero: Tempranillo, Cabernet Sauvignon, and Merlot

SPARKLING WINES	WHITE WINES	ROSÉ WINES	RED WINES	DESSERT WINES
French Champagne the original, in a wide range of styles **Italian Prosecco** **Spanish Cava** **California sparkling wine, etc.**	**Sauvignon Blanc** light bodied, high acid **Pinot Grigio/Gris** light bodied, fruity, low alcohol **Riesling** medium bodied, fruity to off dry, low alcohol **Gewürztraminer** medium bodied, fruity to off dry, low alcohol **Chardonnay** medium to full bodied, crisp-tart to oaky **Chenin Blanc** crisp and acidic to full bodied and lush **Viognier** full bodied, aromatic, and lush **Sémillon** full bodied, aromatic, and lush	**Bordeaux** dry, crisp **Bandol** (mourvèdre) dry, crisp **Languedoc** dry, crisp to fruity, full bodied **Rosado** Spanish, full bodied **Syrah/Shiraz** full bodied, fruity, spicy	**Gamay** light bodied, fruity **Grenache** light bodied to medium bodied **Pinot Noir** medium bodied, can be fruity, low alcohol **Sangiovese** light bodied to medium bodied, high acid **Merlot** medium bodied to full bodied (if oaked) **Tempranillo** medium bodied to full bodied **Syrah/Shiraz** full bodied **Zinfandel** full bodied, fruity, high acid **Nebbiolo** full bodied **Cabernet Sauvignon** full bodied	**Eiswein/ice wine** sweet and crisp **Late-harvest wines** sweet **Muscat** sweet **Tokay** sweet **Sauternes** sweet, lush **Vin santo** sweet, fortified **Port** fortified, fruity or sweet, range of styles **Sherry** fortified, dry to sweet styles **Madeira** fortified, sweet

OPENING AND
POURING WINE

Use the knife on a waiter's corkscrew or a foil cutter to neatly slice the foil. Screw the corkscrew firmly into the centre of the cork, nearly all the way in. Using the lip of the bottle for leverage, pull out the cork with a steady motion. There is no sense in letting a wine "breathe" in the bottle – wine is only aerated by the act of pouring, either into a glass or a decanter. Pour wine into a glass, rotating the bottle as you stop pouring to prevent any drips.

wines are traditionally labelled according to the geographical region in which they are produced, most wines bottled in the New World – the Americas, Australia and New Zealand, and South Africa – are made and labelled as varietals. This shift in labelling was a revolutionary development, making understanding and choosing among these wines much simpler for non-connoisseurs. Luckily, the European regions, as a rule, make their wines from a predominant type of grape, and each wine will also display that grape's varietal qualities, so an understanding of varietals can be applied to European wines once you know which grapes are used in which areas.

The simplest way to start making sense of wine is to focus on the colour and the body. "Body" refers to how the wine feels in the mouth – light or heavy. In simplest terms, white wines, which are made either from white grapes or from red ones with the skins removed at an early stage in the process, are lighter bodied than reds. Among both white and red wines, a range of styles is available. It's up to you to decide what types you like to drink, and when. Another primary consideration is sweetness: "dry" means a wine low in sugar, "off dry" is a little sweet, and "sweet" explains itself.

Serving wine

Serving wine has some seemingly arcane rituals attached, but many of them are grounded in good sense and allow the wine to taste its best. The different shapes of wineglasses are designed to show off the characteristics of the type of wine being served. All wineglasses have a rounded bowl, which captures aromas. The wine's aroma can make up a large part of the pleasure of drinking it. Tall, narrow Champagne flutes are designed to keep the bubbles bubbling up for as long as possible. You'll notice that glasses for Champagne and white wine are fairly straight sided, appropriate for subtler aromas. A balloon-shaped wineglass is perfect for capturing the more complex aromas of a light- or medium-bodied red, allowing you to swirl and sniff. These glasses are also well suited for serving a full-bodied white. A Bordeaux glass, designed for heavy, full-bodied red wines, is large, allowing for more air to be incorporated to soften flavours, and straight sided, to prevent a blast of heady aroma being directed at your nose. The more prominent the personality of the wine, the bigger the glass. Dessert wine and port glasses are smaller than wineglasses, since these wines are served in smaller portions.

The stem of a traditional wineglass acts as a handle, allowing you to hold the glass without touching the bowl. This prevents you from heating up the wine with your hands, which would make the flavours dissipate more quickly. (Cupping the bowl with your palm is a good trick if you are ever served a glass of white wine that is too chilly, and is also part of the ritual of drinking brandy – you want to warm this spirit to bring out its flavours.) Holding a glass by the stem also protects the bowl from greasy fingerprints, which lessens the enjoyment of gazing at the beautiful colour of a wine.

Sometimes a French, Italian, or other ethnic restaurant will serve wine in little tumblers. Obviously, this rustic glass is best suited to a rustic wine – the local red table wine, which in many French and Italian regions is quite good. You can decide how to serve wine at home based on the character of the wine and the mood you want to create. Using alternative wineglasses may create the right ambience for a casual or alfresco supper.

The temperatures for serving wine are also based on maximum enjoyment. Full-bodied red wines should be served at cool room temperature, while light whites benefit from chilling for 20 minutes in iced water or the freezer (don't forget you put the bottle in there, or it will break) or an hour in the fridge. If they are too cold or too warm, their flavours will be dulled. Full-bodied whites, rosés, and lighter-bodied reds fall somewhere in between: a lush Viognier, though white, should not be too cold, which would mask its tropical fruit flavours, while a light rosé, Beaujolais, or even Pinot Noir can be served lightly chilled, especially in summer. Dessert wines and port are generally served at cool room temperature.

Cooking with wine

You might think that wine for cooking calls for a cheaper bottle. While it's true that you would not want to cook with a fine old vintage – since applying heat alters the flavour and structure that the winemaker laboured to produce – neither should the wine be undrinkable. A bad wine is not going to be improved by cooking. Never buy anything labelled "cooking wine". If you're braising a chicken in wine or otherwise using a lot of wine in a dish, you would do well to choose the same varietal to drink at the table, though not necessarily the same bottle or producer.

MATCHING WINE
AND FOOD

Above are possible pairings for the dinner menu on page 14, shown in their proper wineglasses. A simple starter of olives works well with a crisp white wine such as Sauvignon Blanc. A full-flavoured pasta dish, like this carbonara made with bacon, balances with a lighter red wine such as Pinot Noir. And the figs, a dessert that is not overly sweet, can match a sweet dessert wine such as a Muscat without making the wine taste dry.

Pairing wine with food

We believe that matching wine with food is a personal choice. While there are tried-and-true combinations that seem made for one another *(see right)*, it's ultimately a matter of personal taste, the mood of the moment, or simply what you have on hand. Forget the stiff old rules about pairing reds with meat or whites with fish. Try different combinations of varietals with the same dish, and be aware of aromas and flavours that please you. Don't worry about which wine is the "correct" one. The goal is to eat foods you love with wines you love.

We've all been intimidated at one time or another by the task of choosing wine, whether at a restaurant or in a shop. To learn more about which wines you like, you need to find a good shop where you feel comfortable asking questions. This could be a small wine merchant in your area, or even a supermarket with a large selection of wines. When you taste a wine or discuss it with a wine merchant, keep in mind four basic qualities:

BODY: *Does the wine feel light or heavy on the tongue?*

INTENSITY: *Is it bold and assertive, or delicate and mild?*

GENERAL FLAVOUR: *What kinds of tastes and aromas does it bring to mind (citrus, berry, apple, oak)?*

FLAVOUR CHARACTERISTICS: *Is it dry or fruity; what are its levels of acidity and astringency (tannin)?*

Now think about the foods you want to serve. A wine can work with a dish either by mirroring it or contrasting with it. Delicately flavoured foods like sole or halibut are complemented by a delicate, fruity white like Pinot Grigio. A rich, oily salmon may contrast well with a slightly acidic, medium-bodied Pinot Noir — and this fish won't be overwhelmed by this red wine. A spicy chicken stir-fry may overpower a buttery white, but be complemented by the spicy flavour of red Shiraz — or a light white like Riesling. A rich, meaty braise will need a powerful red like Cabernet Sauvignon. And what is the weather like? This may also inform which wine best suits a meal.

As a general rule, wines are better appreciated when they progress from light to heavy over the course of the meal, with whites served before reds, and dry wines before sweet ones. Sweet dessert wines should taste sweeter than the food they are served with.

PAIRING SUGGESTIONS

Salty nibbles
Choose sparkling wines: French Champagne or a fizz from somewhere else in the world

Spicy dishes
Choose fruity, low-alcohol, or spicy wines: Riesling, Pinot Grigio, Pinot Noir, Zinfandel

Rich or fatty dishes
Choose full-bodied wines: Chardonnay, Merlot, Cabernet Sauvignon, Zinfandel, Syrah/Shiraz

Acidic dishes (tomato, citrus, goat's cheese)
Choose high-acid wines: Sauvignon Blanc, Zinfandel, Chianti

Salty or smoked dishes
Choose fruity, low-alcohol wines: Riesling, Gewürztraminer, Pinot Grigio, Pinot Noir

Cheeses
For goat's cheeses, choose high-acid white wines: Australian Sauvignon Blanc, Sancerre

For double- or triple-cream cheeses, choose fruity red or sweet wines: young Pinot Noir, tawny port

For blue cheeses, choose sweet white wines (Sauternes, late-harvest wines) or full-bodied reds

Sweet fruit or dessert
Choose sweet wines, with the wine at least as sweet as the dish

Classic pairings
Caviar with Champagne
Oysters or lobster with Chablis (Chardonnay)
Goat's cheese with Sancerre (Sauvignon Blanc)
Dover sole with white Burgundy (Chardonnay)
Roast lamb with Bordeaux (Cabernet/Merlot)
Charcuterie with Beaujolais (Gamay)
Beef stew or game dishes with Barolo (Nebbiolo)
Roquefort cheese with Sauternes
Stilton cheese with vintage port

About cheese

When and how cheese is served varies from country to country. Traditionally in France, it is usually served after the salad and before dessert, whereas in Britain cheese may be offered before or after the dessert, or take the place of dessert.

Selecting cheese

A good cheese shop, which gives advice and allows you to taste, makes it easy to select your cheeses. Choose just two to four types, depending on the number of people you're serving. You can also offer just one cheese, such as a luxurious ripe Camembert or a buttery blue Gorgonzola, to finish a meal. In any case, you don't want to overwhelm with too much cheese. Rather, you want to intrigue the palate with a few different flavour and texture sensations.

In choosing an assortment of cheeses, aim to offer variety and counterpoint. One approach is to select cheeses made from different

A cheese course is a relaxing way to extend a meal. Pour a little more wine and savour the moment; a cheese course allows everyone to slow down, and lets the conversation wander. Before serving cheese, bring it to room temperature if it has been refrigerated. This will make its texture more appealing on the tongue as well as bringing out its flavours, which are masked by cold. This may take 30 minutes to an hour, depending on the size of the cheese.

A nice way to present cheese is to use a small, smooth wooden board. If you are serving 3 or 4 cheeses, place them on different boards so that guests can pass them round easily.

Different knife shapes work best for different cheese styles. Offer a sharper knife or cheese plane for cutting hard cheeses, and be sure that different cheeses have their own utensils so the cheese flavours remain distinct.

milks: cow's, sheep's, and goat's. Each milk offers a different starting point of flavour, which the cheesemaker develops. Try to include different degrees of pungency. Another consideration is texture. The longer the cheese is aged, the more moisture evaporates from it and the firmer its texture, ranging from fresh, soft, young cheeses to semifirm ones, to long-aged hard cheeses. Including a blue cheese among the choices is a good way to provide range. A last consideration might be appearance. Cheeses are available in so many shapes and colours, with different rinds, leaf wrappers, and ash coatings, that it's easy to create a lovely and varied arrangement that appeals to the eye as well as the palate.

Storing cheese

Cheese does not like the cold. In fact, with the exception of fresh cheeses like ricotta, cheeses actually fare better stored in a cool, dimly lit larder or cellar for a day or two rather than in the fridge. If you do need to put cheese in the fridge for longer storage, wrap it loosely in greaseproof paper and then foil and put it in a large container in the bottom of the fridge.

Accompaniments to cheese

Offer a few simple accompaniments with cheese: good crusty bread and water biscuits or other neutral biscuits provide a plain backdrop, with unsalted butter. Walnuts, toasted for a few minutes to bring out their flavour, are especially good with goat's cheeses, and crisp celery is excellent with a strong cheese. Fruit delivers contrast: classic combinations are apple with Cheddar and pear with Brie. Dried fruits such as apricots or raisins enhance strong-flavoured cheeses such as Comté, Muenster, or Manchego. Pair fresh jams with buttery blue cheeses, or wildflower honeys with semifirm and hard cheeses such as Gruyère and Parmesan.

A versatile wine choice that would complement a range of cheeses is a medium-bodied red. See right and page 37 for some specific suggestions, or let the character of the cheese guide you. For example, with mild fresh cheeses serve a lighter wine, like dry rosé, young Chablis, or Sauvignon Blanc. If the cheeses are stronger, a Chianti, Barolo, or Zinfandel will stand up well. When in doubt, brandy, a lightly chilled sherry, or a sparkling wine is always successful.

A FRENCH CHEESEBOARD

EXPLORATEUR
OR BRILLAT-SAVARIN
(triple-cream)

CHABICHON
(soft, goat's milk)

REBLOCHON
(semifirm, cow's milk)

GRUYÈRE DE COMTÉ
(hard, cow's milk)

*Wine pairing: Viognier or Vouvray
(full-bodied, aromatic white)*
*Accompany with French bread, olives, grapes,
honey or honeycomb*

CHEESE AND FRUIT

PORT-SALUT OR SAINT-ANDRÉ
(double-cream, cow's milk)

LANCASHIRE
(mature, semifirm, cow's milk)

STILTON OR ROQUEFORT
(firm, blue, cow's or sheep's milk)

*Wine pairing: 10-year tawny port or
Poire Williams (pear brandy)*
*Accompany with sliced pears or sharon fruit,
dried figs, toasted raisin-walnut bread*

A SPANISH CHEESEBOARD

MANCHEGO
(firm, sheep's milk)

GARROTXA OR RONCAL
(semifirm, goat's milk)

*Wine pairing: Rioja Crianza
(smooth, medium-bodied Spanish red aged in wood)*
*Accompany with toasted almonds, membrillo (quince
paste), and water biscuits*

Breakfast and Brunch

In this chapter, you'll find homely comfort foods just right for a
cosy breakfast for two. A favourite weekend morning tradition at our
house is custardy French toast, made with a baguette left over from
the night before, or a hearty breakfast hash that never fails to stir
up fond memories of a camping trip we took early in our marriage.
We like to host brunches and here we have several ideas for an easy
yet festive table, including huevos rancheros, an updated version of
eggs Benedict, and ethereal batter puffs that never fail to delight.

Vanilla and Pear Muffins

preparation **15** minutes | cooking **20–25** minutes | **12** muffins

Choose firm, ripe pears with a buttery texture and sweet perfume, such as Comice or Williams', for these American-style muffins, which are perfect for a lazy winter Sunday.

tools | 2 muffin sheets | chef's knife | silicone rubber spatula | skewer | whisk | wire rack

Butter for greasing

FOR THE TOPPING

3 tbsp granulated sugar

2 tbsp finely chopped walnuts

¼ tsp ground cinnamon

FOR THE MUFFINS

300 g (10 oz) flour

115 g (4 oz) caster sugar

2 tsp ground cinnamon

1 tsp freshly grated nutmeg

2 tsp baking powder

½ tsp bicarbonate of soda

¼ tsp fine sea salt

2 eggs

120 ml (4 fl oz) canola (rapeseed) or sunflower oil

175 ml (6 fl oz) buttermilk

2 tsp pure vanilla extract

4 or 5 firm but ripe pears, peeled, cored, and coarsely chopped

115 g (4 oz) walnuts, coarsely chopped

Butter, slightly softened, to serve

Preheat the oven to 180°C (350°F). Grease two 6-cup muffin sheets with butter.

To make the topping, combine the granulated sugar, walnuts, and cinnamon in a small bowl. Set aside.

To make the muffins, stir together the flour, caster sugar, cinnamon, nutmeg, baking powder, bicarbonate of soda, and salt in a bowl. In another bowl, whisk together the eggs, oil, buttermilk, and vanilla extract until blended. Add the dry ingredients to the wet ingredients, stirring just until evenly moistened. The mixture will be slightly lumpy. Using a large rubber spatula, gently fold in the pears and walnuts just until evenly distributed, no more than a few strokes. Take care not to break up the fruit or overmix.

Spoon the mixture into the prepared muffin cups, filling them level with the rim. Sprinkle the muffins with the topping, dividing it evenly. Bake for 20–25 minutes or until golden, dry, and springy to the touch. A wooden skewer inserted into the centre of a muffin should come out clean. Transfer the muffin sheets to a wire rack and allow to cool for 5 minutes before turning out the muffins. Serve warm or at room temperature, with butter.

Banana Bread

preparation **10** minutes | cooking **1** hour | **1** loaf

Banana bread makes a great, wholesome breakfast or afternoon snack with coffee or tea. Try it sliced and toasted, spread with a bit of butter.

tools | loaf tin | chef's knife | box grater | fine-mesh sieve | skewer | wire rack | wooden spoon

Preheat the oven to 180°C (350°F). Grease a 500 g (1 lb) loaf tin with butter.

Sift the flour, baking powder, and salt together into a medium bowl and set aside. In a large bowl, use a wooden spoon to beat the butter with the sugar and lemon zest until soft and creamy. Add one-third of the flour mixture to the butter mixture and stir until fully incorporated. Repeat, adding the remaining flour mixture in 2 more batches. Mix in the eggs and the mashed banana until well blended. Gently fold in the pecans and dates.

Pour the mixture into the prepared loaf tin and smooth the top. Bake for about 1 hour or until a wooden skewer inserted in the centre comes out clean. Remove from the oven and allow to cool in the tin on a wire rack. Turn out onto a plate and serve at room temperature.

Butter for greasing

250 g (9 oz) flour

2¼ tsp baking powder

½ tsp fine sea salt

85 g (3 oz) butter, at room temperature

140 g (5 oz) caster sugar

1 tsp grated lemon zest

2 eggs, lightly beaten

300 g (10 oz) mashed very ripe banana (about 2 large bananas)

60 g (2 oz) pecan nuts, chopped

85 g (3 oz) dates, chopped

Sweet Batter Puffs

preparation **10** minutes | cooking **35** minutes | **12** puffs

Be warned: the aroma of these baking will fill the entire house and create a delicious sense of anticipation – or even impatience! Serve with fresh berries or sliced peaches.

tools | non-stick bun sheets | whisk

Whisk together the eggs and milk in a large bowl. Whisk in the flour, sugar, salt, and butter. Stir the batter until well blended, but don't overbeat, or the eggs will lose their rising power. The batter should have the consistency of double cream.

Divide the batter among the cups of a 12-cup non-stick bun sheet, or two 6-cup sheets, filling the cups two-thirds full. Do not overfill or the puffs will not rise properly. Place in a cold oven and turn it on to 220°C (425°F). After 20 minutes, turn the oven down to 180°C (350°F) and continue baking for 12–15 minutes or until the puffs are billowing out of each cup and golden brown. Serve at once.

3 eggs

360 ml (12 fl oz) milk

175 g (6 oz) flour

2 tbsp caster sugar

1 tsp fine sea salt

45 g (1½ oz) butter, melted

Blueberry Pancakes

preparation **15** minutes | cooking **20** minutes | **4** servings (about **12** pancakes)

The secret ingredient in these American pancakes is whisked egg whites, which gives them a feather-light texture. For tips on separating eggs and whisking egg whites, turn to pages 233 and 234. To give your spouse a treat, cut the recipe in half and serve these pancakes as breakfast in bed. For a nice touch, heat a jug of maple syrup by placing it in a little water in a saucepan over a low heat or by putting it in the microwave for a few seconds.

tools | griddle or frying pan | baking sheet | whisk or electric mixer | ladle | slotted metal turner | silicone rubber spatula | wooden spoon

210 g (7½ oz) flour

2 tbsp caster sugar

1½ tsp baking powder

1 tsp bicarbonate of soda

½ tsp fine sea salt

2 eggs, separated

500 ml (16 fl oz) buttermilk

60 g (2 oz) butter, melted, plus extra melted butter for brushing

175 g (6 oz) blueberries

Maple syrup to serve

Preheat the oven to its lowest setting.

Stir together the flour, sugar, baking powder, bicarbonate of soda, and salt in a large bowl. In another bowl, mix the egg yolks with the buttermilk and melted butter. Add the egg yolk mixture to the flour mixture and stir just until evenly blended.

In another large bowl, whisk the egg whites until soft peaks form. Gently fold the whites into the batter using a spatula, just until no white streaks remain.

Heat a griddle or a 30 cm (12 inch) frying pan, preferably non-stick, over a moderate heat. When the griddle is hot, brush lightly with melted butter. For each pancake, ladle 90 ml (3 fl oz) batter onto the griddle and use the back of the ladle to gently spread into a 10 cm (4 inch) circle. Sprinkle evenly with about 2 tbsp blueberries. Cook for about 2 minutes or until large bubbles form and pop and the edges of the pancakes turn light brown. Turn the pancakes over and cook the other side for 1½–2 minutes or until lightly browned. Transfer to a baking sheet and place in the oven to keep warm. Repeat with the remaining batter.

When all the pancakes are cooked, serve warm with maple syrup.

Buttermilk Waffles with Orange Butter

preparation **15** minutes | cooking **20–30** minutes | **4–8** servings

Waffles turn any weekend morning into a festive occasion. Serve with any topping you like – other possibilities are yogurt and honey or fresh berries and whipped cream.

tools | baking sheet | waffle iron | citrus reamer | wooden spoon

Preheat a waffle iron. Preheat the oven to its lowest setting. Stir together the flour, bicarbonate of soda, and salt in a bowl. In another bowl, stir together the buttermilk, butter, and eggs until well blended. Stir the buttermilk mixture into the flour mixture until it forms a smooth, thick batter.

Spread about 120 ml (4 fl oz) batter evenly in the waffle iron (more or less batter, depending on the size of the waffle iron) and cook following the manufacturer's instructions. Transfer the waffle to a baking sheet and keep warm in the oven. Repeat with the remaining batter. Serve with the orange butter and maple syrup.

orange butter Combine 60 g (2 oz) softened butter, 1 tbsp fresh orange juice, 1 tsp pure vanilla extract, a pinch of fine sea salt, and a pinch of caster sugar in a bowl and beat with a wooden spoon until well blended and fluffy.

275 g (9½ oz) flour

1½ tsp bicarbonate of soda

½ tsp fine sea salt

500 ml (16 fl oz) buttermilk

60 g (2 oz) butter, melted and cooled

2 eggs, lightly beaten

Orange butter to serve *(see left)*

Maple syrup to serve

Breakfast Hash

preparation **10** minutes | cooking **40** minutes | **4** servings

This comforting dish (which gets its name from "haché", the French word for finely chopped) can be made with just about any leftover meat you have on hand, such as grilled steak or roast chicken or pork. Serve with poached eggs (page 214).

tools | medium sauté pan | chef's knife | wooden spoon

Heat the olive oil in a medium sauté pan over a low heat. Add the onion and sauté for about 6 minutes or until softened. Add the potatoes and season with the salt and some pepper. Increase the heat to moderate and add the meat and stock. Stir well, then press the mixture onto the bottom of the pan. Reduce the heat to moderately low. Cover and cook for about 15 minutes or until the hash forms a crust on the base. Stir to mix some of the crust into the rest of the hash. Press onto the bottom of the pan again and cook for a further 10–15 minutes or until crusty, being careful not to overcook the hash and scorch the bottom. Spoon onto 4 warmed serving plates, turning each serving upside down to show off the crusty brown bottom. Garnish with the parsley and serve at once.

3 tbsp olive oil

115 g (4 oz) diced onion

300 g (10 oz) diced floury potatoes

Fine sea salt and pepper

350 g (12 oz) cooked meat, such as steak, finely diced

90 ml (3 fl oz) beef or chicken stock (page 216 or 217)

3 tbsp chopped fresh parsley

French Toast

preparation **10** minutes | resting **15** minutes | cooking **30** minutes | **4** servings

For French toast, or pain perdu, use day-old bread, which absorbs the sweet egg custard mixture better – when fresh bread absorbs egg, it becomes soggy and temperamental. Baguettes and country-style bread give the best results: light and crisp on the surface, custardy and tender on the inside. Top the French toast with icing sugar, mascarpone, fresh fruit, your favourite jam, or honey.

tools | baking sheets | cast-iron frying pan or griddle | serrated bread knife | box grater or citrus zester | citrus reamer

1 day-old baguette

Slice the baguette on a slight diagonal into 20 slices about 2 cm (¾ inch) thick.

4 eggs

1 egg yolk

500 ml (16 fl oz) milk

1 tsp pure vanilla extract

1 tsp grated orange zest

2 tbsp fresh orange juice

4½ tsp caster sugar

½ tsp fine sea salt

In a bowl, beat together the eggs, yolk, milk, vanilla extract, orange juice and zest, sugar, and salt, blending well. Pour the mixture into a large, shallow dish. Submerge the slices of bread and prick their surfaces with a fork so that they can better absorb the egg mixture. If the bread is fairly dry, turn it over a few times and press it into the egg mixture, massaging this into the bread. Leave the bread to soak in the egg mixture for at least 15 minutes, turning once; this ensures a custardlike interior when the bread is cooked.

30 g (1 oz) butter, or as needed

Preheat the oven to its lowest setting. Melt some of the butter in a cast-iron frying pan or on a seasoned griddle over a moderate heat. Place the bread slices, in batches, into the foaming butter and reduce the heat to low. Cook each slice for 3–4 minutes on each side or just until the surface is golden brown. Add more butter to the frying pan if necessary. As the slices are cooked, keep warm in the oven spread in a single layer on baking sheets. Serve on warmed plates.

Courgette and Basil Frittata

preparation **10** minutes | cooking **15** minutes | **2** servings

A fluffy frittata, which begins cooking on the hob and finishes in the oven, makes a great meal any time of day. You can vary this recipe to make use of whatever ingredients you have on hand: leftover cooked greens, roast vegetables, or cheese and herbs. Serve with crusty French bread and sliced Parma ham or salami.

tools | small, non-stick frying pan | chef's knife or mandolin

Preheat the oven to 180°C (350°F).

Beat the eggs in a bowl until blended and season lightly with salt. Set aside. Trim off the ends of the courgettes, then cut into long, narrow matchsticks (see below).

Heat the oil in a 20 cm (8 inch) non-stick, ovenproof frying pan over a moderate heat. Add the courgettes and sauté for 1–2 minutes. Season lightly with salt and pepper. Stir in the ricotta and basil, mixing well, then pour in the eggs.

Reduce the heat to low and stir for 1 minute. Place the pan in the oven and bake for 8–12 minutes or until the frittata has gently risen and is set.

Slide the frittata out of the pan onto a warmed plate and serve at once, or allow to cool to room temperature before serving.

5 eggs

Fine sea salt and pepper

2 medium courgettes

1 tbsp olive oil

75 g (2½ oz) ricotta cheese

Leaves from 2 sprigs fresh basil, torn into small pieces

> **cutting matchsticks** Cutting vegetables into narrow strips of equal size allows them to cook quickly and evenly, and their neat appearance adds a pleasing look to a dish. Small matchsticks – about 3 mm (⅛ inch) thick – are called julienne. To cut matchsticks for this recipe, use a sharp chef's knife or a mandolin. First trim off the courgette's rounded edges, cutting the vegetable into a log that's flat on each side. Cut the courgette across into 5 cm (2 inch) lengths, then cut each piece lengthways into slices 3–5 mm (⅛–¼ inch) thick. Stack the slices and cut lengthways into narrow strips.

Classic French Omelette

preparation **5** minutes | cooking **7** minutes | **1** serving

Omelettes, with a green salad and chilled white wine, can also make an elegant, but easy, midweek supper for two. Use a non-stick pan and brisk heat to create a perfect rolled omelette, tender and plump on the outside and creamy and voluptuous within. Since you can cook only one omelette at a time, keep the first warm by loosely covering it with foil while you prepare the second omelette.

tools | small, non-stick frying pan or omelette pan | chef's knife | silicone rubber spatula

3 eggs

1 tbsp Champagne or sparkling wine

Fine sea salt

2 tbsp mascarpone

2 tsp finely chopped fresh chives

2 tsp finely chopped fresh chervil

1 tsp finely chopped fresh parsley

15 g (½ oz) butter

In a small bowl, beat the eggs lightly with a fork to blend the yolks and whites completely. Stir in the Champagne, a pinch of salt, the mascarpone, and all the herbs. Do not overbeat.

Melt the butter in an 18–20 cm (7–8 inch) non-stick frying pan or omelette pan over a moderately high heat. When the butter stops foaming and just before it begins to brown, add the egg mixture to the pan. The eggs will begin to set on the base within 30 seconds. Begin to pull in the egg mixture from the sides of the pan towards the centre using a small rubber spatula, to allow the raw egg to run underneath the thin sheet of cooked egg. Repeat 2 or 3 times until most of the base is set, while the surface remains moist and creamy. Tilt the pan forwards, sliding the omelette up the side of the pan, and use the spatula to fold in the edge of the omelette, then roll it up. Flip the omelette once or twice with the spatula to secure the roll. Slide the omelette onto a plate and serve at once.

chervil This lacy herb with a delicate parsley-anise flavour is best known as a part of the French herb blend *fines herbes*, a combination of chervil, parsley, tarragon, and chives, commonly used in sauces and omelettes. Chervil wilts quickly, so wrap it in damp kitchen paper, place in a plastic bag, and store in the fridge for no longer than 2 days.

Huevos Rancheros

preparation **10** minutes │ cooking **20–30** minutes │ **4** servings

You can use shop-bought salsa in this dish to make it quicker to prepare, but if possible take a few extra minutes to make the simple and tasty salsa fresca *(fresh salsa). The eggs can be fried in batches; just keep the finished plates in a warm spot until all the eggs are ready.*

tools │ frying pan or griddle │ medium saucepan │ chef's knife │ citrus reamer

To make the salsa, combine all of the ingredients in a bowl and stir to blend. Add 1 tbsp water if the mixture seems dry. Taste the salsa and adjust the seasoning with salt and lime juice. Set aside for 10 minutes to allow the flavours to blend.

In a medium saucepan, combine the refried beans and 4 tbsp water. Heat over a moderately high heat, stirring often, for about 7 minutes or until hot. Remove from the heat and cover to keep warm. Heat a large, heavy frying pan or griddle over a high heat. Add the tortillas one at a time, heating each for a minute or two on each side. Wrap in a clean tea towel to keep warm.

To fry the eggs, coat the frying pan or griddle with a thin film of olive oil. In batches as necessary, break the eggs into the pan and fry over a moderately high heat until the whites are set and the yolks are nearly set.

Place 1 or 2 tortillas on each of 4 warmed plates. Spread each tortilla with 2 or 3 tbsp of beans and top with 1 or 2 eggs. Top the eggs with salsa and slices of avocado. Serve at once.

> **cutting avocados** Preparing an avocado is easier if you know a few tricks. Cut the fruit in half, working around the stone. Twist the halves in opposite directions to separate. To remove the stone, strike it carefully but firmly with the heel of the blade of a large, sharp knife, lodging the knife firmly in the stone, then ease out the stone. Slice the flesh while it's still in the peel, then scoop out the slices with a large spoon.

1 can (about 400 g) refried beans

4–8 corn tortillas

Olive oil for frying

4–8 eggs

1 ripe avocado, sliced

FOR THE SALSA

2 tbsp finely chopped onion

2 ripe, small to medium tomatoes, cored and chopped

2 tbsp chopped fresh coriander

¼ tsp fine sea salt

2 tsp fresh lime juice

1 tbsp finely chopped jalapeño or other fresh green chilli

1 tbsp red wine vinegar

Eggs Benedict

preparation **15** minutes | cooking **15–20** minutes | **4** servings

Serve eggs Benedict for a Mother's Day brunch or an Easter celebration, or treat your houseguests – or yourselves – on a Sunday morning. In the spring, you could substitute sliced steamed asparagus for the spinach.

tools | bain marie pan or double boiler | small saucepans | large sauté pans | paring knife | citrus reamer | slotted spoon | whisk

4 muffins, split

2 tsp olive oil

750 g (1 lb 10 oz) baby spinach leaves, patted dry

¼ tsp fine sea salt

8 eggs

8 slices good cooked ham or Parma ham, at room temperature

FOR THE HOLLANDAISE SAUCE

1½ tbsp fresh lemon juice

60 g (2 oz) butter

3 egg yolks

Fine sea salt

¼ tsp cayenne pepper

To make the hollandaise sauce, warm the lemon juice in a small non-metallic saucepan over a low heat, or in the microwave. Bring 120 ml (4 fl oz) water to the boil in a small saucepan over a high heat. Melt the butter in another small saucepan over a low heat, or in the microwave.

Set up a bain marie pan (page 245) over a low heat. Place the egg yolks in the top pan and place over (but not touching) the barely simmering water in the bottom pan. Whisk the egg yolks constantly until they begin to thicken, then add 1 tbsp of the boiling water and continue to whisk for about 30 seconds or until the yolks have thickened. Add 3 more tbsp boiling water, 1 tbsp at a time, whisking thoroughly after each addition. Whisk in the warm lemon juice and remove the pan from the heat. Pour in the melted butter very slowly, whisking constantly, then add a good pinch of salt and the cayenne. The sauce will thicken. Leave the bowl over the water, off the heat, and cover to keep warm.

Toast the muffins.

Heat the olive oil in a large sauté pan over a moderately low heat. Gently sauté the spinach leaves for about 4 minues or just until tender. Season with the salt. Set aside, covered to keep warm.

To poach the eggs, put 5–7.5 cm (2–3 inches) of water in a large sauté pan. Season the water with salt and bring to a simmer over a moderate heat. One at a time, and working quickly, break each egg into a small ramekin and carefully slip it into the water. Leave space around the eggs. Adjust the heat so that the water is barely simmering. Poach the eggs gently for 3–5 minutes, depending on how you like them cooked. Remove each egg from the water with a slotted spoon. While the egg is still in the spoon, blot the base dry with a clean tea towel and trim off the ragged edges with a paring knife.

Place 2 warm muffin halves, cut side up, on each of 4 plates. Lay a slice of ham on each muffin half. Arrange the warm spinach on the ham, top each bed of spinach with a poached egg, and spoon the hollandaise sauce over the eggs. Serve at once.

Starters

The purpose of a starter is to stimulate the appetite for the meal to come. A dish can be simple and yet play this role perfectly: think of olives gently warmed to awaken their flavours, or crunchy radishes paired with creamy butter. An uncomplicated starter allows you to focus on wonderful flavours and textures and artfully awakens your anticipation for the main course, rather than sating you.

Spicy Almonds

preparation **5** minutes | cooking **15** minutes | **6–8** servings

Toasting almonds fills your kitchen with their sweet fragrance, and you are rewarded with a versatile nibble that goes equally well with a chilled rosé, a classic cocktail, or an ice-cold beer. These almonds can also be added to salads, frittatas, or even pasta.

tools | baking sheet | spatula or wooden spoon

300 g (10 oz) shelled almonds with the skins

½ tsp fine sea salt

2 tsp olive oil

1–2 pinches of red chilli powder or cayenne pepper

¼ tsp garlic granules (optional)

Preheat the oven to 170°C (325°F). In a medium bowl, combine the almonds with 2 tbsp water and the salt, tossing the almonds to coat evenly. Spread the almonds on a baking sheet and bake for 8 minutes. Remove the baking sheet from the oven and drizzle the olive oil over the nuts. Use a spatula or wooden spoon to turn the nuts until they are coated with oil. Sprinkle the chilli powder and garlic granules, if using, over the almonds and toss to coat well. Return the almonds to the oven and bake for a further 5–6 minutes, stirring the almonds after 3 minutes to ensure they cook evenly. Remove from the oven and allow to cool. The almonds will keep in an airtight container for up to 1 week.

Warm Marinated Olives

preparation **10** minutes | cooking **5** minutes | **6–8** servings

For a touch of simple Mediterranean pleasure, fix your mate these warm olives before serving supper. We suggest a combination of olive varieties here, but feel free to choose a selection of flavours, shapes, and colours that appeal to you. Be sure to buy olives with their stones for the best flavour and quality.

tools | medium sauté pan | chef's knife | citrus zester

75 g (2½ oz) Kalamata olives

75 g (2½ oz) Manzanilla olives

75 g (2½ oz) Niçoise olives

1 orange

1 lemon

Leaves from 2 sprigs fresh thyme

1 clove garlic, finely chopped

1½ tbsp extra virgin olive oil

Rinse the olives under cold water to remove any brine. Pat dry with kitchen paper.

Remove half of the orange's zest in long strips using a zester. Remove half of the lemon's zest.

In a bowl, toss the olives with the orange and lemon zests, thyme, garlic, and olive oil. Just before serving, heat the olives in a medium sauté pan over a low heat just long enough to bring out their flavours and gently warm them. Serve in an earthenware crock or dish, with a small ramekin for discarded stones.

Gougères

preparation **20** minutes | cooking **25** minutes | **4** servings

Gougères are golden cheese-laced puffs that bake up crisp yet tender. They are delicious served warm or cold, with white or red wine, and they also make great late-night snacks.

tools | medium saucepan | baking sheets | box grater | baking parchment | wooden spoon

Preheat the oven to 190°C (375°F) and line baking sheets with baking parchment. Combine the butter and 120 ml (4 fl oz) water in a medium saucepan and bring to the boil. Add the flour all at once, quickly stirring with a wooden spoon until the mixture is glossy and smooth and pulls away from the sides of the saucepan. The mixture will form a ball around the spoon.

Remove from the heat and add the eggs, one at a time, beating well after each addition until thoroughly incorporated. Stir in the cheese, cayenne, and salt.

Use 2 spoons or a piping bag without a nozzle to form 2.5 cm (1 inch) balls on the prepared baking sheets. Bake for about 25 minutes or until the balls double in size and turn golden brown, and a thin-bladed knife inserted in the centre comes out clean. Allow to cool slightly or completely before serving.

45 g (1½ oz) butter

125 g (4½ oz) flour

3 eggs

175 g (6 oz) Gruyère cheese, grated

¼ tsp cayenne pepper

¼ tsp fine sea salt, or more to taste

Marinated Goat's Cheese

preparation **5** minutes | resting **1** day | **4** servings

Soft, fresh goat's cheese is satisfying on its own, but marinating the cheese in oil, herbs, and spices makes it completely irresistible. Serve it with water biscuits. Or you could fold it into an omelette or use it to top a green salad, bruschette, or pasta.

tools | chef's knife

Place the goat's cheese in a shallow dish. Drizzle over the olive oil and sprinkle with the thyme, chilli flakes (if using), fennel seeds, and bay leaves. Cover and chill for at least 1 day and up to 3 days. Remove from the refrigerator at least 1 hour before serving to bring the cheese to room temperature.

> **toasting seeds** To toast seeds and bring out their flavour, spread them in a dry frying pan and heat over a moderate heat until fragrant. Watch the seeds carefully to prevent them from getting too brown and burning.

4 rounds fresh goat's cheese, each 1 cm (½ inch) thick, sliced from a log 6 cm (2½ inches) in diameter

175 ml (6 fl oz) extra virgin olive oil

3 or 4 sprigs fresh thyme

¼ tsp dried chilli flakes (optional)

2 tsp fennel seeds, lightly toasted (see left)

2 fresh or dried bay leaves

Aubergine Caviar

preparation **10** minutes | cooking **50** minutes | resting **30** minutes | **4** servings

The name of this aubergine spread may be tongue-in-cheek – a poor man's caviar? – but it's so delicious that it holds its own alongside most luxury foods. With Italian-style cauliflower (page 158) and ginger carrots (page 155) it can make a simple meal for two.

tools | baking sheet | chef's knife | paring knife | citrus reamer

1 large aubergine

1 tbsp olive oil

Fine sea salt and pepper

2 tbsp extra virgin olive oil

1 tbsp fresh lemon juice

1 tbsp balsamic vinegar

1 clove garlic, mashed

Several sprigs fresh mint

Crostini to serve (page 215)

Preheat the oven to 190°C (375°F). Trim the stalk off the aubergine and cut in half lengthways. Rub the cut surfaces with the olive oil and sprinkle with some salt and pepper. Place the halves cut side down on a baking sheet. Roast for 40–50 minutes or until the flesh is soft and cooked through.

Allow the aubergine to cool until it is easy to handle, then peel off the skin with a paring knife. Chop the flesh until it has the texture of a salsa. Combine the chopped aubergine with the extra virgin olive oil, lemon juice, vinegar, and garlic. Taste and adjust the seasoning with salt. Set aside for at least 30 minutes to allow the flavours to blend. When ready to serve, pick the leaves from the mint sprigs, chop coarsely, and stir them into the caviar. Accompany with the crostini.

Radishes with Butter

preparation **10** minutes | **4** servings

Crunchy, raw radishes paired with rich unsalted butter is a French tradition. We like to use French breakfast radishes, with their pretty white and pink colour, oblong shape, and mildly peppery flavour. Choose a French butter for the best flavour. Serve with a rosé.

tools | paring knife | serrated bread knife

1 bunch French breakfast radishes or other mildly spicy radishes

Fine sea salt

60 g (2 oz) butter, cut into 4 portions

1 baguette, cut into slices 1 cm (½ inch) thick

Trim the radish tops, leaving a few of the leaves if they are pretty and green. Trim away and discard the root ends. Submerge the radishes in a small bowl of cold water for 10 minutes to crisp. Drain and pat dry.

On each of 4 small plates, arrange a few radishes, a small pile of sea salt, a pat of butter, and a few baguette slices.

Artichoke Dip

preparation **10** minutes | cooking **30** minutes | **6–8** servings

This savoury dip or spread is rich, even a little decadent, but guests are guaranteed to devour it quickly. Luckily the recipe doubles well! Serve with crostini (page 215) and classic martinis and you'll have an instant party.

tools | small baking dish or soufflé dish | baking sheet | chef's knife | box grater | citrus reamer | colander or sieve | wooden spoon

Preheat the oven to 180°C (350°F). Chop the artichokes into 1 cm (½ inch) pieces and put in a mixing bowl. Add the mayonnaise, lemon juice, 3 tbsp of the Parmesan, and the parsley and mix well with a wooden spoon. Spoon into a small baking dish or soufflé dish and sprinkle with the remaining Parmesan. Place the dish on a baking sheet and bake for 25–30 minutes or until golden on top. Allow to cool slightly before serving with crostini.

1 jar (about 400 g) artichoke hearts packed in olive oil, well drained

90 ml (3 fl oz) mayonnaise

1 tsp fresh lemon juice

3½ tbsp freshly grated Parmesan cheese

1 tbsp chopped fresh parsley

Crostini to serve (page 215)

Guacamole

preparation **10** minutes | **6–8** servings

If you don't have a big mortar and pestle, treat yourself to a Mexican molcajete, *made of volcanic rock. It is so handsome that you can serve the dip in it too. We are purists when it comes to guacamole, relying on the irresistible flavour and texture of perfectly ripe avocado: buttery, nutty, and fruity. Serve with tortilla chips or breadsticks for dipping.*

tools | chef's knife | citrus reamer | mortar and pestle (optional)

Use a mortar and pestle, or a bowl and fork, to mash the onion, chilli, chopped coriander, and a pinch of salt to form a coarse paste. Cut the avocados in half, remove their stones, and scoop out the flesh with a spoon. Add to the mixture and mash until well incorporated. Add salt and lime juice to taste. (The flavours of the lime and salt should be prominent, but the guacamole should not be too salty or acidic.) Set aside for a few minutes to allow the flavours to blend. Garnish the guacamole with the coriander sprigs and serve.

30 g (1 oz) finely chopped onion

1 jalapeño or other fresh green chilli, seeded and finely chopped

4 tbsp coarsely chopped fresh coriander, plus 4 sprigs to garnish

Fine sea salt

2 ripe Hass avocados

1 tbsp fresh lime juice, or to taste

Bruschette Two Ways

preparation **20** minutes | resting **1** hour | cooking **10** minutes | **6** servings

Bruschette – *toasted or grilled bread with savoury toppings – are a fun way to start any social gathering. Halve the recipe to make a light summertime lunch for two with a glass of Chianti or Viognier. The number of bruschetta toppings you can create are infinite, and we hope you will be inspired to create your own with any ingredients that sound appealing to you. The two toppings here are classics.*

tools | large sauté pan | chef's knife | serrated bread knife | colander or sieve

12 slices pugliese or sourdough bread, 1 cm (½ inch) thick

FOR THE TAPENADE AND GREENS TOPPING

150 g (5½ oz) fruity green olives, stoned

5 cloves garlic

2 anchovy fillets, rinsed and patted dry

2 tbsp capers, rinsed and chopped

2 tsp grappa (optional)

Extra virgin olive oil

1 bunch kale, escarole, or Swiss chard

¼ tsp fine sea salt

Pinch of dried chilli flakes (optional)

FOR THE CANNELLINI BEAN TOPPING

325 g (10½ oz) canned cannellini beans *(see note)*

2 fresh sage leaves, chopped

Fine sea salt and freshly ground pepper

Extra virgin olive oil

1 large clove garlic

1 medium, ripe tomato

Toast the bread slices on both sides until golden brown, using a barbecue, ridged cast-iron grill pan, or preheated hot grill.

To make the tapenade and greens topping, roughly chop the olives, keeping the texture slightly coarse. Finely chop 4 of the garlic cloves and the anchovy fillets. Combine the olives, chopped garlic and anchovies, capers, and grappa (if using) in a bowl and drizzle with 4 tbsp extra virgin olive oil. Taste and add more olive oil if needed for flavour or texture. The tapenade should glisten and have a texture similar to that of a salsa, loose but not overly oily. Set aside at room temperature for at least 1 hour to allow the flavours to blend.

When nearly ready to serve, trim the stalks from the greens and chop into bite-sized pieces. Finely chop the remaining garlic clove. Heat 1 tbsp olive oil in a large sauté pan over a moderate heat and add the greens. Sprinkle with 1 tbsp water to create steam. Reduce the heat to low, season the greens with the salt, garlic, and chilli flakes (if using), and cook for 8–10 minutes or until the greens are tender. Taste and adjust the seasoning with salt. Spread the tapenade over 6 of the toasted bread slices and arrange the warm greens on top.

To make the cannellini bean topping, rinse and drain the beans. Combine the beans, sage, a pinch of salt, a grinding of pepper, and 2 tbsp extra virgin olive oil in a bowl and mash with a fork until the beans are pasty and the ingredients are thoroughly combined. Rub the remaining 6 slices of toasted bread lightly and evenly with the garlic clove to flavour well. Slice off the top of the tomato and rub the bread slices with the cut side of the tomato to moisten and give them flavour. Divide the bean mixture among the bread slices and spread evenly. Drizzle each bruschetta with olive oil and serve at once.

Note: If you have leftover white beans and sage (page 189), you can use this in place of canned cannellini beans.

Prawns with Parsley-Garlic Butter

preparation **30** minutes | cooking **5** minutes | **6–8** servings

This starter almost immediately disappears as soon as it is placed on the table. The prawns are butterflied, or cut almost in half and opened flat, while still in their shells, then topped with a flavoured butter and quickly grilled. When prepared like this, the prawns are easy to peel, and very flavourful and attractive.

tools | baking tray or roasting tin | chef's knife | paring knife | box grater or citrus zester | wooden spoon

Make the parsley-garlic butter.

Preheat the grill. Remove the legs from the prawns. With a sharp paring knife, make an incision 5 mm (¼ inch) deep all the way along the curved back of each prawn up to the last tail section. Don't cut all the way through the prawn; cut just enough to open it up, or butterfly it. Lift any dark vein with the tip of the knife and pull it out, then press down on the opened prawn to flatten it without separating the halves. Rinse the prawns under cold water and pat dry.

Arrange the butterflied prawns in a single layer in a baking tray or roasting tin (you may need to cook in batches). Place 1–2 tsp of the parsley-garlic butter (depending on the size of the prawns) in the centre of each one. Slide the tray under the grill and cook for 4–5 minutes or until the prawns turn pink and are just cooked through. Transfer the prawns to a serving platter or individual plates and pour over any drippings from the tray. Serve with plenty of napkins and a plate for the shells.

Parsley-garlic butter *(see below)*

1 kg (2¼ lb) raw king or tiger prawns in shell without heads (about 28)

> **parsley-garlic butter**   The ingredients in this flavoured butter can be changed to suit your taste – try chives instead of parsley, or orange zest instead of lemon zest. In a bowl, combine 225 g (8 oz) butter, slightly softened; leaves from 1 bunch fresh parsley, finely chopped; 5 or 6 medium to large cloves garlic, finely chopped; 1 tbsp grated lemon zest; 2 tsp fine sea salt; and 1 tsp pepper. Mash together well with a wooden spoon. The butter can be refrigerated for up to 3 days before using, and any leftover butter will keep for up to 1 month in the freezer.

Grilled Mozzarella Sandwiches

preparation **10** minutes | cooking **8** minutes | **6** servings

The keys to a sensational starter are simplicity, an appealing texture, and a savoury taste that sharpens the appetite. These little sandwiches fit the bill perfectly, and they go very well with rustic tumblers of red or white wine.

tools | cast-iron frying pan or non-stick griddle | chef's knife | serrated bread knife | brush (optional)

1 loaf pugliese or sourdough bread, preferably day-old

750 g (1 lb 10 oz) fresh mozzarella cheese (*mozzarella di bufala*, if you like)

Fine sea salt

2 tbsp olive oil

1 tbsp chopped fresh parsley

Cut the bread into 12 slices 5 mm (¼ inch) thick. Arrange half of the slices on your work surface. Cut the mozzarella into slices 5 mm (¼ inch) thick and place on top of the arranged bread slices. Season the mozzarella with salt and cover with the remaining bread slices. Make sure the top bread slices fit the bottoms so that the cheese is not exposed or falling out of the sandwich.

Brush the surface of a cast-iron frying pan or non-stick griddle with a thin film of olive oil and heat over a moderate heat. Brush the tops of the sandwiches with oil as well. When the pan is hot, add the sandwiches oiled side down, in batches as necessary, and cook for 3–5 minutes or until the base is golden and the cheese starts to melt. Brush the top slices of bread with oil and turn the sandwiches over, adding a little more oil to the pan if needed. Cook for a few more minutes. The sandwiches should be golden on both sides and the cheese should be melted.

Remove the sandwiches from the pan and cut into neat, bite-sized pieces (triangles or rectangles, depending on the shape of the bread). Sprinkle with the chopped parsley and serve warm on a serving platter lined with a cloth napkin.

Crab Cakes

preparation **30** minutes | cooking **15** minutes | **4** servings

Once you master the knack of making crab cakes, you'll see how easily you can vary them. Try adding finely chopped fresh ginger, diced red pepper, or chopped sautéed spinach. If you want truly fabulous crab cakes, make spicy mayonnaise to top them with, and use some of the unflavoured home-made mayonnaise in the crab cakes as well. This recipe yields an excellent starter for four, or will serve two as a main course with a green salad (page 82) and a bowl of sweetcorn soup (page 81).

tools | small and large sauté pans | chef's knife | citrus reamer | slotted metal turner or tongs

Heat the olive oil in a small sauté pan over a moderately low heat. Add the onion and celery and sauté for about 10 minutes or until tender; do not brown. Season lightly with salt, then remove from the heat and leave to cool completely.

Meanwhile, in a medium bowl, combine the crabmeat, fresh breadcrumbs, mashed potatoes, mustard, mayonnaise, chives, tarragon, cayenne, and lemon juice. Season with salt and pepper. Mix together gently with a fork to keep the mixture fluffy. Carefully stir in the cooled onion mixture. Taste and add a little more lemon juice, cayenne, or salt if needed.

Spread the toasted breadcrumbs on a plate. Scoop out a ball of the crab mixture (about 4 tbsp) and drop into the crumbs. Shape into a compact cake about 2 cm (¾ inch) thick and coat lightly with crumbs, patting them on so they adhere. You should be able to make 8 crab cakes. At this point, you can refrigerate the cakes until just before you are ready to cook them.

Preheat the oven to its lowest setting. Heat half of the oil in a large sauté pan over a moderate heat. Place 4 of the crab cakes in the pan and cook for 3 minutes or until a golden crust forms on the base. Use tongs or a slotted turner to turn the cakes over. Cook for another 3 minutes or until a golden crust forms on the other side. Remove the cakes from the pan and keep warm in the oven while cooking the remaining crab cakes, using the rest of the oil.

To serve, place the crab cakes on individual plates with a dollop of spicy mayonnaise, if using, and a sprinkling of rocket leaves.

1 tbsp olive oil

60 g (2 oz) finely chopped onion

60 g (2 oz) finely chopped celery

Fine sea salt and pepper

500 g (1 lb 2 oz) fresh or thawed frozen white crabmeat, picked over for shell pieces and cartilage

45 g (1½ oz) fine fresh breadcrumbs (page 215)

115 g (4 oz) mashed potatoes, cooled (page 178)

3 tbsp Dijon mustard

4 tbsp mayonnaise

2 tbsp chopped fresh chives

2 tbsp chopped fresh tarragon

¼ tsp cayenne pepper

Juice of ½ lemon, or to taste

115 g (4 oz) fine toasted breadcrumbs (page 215)

4 tbsp grapeseed or olive oil

Spicy mayonnaise to serve (page 213; optional)

Rocket leaves to serve

Soups and Salads

These versatile recipes can start a multi-course dinner or double as
light meals, lunches for two, or late-night snacks. Fun to assemble
salads such as tomato, mozzarella, and basil require some timely
shopping, but they make up for it by coming together in minutes.
Some of the soups, such as gazpacho or butternut squash, can be
made ahead of time and served as a weeknight supper. Clam chowder
can be the centrepiece of any gathering, and frisée with lardons
and poached egg is a perfect brunch main course.

Gazpacho

preparation **15** minutes | chilling **2** hours | **4** servings

Don't attempt to make gazpacho with canned tomatoes. Wait until summertime, then visit your local farmers' market and buy the ripest tomatoes you can find.

tools | chef's knife | food mill, food processor, or blender

1 cucumber

1 small red pepper

8 ripe tomatoes

30 g (1 oz) chopped red onion

1 tsp finely chopped garlic

Extra virgin olive oil

Red wine vinegar

6 tbsp fresh breadcrumbs (page 215)

Fine sea salt

Peel the cucumber and slice in half lengthways, then scoop out any seeds with a small spoon. Finely dice enough cucumber to measure out 2 tbsp; set aside for the garnish. Chop the rest of the cucumber. Remove the core and seeds from the red pepper. Chop the pepper and tomatoes.

Combine the chopped cucumber, red pepper, tomatoes, onion, garlic, 4 tbsp olive oil, and 2 tbsp vinegar and purée until smooth using a food mill, food processor, or blender. Stir in the breadcrumbs. Taste for salt and vinegar and adjust according to your taste. Cover and refrigerate for at least 2 hours or up to 2 days.

Serve cold in chilled bowls, drizzled with extra virgin olive oil and garnished with the reserved diced cucumber.

Leek and Potato Soup

preparation **15** minutes | cooking **15** minutes | **4** servings

The arrival of stormy days and chilly nights is your cue to simmer up a pot of this soup. It can be made some days in advance, so it's ready and waiting when you need a quick meal.

tools | medium saucepan | chef's knife | colander | ladle | vegetable peeler

5 medium leeks

2 large boiling potatoes, such as Maris Piper or Desirée

2 litres (3½ pints) vegetable stock

½ tsp fine sea salt, or to taste

3 sprigs fresh thyme

1 clove garlic, lightly crushed

4 tbsp crème fraîche or soured cream

1 tbsp chopped fresh chives

Clean the leeks by trimming off their roots and green tops. Peel away the tough outer green leaves, exposing the tender stalk. Quarter each stalk lengthways, and cut into 5 mm (¼ inch) dice. Rinse the leeks under cold water in a colander to remove any sand or dirt, then leave to drain. Peel the potatoes and dice finely.

Bring the stock to the boil in a saucepan over a moderately high heat. Add the salt, potatoes, thyme, and garlic. Bring back to the boil, then cover the pan and cook for 5 minutes. Add the leeks, lower the heat, and simmer, uncovered, for 10 minutes or until the leeks and potatoes are tender. Taste and adjust the seasoning.

Remove the thyme sprigs. Ladle the soup into warmed bowls, garnish each with a dollop of crème fraîche and a sprinkle of chives, and serve at once.

New England Clam Chowder

preparation **20** minutes | cooking **30** minutes | **6–8** servings

There is something comforting in creating and serving supper out of a single pot – not to mention what a gift it is to the person doing the washing-up. Serve this classic American chowder with warm crusty French bread and lemony Caesar salad (page 88). For a dinner party, make the chowder base ahead of time and add the clams just before serving.

tools | medium and large sauté pans | large saucepan | chef's knife | muslin | fine-mesh sieve | ladle | vegetable peeler | wooden spoon

To make the roux, melt the butter in a medium sauté pan over a low heat. Add the flour and cook the mixture, stirring constantly with a wooden spoon, for about 4 minutes or until it is beige in colour. Do not allow it to brown. Remove from the heat and set aside.

To open the clams and make the clam stock, combine 600 ml (1 pint) water and the clams in a large sauté pan, discarding any clams that do not close to the touch. Place over a moderate heat, cover, and cook for 2–5 minutes or until the clams open. Remove from the heat and allow the clams and their liquid (now clam stock) to cool slightly. Discard any clams that failed to open. Use your fingers or a small spoon to pick the clams out of their shells, letting any juices drip back into the pan. Put the clams on a chopping board and discard the shells. Pour the stock through a fine-mesh sieve lined with damp muslin to remove any grit. Chop the clams coarsely for a finer texture in the final chowder. Set the clams and stock aside.

To make the chowder, melt the butter in a large saucepan over a low heat. Gently sauté the bacon, onions, celery, and carrot, stirring constantly, for 10 minutes or until tender. Do not brown. Add the clam stock, cream, milk, potatoes, thyme, and bay leaf. Bring to a gentle simmer and cook for 5 minutes. Stir 1 tbsp of the chowder liquid into the roux until smooth. Add the roux mixture to the rest of the chowder in the pan, stirring thoroughly to incorporate. Simmer, stirring constantly, for 4–5 minutes to thicken the chowder.

When just about ready to serve, add the chopped clams to the chowder and simmer for a further 2 minutes. Add the salt, taste, and adjust the seasoning. Ladle into warmed bowls, sprinkle with the parsley, and serve.

FOR THE ROUX

15 g (½ oz) butter

2½ tbsp flour

FOR THE CLAMS AND CLAM STOCK

1.25 kg (2½ lb) fresh clams, scrubbed well

FOR THE CHOWDER

30 g (1 oz) butter or 2 tbsp olive oil

2 thick rashers streaky bacon, finely chopped

2 small onions, finely diced

1 large stick celery, finely diced

1 large carrot, peeled and finely diced

250 ml (8 fl oz) double cream

360 ml (12 fl oz) milk

1 large or 2 small boiling potatoes, such as Maris Piper or Desirée, peeled and finely diced

Leaves from 3 sprigs fresh thyme

1 bay leaf

¼ tsp fine sea salt

1 tbsp chopped fresh parsley

Black Bean Soup

soaking **4** hours | preparation **20** minutes | cooking **2** hours | **6–8** servings

Plan ahead and start soaking the beans the night before you prepare this recipe, which makes enough soup for more than one delicious meal. If you live in an area where there are Latin American markets, look for epazote, a herb commonly used in Mexican cooking, to give the soup an authentic flavour. See if they have tomatillos too, so you can make a delicious salsa topping to dress up the soup.

tools | large saucepan | chef's knife | food processor or blender | citrus zester | ladle | large metal spoon

500 g (1 lb 2 oz) dried black beans

1 large onion, diced

1 large carrot, peeled and diced

1 stick celery, diced

4 cloves garlic, lightly crushed

1 sprig fresh epazote or coriander

½ small bacon hock

2.5 litres (4½ pints) chicken or vegetable stock (page 216), or as needed

1 tbsp ground ancho chilli powder

1 tbsp ground cumin

1½ tsp fine sea salt

120 ml (4 fl oz) crème fraîche or soured cream

Thin strips of lime zest to garnish

Tomatillo salsa to garnish (*see right*; optional)

Rinse and pick over the beans, discarding any debris and any discoloured beans. Put them in a bowl, add water to cover by 7.5 cm (3 inches), and leave to soak for 4 hours or up to overnight.

Drain the beans and put them in a large saucepan with the onion, carrot, celery, garlic, epazote, bacon hock, and stock. Bring to the boil and skim off any foam with a large metal spoon. Reduce the heat to low and simmer slowly, uncovered, for about 2 hours or until the beans are creamy and tender. Add more stock to the beans if needed to keep them just covered. Stir often so that the beans cook evenly.

When the beans are tender, remove the bacon hock and epazote and discard them. Allow the bean mixture to cool slightly, then ladle into a food processor or blender in small batches, adding some of the cooking liquid as necessary, and process to an even and smooth purée. Return the soup to the pan and stir in the chilli powder and cumin. The soup should be smooth with a pouring consistency, without being too runny or too thick. Add water to thin the soup, if necessary; if it is too runny, simmer over a moderate heat until slightly thickened. Add the salt (if you are using stock made with a stock cube, you may not need as much salt). Taste the soup and adjust the seasoning.

When ready to serve, reheat the soup over a moderate heat and ladle into warmed bowls. Garnish with the crème fraîche, lime zest, and the tomatillo salsa, if using.

tomatillo salsa Tomatillos look like miniature green tomatoes in a papery husk, but they are actually unrelated to tomatoes and instead are in the same family as the cape gooseberry or physalis. Remove the husks from 10 tomatillos, rinse, and finely chop. Finely chop 1 small red onion. Remove the seeds from 1 serrano chilli and finely chop. In a non-metallic bowl, combine the tomatillos, onion, chilli, 4 tbsp chopped fresh coriander, 1 tbsp olive oil, 1 tsp champagne vinegar or white wine vinegar, and ½ tsp fine sea salt. Mix well, then leave aside for 30 minutes to allow the flavours to blend.

Butternut Squash Soup

preparation **20** minutes | cooking **1½** hours | **4–6** servings

Butternut squash soup is velvety in texture, restorative, and delicious. You can also substitute other squash varieties, such as acorn or kabocha, or use pumpkin. Garnish the soup with cumin seeds, toasted for a minute in a dry pan, or top it with mascarpone or whipped cream flavoured with a pinch of cayenne or nutmeg.

tools | large saucepan | baking tray or roasting tin | chef's knife | food processor or blender | ladle | whisk

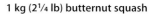

Preheat the oven to 190°C (375°F). Cut the butternut squash in half lengthways and scrape out the seeds and fibrous pulp with a large spoon. Coat the cut surfaces with 1 tbsp of the olive oil and season generously with salt and pepper. Place the halves cut side down in a baking tray or roasting tin and slip 2 sage leaves and 2 garlic cloves under each cavity. Roast the squash for 40–50 minutes or until the flesh is tender to the touch.

Allow the squash to cool completely. Peel off the skin and discard. Chop the flesh coarsely and set aside. Squeeze the roasted garlic from its skins and reserve.

Heat the remaining 2 tbsp olive oil in a large saucepan over a low heat. Add the onions and cook, stirring occasionally, for about 15 minutes or until tender and translucent. Add the butternut squash, roasted garlic, vegetable stock, mace, cloves, and salt and pepper to taste. Whisk until the soup is well mixed. Partly cover and simmer, stirring often, for about 20 minutes.

Remove from the heat and allow to cool slightly. Ladle into a food processor or blender in small batches and process until very smooth. Return the soup to the pan and add warm water to thin, if necessary.

When ready to serve, reheat the soup over a low heat and stir in the cream. Taste and adjust the seasoning with salt. Ladle into warmed bowls and serve with a little cream on top of each serving, if you like. Serve at once.

> **butternut squash purée** Follow the instructions above to roast a butternut squash. When cool enough to handle, scoop the squash flesh from the skin and purée using a food mill or potato ricer. Reheat the purée in a saucepan and add 60 g (2 oz) butter. Season with salt and pepper to taste. Serve with brined pork chops (page 105).

1 kg (2¼ lb) butternut squash

3 tbsp olive oil

Fine sea salt and pepper

4 fresh sage leaves

4 small unpeeled cloves garlic

2 large onions, diced

1 litre (1¾ pints) vegetable stock (page 216) or water

½ tsp ground mace

¼ tsp ground cloves

120 ml (4 fl oz) double cream, plus extra to garnish (optional)

Minestrone Thickened with Bread

preparation **30** minutes | cooking **1½–2** hours | **6** servings

Many traditional Italian dishes, like this one, are vehicles for using up stale bread, which comes in handy because a fresh-baked loaf doesn't keep long. Here, toasted day-old bread absorbs flavourful liquid and thickens this substantial soup, which makes a hearty meal in autumn or winter.

tools | medium and large saucepans | baking sheet | chef's knife | serrated bread knife | ladle | box grater or vegetable peeler

1 loaf day-old pugliese or other country-style bread

5 tbsp extra virgin olive oil, plus oil for drizzling

Fine sea salt and pepper

500 g (1 lb 2 oz) fresh borlotti, cannellini, or flageolet beans, or 1 can (about 400 g) cannellini beans

2 small onions, diced

3 thin slices pancetta or streaky bacon

1 bay leaf

1 tsp chopped fresh sage

3 sticks celery, diced

2 carrots, peeled and diced

1 small bulb fennel, diced

4 cloves garlic, thinly sliced

1 bunch kale or other hearty greens, coarsely chopped

6 drained canned plum tomatoes

85 g (3 oz) Savoy cabbage, sliced

1.5 litres (2¾ pints) chicken stock (page 216) or water, or as needed

Parmesan cheese to garnish

Preheat the oven to 180°C (350°F). Cut the crust off the bread and tear the bread into bite-sized pieces. Toss the bread pieces with 3 tbsp of the olive oil and salt to taste until evenly coated, spread on a baking sheet, and bake for 10–12 minutes or until lightly golden.

If using fresh beans, pod them and put them in a medium saucepan. Add water to cover by 5 cm (2 inches), a little olive oil, and salt to taste. Simmer over a low heat for about 30 minutes or until the beans are soft but not falling apart. Set them aside in their cooking liquid. If using canned beans, rinse and drain.

Heat the remaining 2 tbsp olive oil in a large saucepan over a moderately low heat. Add the onions, pancetta, bay leaf, and sage and sauté for about 10 minutes or until the pancetta and onions soften slightly. Stir in the celery, carrots, fennel, and garlic. Add the kale, tomatoes, and cabbage and sauté the vegetables for 3–4 minutes or until softened. Season with salt. Add the stock, increase the heat to high, and bring to the boil. Reduce the heat to low and simmer for about 40 minutes or until all the vegetables are tender.

Add the beans and half of their cooking liquid, or 250 ml (8 fl oz) water if using canned beans. Simmer for a further 10 minutes. Add the toasted bread and stir, then cover and continue to simmer for about 15 minutes or until the bread absorbs the liquid and melts into the soup. If the soup is too thick, thin with water, stock, or additional bean cooking liquid.

To serve, ladle the soup into warmed bowls and garnish each bowl with grated or shaved Parmesan, a drizzle of olive oil, and a grinding of pepper.

Sweetcorn Soup

preparation **10** minutes | cooking **40** minutes | **6** servings

Sweetcorn is inherently a little starchy, so it gives both flavour and body to this simple soup. Try to buy recently picked sweetcorn for the sweetest flavour.

tools | large saucepan | baking sheet | chef's knife | bread knife | blender | ladle | sieve

Preheat the oven to 190°C (375°F). Melt 30 g (1 oz) of the butter. Cut the bread into 1 cm (½ inch) cubes and toss with the melted butter and a pinch of salt. Spread on a baking sheet and bake for about 10 minutes or until golden.

Heat the olive oil and remaining butter in a large saucepan and add the onions. Sauté over a low heat for about 30 minutes or until the onions are very soft. Add 1 litre (1¾ pints) water, increase the heat to high, and bring to the boil. Reduce the heat to moderate and add the sweetcorn. Simmer for 5 minutes. Season with salt. Remove from the heat. Allow to cool slightly, then purée in a blender, in batches as needed. Pass the soup through a sieve to achieve a uniform smooth texture. Press the solids with the back of a spoon to extract as much liquid as possible. Reheat gently, stirring, then taste and adjust the seasoning. Ladle into warmed bowls and garnish each serving with the croûtons and a dollop of crème fraîche.

4 slices day-old sourdough bread

75 g (2½ oz) butter

Fine sea salt

3 tbsp olive oil

2 large onions, coarsely chopped

Kernels cut from 8 cobs sweetcorn

4 tbsp crème fraîche or soured cream

French Onion Soup

preparation **20** minutes | cooking **1** hour | **6–8** servings

On a cold winter's night, nothing is more satisfying than soup made from onions slowly cooked until caramelized and fortified with bread and melted cheese.

tools | large saucepan | chef's knife | serrated bread knife | box grater | ladle | kitchen string

Melt the butter in a large saucepan over a moderately low heat. Add the onions and cook, stirring occasionally, for about 15 minutes or until softened but not browned. The onions will exude their moisture and then reabsorb it. Season the onions liberally with salt and pepper. Continue to cook for 10 minutes or until the onions start to caramelize slightly.

Add the sherry, beef and chicken stocks, and thyme. Reduce the heat to low and simmer, partly covered, for 20–30 minutes or until the onions are very tender. Taste and adjust the seasoning with salt and pepper.

Preheat the grill. Ladle the soup into individual flameproof soup bowls. Place 2 slices of bread on top of each bowl and sprinkle evenly with the cheese. Slide under the grill and grill for 3–4 minutes or until the cheese is bubbly and lightly browned. Serve at once.

45 g (1½ oz) butter

4 large onions, thinly sliced

Fine sea salt and pepper

2½ tbsp cream sherry

1 litre (1¾ pints) beef stock

1 litre (1¾ pints) chicken stock

6 sprigs fresh thyme, tied in a bundle

12–16 slices baguette, 5 mm (¼ inch) thick, toasted

85 g (3 oz) Gruyère cheese, grated

Tossed Green Salad

preparation **10** minutes | **4** servings

Rather than buying bagged salad mixes, assemble your own blend of greens, balancing different flavours and textures to suit the season and your taste. To allow the flavour of the greens to shine through, dress them simply with fruity olive oil, a hint of vinegar, salt, and pepper. Spin or pat the the greens completely dry to avoid diluting the vinaigrette.

tools | salad spinner

FOR AUTUMN AND WINTER SALADS

1 small bunch watercress, stalks discarded

1 large handful rocket leaves

2 heads chicory, 1 medium or 2 small heads frisée, or 1 small head radicchio

1 bunch fresh chervil (optional), stalks discarded

FOR SPRING AND SUMMER SALADS

350 g (12 oz) mixed lettuces and other salad greens and herbs, such as cos lettuce, Oak Leaf lettuce, dandelion greens, lamb's lettuce, chervil, and/or butterhead lettuce

Basic vinaigrette (page 212)

Separate any heads of lettuce, chicory, and radicchio into individual leaves. Swish all the greens in a large bowl of cold water. Lift the greens out, allowing the dirt to settle to the bottom of the bowl, and spin dry in a salad spinner, then place the greens between layers of kitchen paper to dry completely.

Combine all the greens in a large bowl, cover, and keep in the fridge until needed, or roll up the greens in the kitchen paper, place in plastic bags, and chill.

Just before serving, tear the greens into bite-sized pieces as necessary and put them in a serving bowl. Pour some of the vinaigrette over the greens and toss gently, using your hands, which are the best tools for gently coating the leaves without damaging them. Taste the greens; they may need a pinch of salt or more vinaigrette, but do not overdress. Serve at once.

Panzanella

preparation **15** minutes | cooking **10** minutes | resting **30** minutes | **8** servings

Here, rustic bread meets juicy tomatoes and aromatic vegetables for simple summertime pleasure. Make this a few hours in advance for a slightly softer texture.

tools | baking sheet | chef's knife | serrated bread knife

Preheat the oven to 230°C (450°F). Cut the crust off the bread and tear the bread into bite-sized pieces. Arrange in a single layer on a baking sheet and toast in the oven for about 10 minutes or until the bread is crisp and golden. Core the tomatoes and cut into wedges. Put the toasted bread in a large bowl, add the tomatoes, and toss together. Set aside for 30 minutes or up to 3 hours.

Meanwhile, combine the celery and onions in a bowl and season with 1 tsp salt, which will draw moisture from the vegetables and tenderize them.

Drain the excess moisture from the celery mixture, then add to the tomato and bread mixture. Add the basil, tearing the leaves into pieces. Add 6 tbsp olive oil, 3 tbsp vinegar, the capers, and several grindings of pepper and toss well. Taste and adjust the seasoning, adding more oil, vinegar, pepper, or salt to taste.

500 g (1 lb 2 oz) country-style bread, preferably stale

750 g (1 lb 10 oz) ripe tomatoes

500 g (1 lb 2 oz) celery, finely diced

500 g (1 lb 2 oz) red or large yellow onions, thinly sliced

Fine sea salt and pepper

15 g (½ oz) fresh basil leaves

Extra virgin olive oil

Red wine vinegar

3 tbsp capers, rinsed and chopped

Winter Chicory and Apple Salad

preparation **15** minutes | cooking **7** minutes | **4** servings

Your bowl of salad will brighten a winter meal with a beautiful mixture of colours. The creamy white dressing that lightly coats it also makes a great dip for raw vegetables.

tools | baking sheet | chef's knife | paring knife | salad spinner | whisk

Preheat the oven to 180°C (350°F). Spread the pecans on a baking sheet and toast in the oven for about 7 minutes or until fragrant. Coarsely chop and set aside.

Combine the cream and 1 tbsp vinegar in a serving bowl and whisk lightly. Crumble in the cheese. Add 1 tsp salt and pepper to taste and whisk until the dressing is smooth. Taste and adjust the seasoning with additional vinegar, salt, or pepper if necessary. The dressing should taste fairly bold to complement the bitter salad leaves. Tear the leaves into bite-sized pieces, discarding any wilted outer leaves, and add to the bowl. Sprinkle with salt, then toss with the dressing.

Peel the apple if you like, then core and slice. Add the slices to the salad, tossing gently. Arrange the dressed salad on chilled plates. Sprinkle each salad with the toasted pecans and serve at once.

30 g (1 oz) pecan nuts

6 tbsp double cream

Cider vinegar

85 g (3 oz) Roquefort cheese

Fine sea salt and pepper

500 g (1 lb 2 oz) mixed radicchio, hearts of escarole, and frisée

1 Gala or Fuji apple

Smoked Trout and Grapefruit Salad

preparation **15** minutes | **6** servings

Though they may seem an unlikely combination, the ingredients in this salad marry harmoniously. Serve for brunch with toasted bagels, radishes (page 62), and fluffy scrambled eggs.

tools | chef's knife | whisk

2 ruby grapefruits

1 tbsp champagne vinegar

1 tbsp finely chopped shallot

3 tbsp crème fraîche or soured cream

2 tbsp extra virgin olive oil

Fine sea salt and pepper

4 large heads chicory

2 Hass avocados, diced (page 53)

500 g (1 lb 2 oz) smoked trout fillets, skinned

Cut the peel off the grapefruits with a chef's knife and cut out the segments over a bowl to catch the juices (page 233). Transfer the segments to a plate. Squeeze the membranes over the bowl to extract any extra grapefruit juice. Stir in the vinegar and shallot, then whisk in the crème fraîche and olive oil. Season the dressing with salt and pepper to taste and pour into a small jug.

Trim the end from the chicory and separate into individual leaves. Arrange the leaves on a large platter. Nestle in the grapefruit sections, alternating with the diced avocado and pieces of smoked trout, flaked by hand into bite-sized pieces. Assemble this salad freely like a mosaic, but aim to offer a taste of all the ingredients with each bite. Serve with the dressing.

Tomato, Mozzarella, and Basil Salad

preparation **10** minutes | **4–6** servings

This simple salad relies on two perfect allies: ripe, juicy summer tomatoes and sweet fresh mozzarella. Use your best extra virgin olive oil here, since its flavour will shine. If your local tomatoes are good, you may find yourselves eating this every day all summer.

tools | chef's knife | serrated small knife

8 very ripe red or gold tomatoes

500 g (1 lb 2 oz) fresh mozzarella cheese (*mozzarella di bufala*)

15 g (½ oz) fresh basil leaves

4 tbsp best-quality extra virgin olive oil

Fine sea salt and ground pepper

Slice the tomatoes 5 mm (¼ inch) thick with a serrated knife. Slice the mozzarella into thin slices.

On a serving platter, arrange overlapping slices of tomato and mozzarella in an alternating pattern. Garnish the platter generously with basil leaves, tucking some underneath the tomatoes. Drizzle the olive oil over everything and sprinkle generously with salt and pepper. Serve at once.

Frisée with Lardons and Poached Egg

preparation **10** minutes | cooking **15** minutes | **4** servings

This classic French bistro salad is too good, simple, and satisfying not to become a staple at home. Frisée is a bitter-flavoured salad green, also called curly endive, and lardons *are small pieces of bacon. Here we offer a slight variation on the classic, adding a touch of reduced balsamic vinegar to enhance the poached egg on top.*

tools | small saucepan | small and large sauté pans | chef's knife | paring knife | salad spinner | slotted spoon | whisk

Pat the frisée leaves dry and tear into bite-sized pieces, if you like. Put them in a medium bowl.

In a small bowl, combine the shallot with the sherry vinegar, a good pinch of salt, and a few grindings of pepper. Set aside to "pickle" for 10 minutes. Drizzle in the olive oil while whisking, to make a vinaigrette. Taste and adjust the seasoning with salt and pepper.

Put the bacon in a sauté pan over a moderate heat and fry for about 5 minutes or until crisp. Using a slotted spoon, transfer the bacon to the bowl with the frisée. (If you like, add a little of the bacon fat to the frisée to enhance the flavour of the salad.) Add the vinaigrette and toss the salad to combine all the ingredients. Taste and add a pinch of salt, if necessary. Divide the salad among serving plates.

Put the balsamic vinegar in a small saucepan over a moderate heat. Simmer for 3–4 minutes or until reduced by half. Set aside.

Meanwhile, poach the eggs. Put 5–7.5 cm (2–3 inches) of water in a large sauté pan. Season the water with salt and bring to a simmer over a moderate heat. One at a time, and working quickly, break each egg into a small ramekin and carefully slip it into the water. Leave space around the eggs. Adjust the heat so that the water barely simmers. Poach the eggs gently for 3–5 minutes, depending on how you like them cooked. Remove each egg from the water with a slotted spoon. While the egg is still in the spoon, blot the base dry with a tea towel and trim off the ragged edges with a paring knife.

Gently place an egg on each salad. Drizzle an equal amount of the balsamic reduction over each salad and serve at once.

2 heads of frisée, leaves separated

1 small shallot, finely chopped

2 tbsp sherry vinegar or red wine vinegar

Fine sea salt and pepper

120 ml (4 fl oz) extra virgin olive oil

4 thick rashers streaky bacon, cut into 1 cm (½ inch) pieces

4 tbsp balsamic vinegar

4 eggs

Caesar Salad with Garlic Croûtons

preparation **20** minutes | cooking **12** minutes | **4** servings

A Caesar salad is hearty enough to constitute a lunch by itself, especially when served with warm fresh bread. Though you'll often see chicken and other items thrown into this classic salad, we like the traditional version. Since this recipe uses so few ingredients, don't skimp on the quality: this is the time to use your very best olive oil and well-aged Parmesan cheese. Look for hearts of romaine in the supermarket. You can also use cos lettuce, removing the outer leaves to reach the tender inner leaves.

tools | baking sheet | chef's knife | box grater | citrus reamer | salad spinner | vegetable peeler | whisk

2 hearts romaine lettuce, about 250 g (9 oz) each, leaves separated and cut into bite-sized pieces

Garlic croûtons (*see right*)

A hunk of good Parmesan cheese for shaving

FOR THE DRESSING

1 egg

2 tbsp fresh lemon juice

½ tsp Worcestershire sauce

1 tsp red wine vinegar

1½ tbsp chopped anchovy fillets

1 small clove garlic, finely chopped

120 ml (4 fl oz) extra virgin olive oil

60 g (2 oz) Parmesan cheese, freshly grated

Fine sea salt and ground pepper

To make the dressing, break the egg into a small bowl. Add the lemon juice, Worcestershire sauce, vinegar, anchovies, and garlic and whisk to combine well. Gradually whisk in the olive oil. Stir in the grated cheese. Season to taste with salt and pepper.

In a large bowl, combine the lettuce, croûtons, and dressing and toss well. Divide the salad among 4 chilled plates. Using a vegetable peeler, shave thin curls of Parmesan over each salad. Serve at once.

Note: This recipe includes uncooked egg. For more information, see page 226.

garlic croûtons These croûtons are torn instead of cubed for a more homely, rustic look. Preheat the oven to 180°C (350°F). In a small bowl, whisk together 2 tbsp extra virgin olive oil and 1 large clove garlic, finely chopped. Tear ¼ loaf of day-old rustic sourdough or French bread into about 20 bite-sized pieces and toss in a large bowl with the garlic oil and a pinch of fine sea salt. Spread the pieces on a baking sheet in a single layer. Toast in the oven, stirring occasionally, for 9–12 minutes or until the pieces are golden brown. Allow to cool completely before using.

Salade Niçoise

preparation **30** minutes | cooking **15** minutes | **2** servings

"Niçoise" refers to the cooking style of the city of Nice; dishes with this name typically include tomato, garlic, anchovies, and the famous purple-black, briny olives from the south of France. Make sure that each ingredient is of the best quality and appealing, and you will have a simple and sparkling brunch, lunch, or light summer supper.

tools | large saucepan | chef's knife | paring knife | salad spinner | slotted spoon | whisk

Bring a large saucepan of salted water to the boil. Add the potatoes and cook for about 10 minutes or just until tender. Scoop the potatoes out with a slotted spoon and set aside to drain and cool. Add the French beans to the boiling water and cook for 3–5 minutes or until tender but firm. Drain, rinse with cold running water, and leave to cool.

Use a paring knife to peel the potatoes and cut them into wedges. Combine the potatoes in a mixing bowl with the French beans, tomatoes, and olives. Season with salt and toss with a few tablespoons of the vinaigrette. Break the tuna into bite-sized pieces into a separate small bowl. Lightly season with salt and pepper and toss with a few teaspoons of the vinaigrette. In another bowl, toss the salad greens with some of the remaining vinaigrette to taste.

Divide the salad greens between serving plates. Tuck the vegetables in and around the greens, then scatter over the tuna. Cut the anchovy fillets into thin strips and arrange on top of the salad. Moisten the salads with more vinaigrette, if necessary. Garnish with the eggs, tucking the wedges into each salad. Serve at once.

> **stoning olives** To stone a quantity of olives quickly, put them in a plastic bag and crush with a pan. This will expose the stones and make them easier to cut out.

6 small new potatoes

1 handful French beans

2 small ripe tomatoes, diced and lightly salted

15 Niçoise olives, rinsed and stoned

Fine sea salt and pepper

Basic vinaigrette (page 212)

1 can (about 200 g) good-quality tuna, packed in olive oil or spring water, drained

1 handful mixed salad greens, 75–90g (2½–3 oz)

Anchovy fillets, rinsed in cold water and patted dry

2 hard-boiled eggs (page 214), peeled and cut into wedges

Roast Beetroot and Feta Salad

preparation **10** minutes | cooking **1** hour | **4** servings

Vegetable salads are a colourful way to begin a meal. Here, roast beetroot contributes substance, richness, and texture to tender salad greens. Substitute lamb's lettuce for the butterhead lettuce, or try crisp, mildly bitter chicory.

tools | baking dish | chef's knife | paring knife | salad spinner | whisk

1 tbsp sherry vinegar

1 tbsp red wine vinegar

4 tbsp extra virgin olive oil

Fine sea salt and freshly ground pepper

1 small butterhead lettuce, 250 g (9 oz) lamb's lettuce, or 1 head chicory, patted dry

50 g (1³⁄₄ oz) feta cheese, crumbled

FOR THE BEETROOT

500 g (1 lb 2 oz) small to medium red or gold beetroots

2 tsp red wine vinegar

2 tsp olive oil

Fine sea salt

To prepare the beetroot, preheat the oven to 200°C (400°F). Trim the stalks, leaving about 1 cm (½ inch) intact. Leave the root ends untrimmed. Wash the beetroots thoroughly and put them in a baking dish with enough water to cover the bottom of the dish. Cover the dish with foil and roast for 45–60 minutes or until the beetroots can be easily pierced with a sharp knife. Do not overcook or the beetroots will be mushy. Leave to cool.

Using a small paring knife, trim off the tops and bottoms of the beetroots, then peel away the skins with the knife. Cut the beetroots in half, then into quarters or wedges. Sprinkle the beetroot with the red wine vinegar, olive oil, and a pinch of salt. At this point the beetroot can be kept in the fridge, covered, for several days.

In a non-metallic bowl, whisk together the sherry and red wine vinegars and the extra virgin olive oil, then season with salt and pepper. Taste and adjust the seasoning to your liking.

Separate the lettuce leaves and tear into bite-sized pieces. Toss in a bowl with the vinaigrette to coat thoroughly. Divide the greens among salad plates and nestle the roast beetroot into the greens. Sprinkle the feta evenly over each salad and serve at once, with a pepper mill on the table.

Meat, Poultry, and Seafood

Whether you're serving a midweek supper or a celebratory meal,
the recipes in this chapter will help you answer the eternal question of
what to make for dinner. We find that having a great dish in mind as the
centrepiece for a meal makes it easy to round out the menu — and this
chapter is packed with memorable menus. We share some recipes here
that are family traditions for us — from oven-fried chicken with lots of
garlic to the roast turkey we feast on every Christmas.

Rib-eye Steak with Pan Jus

preparation **5** minutes | cooking **25** minutes | **2** servings

This is a nice way to prepare a rib-eye for two: ask the butcher to cut the steak thick, then sear it, roast it, and thinly slice it to serve. The pan juices are used to create a rich yet simple sauce to accompany the meat. Serve this with mashed potatoes (page 178) and a tossed green salad (page 82).

tools | ovenproof sauté pan | chef's knife | tongs | wooden spatula

1 rib-eye steak, cut about 4 cm (1½ inches) thick, about 500 g (1 lb 2 oz)

Fine sea salt and pepper

1 sprig fresh rosemary

1 tbsp olive oil

4 tbsp dry red wine

120 ml (4 fl oz) beef or chicken stock (page 216 or 217)

2 small sprigs fresh thyme

Preheat the oven to 200°C (400°F). Season the steak liberally with salt and pepper. Pick the rosemary leaves from the stalk and press them into the steak. Heat the olive oil in an ovenproof sauté pan over a moderately high heat. When the oil is quite hot, but before it starts to smoke, add the steak and sear and brown on one side for about 1 minute. Turn the steak over to sear the other side for 1 minute. Use tongs to hold the steak upright and sear the sides for 1 minute per side.

Place the pan with the steak in the oven and roast for 10–12 minutes for medium-rare, or until it is cooked to your liking (see page 225). Press the centre of the steak to gauge this; it will still have some give for medium-rare and feel more firm for medium. Remove the pan from the oven and transfer the meat to a carving board. Leave to rest for 10 minutes.

Meanwhile, add the wine, stock, and thyme to the drippings in the pan and place over a moderately high heat. (Be careful not to burn yourself on the hot pan.) Deglaze the pan by stirring with a wooden spatula and loosening any caramelized bits stuck to the bottom. Simmer until reduced by half. Taste and adjust the seasoning with salt and pepper. Remove the thyme sprigs.

Using a chef's knife, carve the steak across the grain into thin slices. Arrange the slices on warmed plates and spoon the pan juices over the top.

Note: This is a large portion of steak for 2 people, but using a big, thick piece makes for better end results – wide, perfectly cooked slices still rare in the centre. Save any leftover steak to use in breakfast hash (page 47). Keep in the fridge for up to 3 days, or wrap well and freeze for up to 1 month.

Barbecued T-bone with Garlic Butter

preparation **15** minutes | cooking **12** minutes | resting **5** minutes | **4** servings

On a summer night when when you are hosting an intimate gathering for close friends, barbecuing sets a relaxed mood. Thick T-bone steaks cook up succulent and juicy, and they taste especially savoury when they absorb charcoal or wood smoke flavours. Serve with Tuscan farro (page 190), or accompany with handfuls of fresh rocket leaves placed underneath each steak. The juices from the steak will provide all the dressing the rocket needs. To serve two, simply cut the recipe in half.

tools | barbecue | tongs

Make the garlic butter.

Season the steaks by rubbing them with the olive oil, thyme, salt, and pepper to taste. Prepare a charcoal fire in the barbecue (page 228). When the coals are ready, they will have burned down to glowing embers covered with grey ash. Place the steaks on the barbecue grill and cook for 5–6 minutes on each side for medium-rare, or until they are cooked to your taste (see page 225). Press the centre of a steak to gauge this; it will still have some give for medium-rare or be more firm for medium. Remove the steaks from the barbecue and place them on a platter.

Place a knob or two of garlic butter on each steak and sprinkle over the parsley. Allow to rest for 3–5 minutes, then serve.

Garlic butter (*see below*)

4 T-bone steaks, 300 g (10 oz) each

2 tbsp extra virgin olive oil

Leaves from 3 sprigs fresh thyme

¾ tsp fine sea salt

Freshly ground pepper

2 tbsp chopped fresh parsley

> **garlic butter** Topping a steak with garlic butter is a quick way to add delicious flavour. Allow 125 g (4½ oz) salted butter to come to room temperature. Use a fork to blend in 1 tbsp finely chopped fresh thyme, 4 cloves garlic, minced, 1–2 dashes of Worcestershire sauce, and 1–2 dashes of Tabasco sauce. Roll into a log in greaseproof paper and chill.

Roast Beef with Yorkshire Pudding

seasoning **12** hours | preparation **10** minutes | cooking **2** hours | **8** servings

This is the perfect recipe for the first Sunday lunch you host as a married couple. It's impressive, but it's also extremely easy to prepare. The Yorkshire pudding uses dripping from the meat, so it needs to be prepared while the joint is resting. You may want to make two Yorkshire puddings, because you can never have enough!

tools | 23 cm (9 inch) baking tin | large roasting tin | brush | fine-mesh sieve | instant-read thermometer | carving knife and fork | whisk | wooden spoon

FOR THE ROAST BEEF

2.5 kg (5½ lb) beef rib joint

1¼ tsp fine sea salt

Freshly ground pepper

FOR THE YORKSHIRE PUDDING

2 eggs

300 ml (10 fl oz) milk

140 g (5 oz) flour

pinch of fine sea salt

One day before serving, season the joint with the salt and pepper to taste. Cover and return to the fridge. The next day, 1–2 hours before roasting, remove the joint from the fridge so it can come to room temperature.

Preheat the oven to 220°C (425°F). Set the beef in a large roasting tin and place in the oven. Roast for 15 minutes, then lower the heat to 190°C (375°F). Continue roasting, basting the meat frequently with the pan juices, for about 1¼ hours or until an instant-read thermometer inserted into the centre of the joint away from the bone registers 57°C (135°F) for medium-rare. (The temperature of the meat will continue to rise after it is removed from the oven.)

Transfer the beef to a carving board and leave to rest, loosely covered with foil, for 30 minutes. This allows time for the juices to be redistributed evenly throughout the meat and makes carving easier. Reserve the roasting tin with the brown sediments and keep the oven on.

While the beef is resting, make the Yorkshire pudding. Place a 23 cm (9 inch) baking tin in the oven to heat. Meanwhile, in a bowl, whisk the eggs and milk together until blended. Add the flour a little at a time, whisking constantly until smooth. The batter should have the consistency of double cream. Add the salt. Remove the baking tin from the oven and add 2 tbsp of the beef dripping from the roasting tin. (Tilt the roasting tin and spoon off the clear fat from the brown sediments.) Pour the batter into the baking tin and return to the oven. Bake for about 25 minutes or until the pudding is puffy and crisp.

To serve, carve the beef into 5 mm (¼ inch) slices, cutting close to the bones. Cut the Yorkshire pudding into wedges and serve at once with the beef.

beef jus While the Yorkshire pudding bakes, you can make a beef jus with the brown sediments left in the roasting tin. Skim off any excess clear dripping, then add 500 ml (16 fl oz) chicken stock (page 216) to the tin. Place the tin over a moderate heat and deglaze by stirring and loosening any caramelized bits stuck to the bottom of the tin using a wooden spatula. Cook for about 4 minutes, stirring constantly. Strain the jus through a fine-mesh sieve. Keep warm until serving.

Beef Daube

preparation **20** minutes | cooking **3** hours **40** minutes | **4–6** servings

In this version of daube, a traditional French stew, we use white wine for a lighter touch, and add tomatoes and Dijon mustard for a Provençal accent. To finish the dish, we whisk in a little crème fraîche to add body and sweetness. Serve with warm buttered noodles such as fettuccine or pappardelle. This dish tastes even better the next day.

tools | flameproof casserole | chef's knife | wooden spatula | slotted spoon | kitchen string | tongs | whisk

Season the beef liberally with salt and pepper. In a flameproof casserole with a tight-fitting lid, heat the olive oil over a moderate heat. In several small batches to avoid crowding, brown the pieces of beef on all sides. Watch carefully and adjust the heat if necessary to avoid scorching the meat. With tongs, remove each batch as it is browned and set aside on a platter. Don't rush this step: browning the meat well all over imparts flavour to the stew.

Preheat the oven to 150°C (300°F). Pour off and discard any excess fat left in the casserole, leaving only a thin film. While the pot is off the heat (to avoid flare-ups), add the brandy and wine to it. Return to a moderate heat and deglaze by stirring and scraping with a wooden spatula to loosen any caramelized bits from the pot. Bring the liquid to a simmer, then simmer for about 8 minutes to evaporate most of the alcohol. Whisk in the mustard until thoroughly blended.

Add the browned beef and any juices that have accumulated on the platter, the tomatoes with their liquid, the onions, and the garlic. Tie the thyme, tarragon, and savory tightly together with kitchen string and add to the pot. Cover the pot and transfer to the oven. Braise for 2½–3 hours or until the meat is tender. Remove and discard the bundle of herbs. (The daube can be prepared to this point up to 2 days in advance.)

Using a slotted spoon, transfer the beef, tomatoes, and onions to a platter. Bring the liquid to the boil over a high heat and cook for 8–10 minutes or until reduced by about one-third. Stir in the crème fraîche until blended. Taste and adjust the seasoning, then return the beef, tomatoes, and onions to the sauce to heat through. Spoon into warmed bowls to serve.

beef for braising The best beef for braising and stewing contains plenty of fat and connective tissue, which contribute flavour and keep the meat succulent during its long cooking time. Topside is often braised, but it is very lean and so can become dry and chewy with lengthy simmering. For this dish, it is better to use chuck or blade from the shoulder or brisket. Buy a large piece and ask the butcher to cut it into 5 cm (2 inch) pieces for you, or do this yourself at home.

---

1 kg (2¼ lb) boneless braising beef such as beef chuck or brisket, cut into 5 cm (2 inch) pieces

Fine sea salt and pepper

3 tbsp olive oil

4 tbsp brandy

1 bottle (750 ml) dry white wine

2 tbsp Dijon mustard

1 can (about 400 g) plum tomatoes

3 small onions, thinly sliced

6 cloves garlic, lightly crushed

3 sprigs fresh thyme

3 sprigs fresh tarragon

2 sprigs fresh winter or summer savory

5 tbsp crème fraîche or 4 tbsp soured cream

Osso Buco

preparation **30** minutes | cooking **2** hours **40** minutes | **4** servings

Osso buco, which literally means "bone with a hole", refers to the thick round slices of veal shin that are braised with aromatic vegetables. The highlight of this wintertime feast is scooping out the flavourful bone marrow lodged in the centre of each slice – considered a delicacy by the Italians. Serve with orzo or risotto (page 149).

tools | ovenproof sauté pan with tight-fitting lid | large baking sheet | chef's knife | citrus reamer | wooden spatula | kitchen string | tongs

115 g (4 oz) flour

Fine sea salt

½ tsp freshly ground pepper

4 centre-cut slices veal shin, each about 4 cm (1½ inches) thick, tied around the middle with kitchen string

5 tbsp olive oil

1 small onion, finely diced

1 large carrot, peeled and finely diced

2 small to medium sticks celery, finely diced

3–4 cloves garlic, finely chopped

2 bay leaves

175 ml (6 fl oz) white wine

250 ml (8 fl oz) beef stock (page 217), or more as needed

2 cans (about 400 g each) chopped plum tomatoes, drained

2 tsp chopped orange zest

2 sprigs fresh thyme

1 small sprig fresh rosemary

Orange *gremolata* to serve (see right)

Preheat the oven to 180°C (350°F). Combine the flour with ¼ teaspoon salt and the pepper and spread on a plate. Dredge the veal slices in the flour mixture, turning them to coat evenly. Shake off the excess flour. Select a heavy, ovenproof sauté pan with a tight-fitting lid large enough to hold the veal slices in a single layer and heat 3 tbsp of the olive oil over a high heat. When the oil is hot, place the veal in the pan and brown evenly for about 3 minutes on each side. Using tongs, transfer the veal to a plate and set aside.

Without cleaning the pan, add the remaining 2 tbsp olive oil. When the oil is hot, add the onion, carrot, celery, garlic, bay leaves, and a pinch of salt. Cook, stirring occasionally, for about 8 minutes or until the onion is golden; watch carefully to avoid burning the vegetables. Add the wine and deglaze the pan by stirring and scraping with a wooden spatula to loosen any caramelized bits on the bottom. Add the stock and cook for about 5 minutes or until reduced by half. Add the tomatoes, orange zest, thyme, and rosemary. Cook, stirring occasionally, for 5 minutes. Season with ½ tsp salt.

Return the veal slices to the pan. The tomato mixture should come about two-thirds of the way up the slices. If it doesn't, add a little more beef stock or water. Cover the pan with the lid and place in the oven on a large baking sheet. Braise for 2 hours, turning the slices every 30 minutes to ensure that they cook evenly. Add extra stock or water if the liquid in the pan is getting too low or too thick. When the veal is done, the meat should be extremely tender and be falling away from the bone. Remove from the oven and place the veal slices on a large platter; keep warm. Remove and discard the bay leaves from the pan, then place over a moderate heat and simmer for 10 minutes or until the liquid is reduced to a saucelike consistency – it should have a velvety texture, but not be too thick. Taste and adjust the seasoning with salt and pepper. To serve, spoon the sauce over the warm veal slices and sprinkle with orange *gremolata*.

orange gremolata   To make this variation on the traditional lemon and parsley accompaniment to osso buco, combine 2 tbsp chopped fresh parsley, 1 tsp finely chopped garlic, and 2 tsp chopped orange zest in a bowl and mix well.

Rack of Lamb with Mustard and Herbs

preparation **10** minutes | cooking **30** minutes | resting **10** minutes | **6–8** servings

Rack of lamb is another name for best end of neck. When the rack is seared in a pan and then roasted in the oven, the meat stays juicy and succulent. Carve the rack into cutlets to serve. To make carving easy, ask the butcher to chine the joint for you and to remove all but a thin layer of fat from each rack. This is a good dish for a celebratory meal.

tools | large sauté pan | large baking dish | chef's knife | instant-read thermometer | tongs | brush (optional)

Preheat the oven to 200°C (400°F). Season the lamb with salt and pepper. Heat the olive oil in a large sauté pan over a moderately high heat. Sear the lamb, one joint at a time, browning on each side (about 2½ minutes per side). Using tongs, hold each rack upright and sear the ends for about 20 seconds each. The racks should look golden all over. Transfer them to a baking dish that will hold them side by side, placing them meaty side up.

Stir together the breadcrumbs, garlic, thyme, rosemary, and melted butter in a bowl. Season with a pinch of salt and mix well. Brush or smear the seared lamb thoroughly with a thin layer of mustard. Sprinkle the breadcrumb mixture over the mustard, gently pressing it onto the lamb so that it adheres.

Roast the lamb for 20–30 minutes or until an instant-read thermometer inserted into the centre of the meat but not touching bone registers 49°C (120°F) for rare, or 54°C (130°F) for medium-rare. (The temperature of the meat will continue to rise after it is removed from the oven.) Transfer the lamb to a carving board or serving platter. Allow to rest for 10 minutes to allow the juices to be redistributed before slicing into cutlets and serving.

2 racks of lamb, each with 8 cutlet bones, about 750 g (1 lb 10 oz) each, trimmed of all but a thin layer of fat

Fine sea salt and freshly ground pepper

1 tbsp olive oil

45 g (1½ oz) fine fresh breadcrumbs (page 215)

1 clove garlic, finely chopped

1 tsp chopped fresh thyme

½ tsp chopped fresh rosemary

30 g (1 oz) butter, melted

3 Tbsp Dijon mustard

Provençal Roast Leg of Lamb

preparation **10** minutes | cooking **1** hour **35** minutes | resting **20** minutes | **6–8** servings

Rosemary, thyme, and bay leaves grow wild in the south of France. In this recipe, we use these herbs, along with a generous amount of garlic, to infuse the fragrances of Provence into a leg of lamb as it roasts. If time permits, season the lamb the day before cooking it. Serve with soft or grilled polenta (page 186) or rosemary roasted potatoes (page 177).

tools | roasting tin | small roasting rack | chef's knife | fine-mesh sieve | wooden spatula | instant-read thermometer

1 leg of lamb, 3–3.5 kg (6–8 lb), boned, trimmed, rolled, and tied

Fine sea salt and pepper

4 tbsp extra virgin olive oil

1 small bunch fresh rosemary

1 small bunch fresh thyme

6 heads garlic

2 bay leaves

Remove the lamb from the refrigerator up to 2 hours before cooking to bring it to room temperature (this ensures even roasting). Preheat the oven to 220°C (425°F). Season the lamb generously with 1 tsp salt and pepper to taste and rub with 3 tbsp of the olive oil. Pick a few of the leaves from the rosemary and thyme sprigs and rub them into the lamb.

Trim off the top one-third of each head of garlic with a sharp chef's knife. Place the garlic heads in a roasting tin with the remaining rosemary and thyme leaves, and the bay leaves. Drizzle the remaining 1 tbsp olive oil over the garlic. Nestle a small rack on top of the herbs and garlic and place the lamb on the rack.

Roast the lamb for 20 minutes, then reduce the oven temperature to 180°C (350°F). Continue roasting, turning occasionally, for about 1¼ hours or until an instant-read thermometer inserted into the thickest part of the lamb registers 49°C (120°F) for rare or 54°C (130°F) for medium-rare. (The temperature will continue to rise.) Cooking time is about 15 minutes per 450 g (1 lb). Transfer the lamb to a platter and leave it to rest for 20 minutes.

Carve the meat thinly and serve with the roasted garlic, which will be mellow in flavour and softened. Encourage your guests to squeeze the softened garlic out of its skin and spread it on the lamb.

> **lamb jus** To create a simple sauce to serve with the lamb, remove the garlic and herbs from the roasting tin and spoon off the excess clear fat from the brown sediment. Place the tin over a moderately low heat and add 250 ml (8 fl oz) chicken stock (page 216), 2 tbsp water, and 2 tbsp dry white wine. Deglaze the roasting tin by stirring and loosening any caramelized bits stuck to the bottom using a wooden spatula. Cook for about 5 minutes. Strain the jus through a fine-mesh sieve. Keep warm until serving.

Brined Pork Chops

preparation **10** minutes | cooking **12** minutes | **2** servings

Pork has been bred to be so lean nowadays that it tends to dry out easily during cooking. Soaking pork in brine is our secret weapon for juicy chops. It's also better to buy thicker chops as they are less likely to dry out during cooking as thinner, boneless ones. Put the chops in the brine in the morning, and you'll have a quick dinner ready to go at the end of the day. Serve with braised fennel (page 167) or butternut squash purée (page 77).

tools | cast-iron frying pan | large bowl

To make the brine, combine the sugar and salt with 1 litre (1¾ pints) cold water in a large bowl and stir to dissolve. Add the thyme leaves, bay leaf, peppercorns, cloves, and chilli flakes.

Place the pork chops in the brine. Cover and leave in the refrigerator, turning occasionally, for at least 8 hours but no longer than 2 days.

When ready to cook, lift the chops out of the brine and pat dry thoroughly with kitchen paper. Heat the olive oil in a cast-iron frying pan. Add the chops and cook over a moderate heat for about 8 minutes or until brown on one side.

Turn the chops over and cook the other side for about 4 minutes or until just cooked through. Press the centre of a chop to gauge this; it should still have some give for medium-rare chops that are juicy in the middle. Leave the chops to rest for a minute or two, then serve.

Note: If thick chops aren't available, reduce the cooking time by a few minutes.

2 centre-cut pork loin chops,
4 cm (1½ inches) thick

2 tbsp olive oil

FOR THE BRINE

60 g (2 oz) sugar

2½ tsp fine sea salt

½ tsp fresh thyme leaves

1 bay leaf

6 black peppercorns

4 whole cloves

Good pinch of dried chilli flakes

Roast Pork Loin with Apricots

seasoning **6** hours | preparation **10** minutes | cooking **35** minutes | resting **15** minutes | **4** servings

Stuffing a pork joint is easy, and you can use almost any dried fruit you like. Dried figs, cherries, cranberries, or prunes – or a combination of two or three of these – are all classic accompaniments for roast pork and yield a juicy stuffing. Serve with braised fennel (page 167) and soft polenta (page 186) for a classic autumn meal.

tools | roasting tin | roasting rack | boning knife | mortar and pestle | wooden spatula | instant-read thermometer

1 boned centre-cut loin of pork, about 1 kg (2¼ lb)

85 g (3 oz) dried apricots

1¼ tsp fine sea salt

Freshly ground pepper

Leaves from 2 sprigs fresh rosemary

1 tsp cumin seeds, lightly toasted (page 61) and crushed

2 tsp fennel seeds, lightly toasted (page 61) and crushed

Creamy pan sauce (*see below*; optional)

One day or at least 6 hours before cooking, stuff and season the pork loin. Use a thin boning knife to make an incision from each end that runs the length of the joint through its centre. The incision should be no wider than 2.5 cm (1 inch). Stuff the dried apricots into the centre, one at a time, until the incision is completely filled with apricots. Season the pork liberally with the salt and pepper to taste. Rub with the rosemary, cumin seeds, and fennel seeds.

Preheat the oven to 230°C (450°F). Place the pork on a rack in a roasting tin and put it into the oven. Roast for 10 minutes, then lower the oven temperature to 190°C (375°F). Roast for a further 25 minutes or until an instant-read thermometer inserted into the centre of the joint registers 57°C (135°F) for medium-rare. Remove from the oven and leave to rest for 15 minutes. This allows time for the juices to be redistributed evenly throughout the joint.

Carve the pork into slices about 5 mm (¼ inch) thick, in order to show off the centre stuffing. Arrange on a large platter or on individual plates and serve, with the optional creamy pan sauce.

> **creamy pan sauce** To make a light pan sauce, after removing the pork from the roasting tin, place the tin over a moderately low heat. Add 120 ml (4 fl oz) dry white wine and deglaze the tin by stirring and loosening any caramelized bits stuck to the bottom using a wooden spatula. Simmer for 1–2 minutes to reduce the liquid by half. Add 250 ml (8 fl oz) chicken stock (page 216) and continue to simmer, stirring once or twice, for about 3 minutes or until reduced by half again. Add 4 tbsp double cream and stir once more. Serve warm in a small gravy boat or jug.

"Barbecued" Spareribs

preparation **10** minutes | marinating **5** hours | cooking **1** hour **35** minutes | **4–6** servings

Although this recipe requires marinating the spareribs in advance – preferably the day before cooking – the results are well worth the wait. The ribs are slowly cooked in the oven until the succulent, flavoursome meat is falling off the bones, making them reminiscent of spareribs cooked in a covered barbecue over slow-burning coals.

tools | baking dish | large saucepan | sauté pan | chef's knife | blender or food processor | large brush

To make the marinade, trim the root ends from the garlic cloves. Combine all the marinade ingredients in a blender or food processor and purée until smooth. Rub the marinade liberally all over the spareribs at least 5 hours before cooking or, preferably, the day before.

Meanwhile, make the barbecue sauce. Heat the olive oil in a sauté pan over a moderate heat. Add the onion and cook for 10–15 minutes or until softened. Transfer to a blender or food processor and purée until smooth. Put the onion purée in a large saucepan and add all of the remaining barbecue sauce ingredients and 5 tbsp water. Cook over a low heat, stirring frequently, for 15 minutes to blend the flavours. Watch the sauce carefully as it can stick and burn.

Preheat the oven to 190°C (375°F). Place the marinated spareribs in a shallow baking dish and cover with foil. Bake for 45–60 minutes or until the meat starts to soften but is not falling off the bone.

Remove the spareribs from the oven and uncover. Coat the ribs liberally on all sides with the barbecue sauce. Cover again and return to the oven. Bake for a further 15 minutes. Remove from the oven and slice into individual ribs. Toss in the sauce in the baking dish, then return to the oven, covered, to bake for 10 minutes. Allow to cool slightly before serving, garnished with coriander sprigs.

Note: You will have leftover barbecue sauce. Store it in the refrigerator for up to 10 days, or freeze for up to 2 months.

2 kg (4½ lb) meaty pork spareribs, in sheets

Fresh coriander sprigs to garnish

FOR THE MARINADE

8–10 cloves garlic

10 g (⅓ oz) fresh coriander leaves

2 tbsp olive oil

1 tbsp dark soft brown sugar

2 tbsp soy sauce

1 tbsp Chinese five-spice powder

1 tbsp fine sea salt

FOR THE BARBECUE SAUCE

4 tbsp olive oil

125 g (4½ oz) diced onion

350 g (12 oz) tomato purée

175 ml (6 fl oz) cider vinegar

1 tbsp dry mustard

1 tbsp ground ginger

120 ml (4 fl oz) soy sauce

115 g (4 oz) honey

100 g (3½ oz) dark molasses or treacle

1 tbsp Chinese five-spice powder

Goat's Cheese-stuffed Chicken Breasts

preparation **15** minutes | cooking **10** minutes | **4** servings

This savoury chicken dish is quite fun to assemble once you get the hang of it. Accompany these tender stuffed chicken breasts with braised red cabbage (page 158) in the winter or a simple tomato and mozzarella salad (page 84) in the summer.

tools | large sauté pan | boning knife | meat mallet or small frying pan | tongs |

4 skinless, boneless chicken breasts (fillets)

Fine sea salt and pepper

60 g (2 oz) fresh goat's cheese

4 thin slices Parma ham

8 fresh sage leaves

300 g (10 oz) flour

2 eggs, lightly beaten with 2 tbsp water

225 g (8 oz) fine dried breadcrumbs

4 tbsp olive or grapeseed oil, or as needed

Season the chicken breasts with salt and pepper on both sides. Use a boning knife to cut a horizontal incision into each breast, without cutting the breasts in half, creating a pocket for stuffing.

Place each chicken breast between 2 pieces of baking parchment or greaseproof paper. Pound lightly with a mallet or small frying pan until each breast is about 2 cm (¾ inch) thick. When all the breasts have been pounded, rub each one lightly all over with a little of the oil.

Stuff each pocket with about 1½ tbsp of the goat's cheese, spreading evenly, then follow with a slice of Parma ham and 2 sage leaves.

Arrange a plate with the flour, a bowl with the eggs, and another plate with the breadcrumbs on the work surface. Dredge each stuffed breast in the flour, shaking off the excess. Dip it into the beaten eggs, then dredge in the breadcrumbs.

Heat 2 tbsp of the oil in a large sauté pan over a moderate heat. When the oil is hot but not smoking, add 2 of the chicken breasts to the pan, placing them side by side. Cook for 1 minute, then reduce the heat to low and continue to cook for 2 more minutes. Using tongs, carefully turn the breasts and cook for about 2 minutes on the other side or until golden and just becoming firm to the touch.

Transfer the chicken breasts to a plate and cover loosely with foil to keep warm while you cook the other breasts in the same way, adding more oil to the pan as needed. Serve at once.

Grandmother's Oven-fried Chicken

preparation **30** minutes | cooking **1** hour **20** minutes | **8** servings

This recipe, passed down in our family, calls for studding chicken with garlic, coating it with egg and crumbs, and baking it slowly with butter until it is crisp and golden, almost like fried chicken. If you're watching your waistline (or your spouse's!), you can remove the skin from the chicken. We find the dish more succulent with the skin intact, but the recipe works fine without it. Leftovers are excellent cold for a picnic.

tools | large glass baking dish | chef's knife | paring knife | whisk or fork

Preheat the oven to 180°C (350°F). Separate the garlic heads into cloves. Peel the garlic cloves, then cut them lengthways into at least 32 small slivers about 3 mm (inch) thick. Place the chicken legs on a large platter and season them liberally with salt and pepper. Pierce each leg with the tip of a paring knife to make 4 small incisions just large enough to hold a garlic sliver. Insert a sliver into each incision. Reserve any leftover garlic.

Stir together the parsley, oregano, and breadcrumbs in a shallow bowl large enough to hold a chicken leg. Put the flour in a separate shallow bowl of similar size. In a third bowl of the same size, beat the eggs with 2 tbsp water until well blended.

Put the butter in a large glass baking dish and place it in the preheated oven to melt. Meanwhile, dredge each piece of chicken in the flour, shaking off any excess, then coat it in the egg mixture, and finally dredge it in the herbed breadcrumbs.

When the butter has melted, remove the dish from the oven and nestle the crumbed chicken pieces, skin side down, in the warm butter, arranging the pieces to fit tightly. Tuck any leftover garlic between the chicken pieces.

Bake for 45 minutes, then carefully turn over each piece of chicken. Continue baking for about 35 minutes or until the chicken is well browned and crisp on the edges. Remove the chicken from the oven and allow to cool slightly before serving, with any caramelized garlic slivers sprinkled on top.

2 heads garlic

8 chicken legs (drumsticks and thighs), with the skin or without

Fine sea salt and pepper

1 tbsp chopped fresh parsley

1 tbsp chopped fresh oregano

175 g (6 oz) fine toasted breadcrumbs (page 215)

150 g (5½ oz) flour

3 eggs

125 g (4½ oz) butter

Roast Chicken with Lemon and Herbs

seasoning **5** hours | preparation **10** minutes | cooking **45–55** minutes | resting **10** minutes | **4** servings

The trick to making a great roast chicken is to choose a chicken that isn't too large. A 1.5 kg (3 lb 3 oz) bird is just about the right size for four, or for two with leftovers, and it roasts evenly: the centre cooks through before the outer parts are overdone and dry, as is sometimes the problem with larger birds. Serve with crisp rosemary roasted potatoes (page 177) and a tossed green salad (page 82). Use leftovers to make fried rice (page 128) or a chicken pie (page 118).

tools | small roasting tin

1 chicken, about 1.5 kg (3 lb 3 oz)

½ tbsp fine sea salt

½ tsp pepper

3 cloves garlic, lightly crushed

4 small sprigs fresh rosemary

½ scrubbed lemon

If possible, season the chicken 3–5 hours or a day before you roast it, for more tender, succulent results. Remove any giblets from the cavity. Rub the salt and pepper over the entire surface of the chicken, including inside the cavity and on the back, wings, and inner and outer thighs. Using your forefinger, separate the skin from the breast meat without tearing it. Cut 1 garlic clove in half and place the halves and 1 rosemary sprig under the skin. Place the other 2 garlic cloves and remaining 3 rosemary sprigs inside the cavity. Cover and refrigerate until about 1 hour before you are ready to cook the chicken, then take the chicken out of the fridge. Allowing the bird to come closer to room temperature will help the meat cook more evenly.

Preheat the oven to 230°C (450°F). Just before roasting, squeeze the juice from the lemon half over the chicken and place the squeezed lemon half inside the cavity to perfume the meat. (If you have any extra lemon and rosemary, you can add them to the tin.) Put the chicken in a small roasting tin.

Place the chicken in the oven and roast for 10 minutes. Reduce the temperature to 180°C (350°F) and continue to roast for about 35 minutes or until the skin is crispy and golden brown, turning the tin around halfway through to ensure that the chicken cooks evenly. An instant-read thermometer inserted in the thigh away from the bone should register 80°C (175°F).

Remove from the oven and leave the chicken to rest for 10 minutes before carving. The temperature of the bird will continue to rise after it has been removed from the oven, and the resting time allows the juices to be redistributed evenly throughout the bird for more succulent meat.

Chicken Braised in Red Wine

preparation **20** minutes | cooking **50** minutes | **4–6** servings

This hearty and restorative dish is perfect for a cosy cold weather get-together. For the best results, choose a good bottle of fruity red wine such as a Pinot Noir or any Burgundian-style red. Avoid wines with heavy oak or other wood flavours. Serve with celeriac purée (page 169) and caramelized Brussels sprouts (page 164).

tools | large sauté pan or cast-iron frying pan | 2 large saucepans | chef's knife | ladle | slotted spoon | whisk

Pour the wine into a large saucepan and bring to the boil over a moderate heat. Cook until reduced by half. Set aside.

Season the chicken pieces with salt and pepper. Spread the 75 g (2½ oz) flour in a shallow dish. Lightly dredge the chicken pieces in the flour, shaking off any excess. In a large sauté pan or cast-iron frying pan, melt 30 g (1 oz) of the butter over a moderate heat. In batches as necessary to avoid crowding, brown the pieces of chicken on all sides. Transfer the chicken to a platter and set aside.

Add the remaining 30 g (1 oz) butter to the pan and melt, then add the onion, bacon, and garlic. Sauté for about 10 minues or until the onion is soft. Add the mushrooms, thyme, bay leaves, ¼ tsp salt, and a little pepper. Increase the heat to moderate and sauté for about 5 minutes or until the mushrooms release their moisture. Add the brandy and continue cooking for 1 minute.

Transfer the bacon and mushroom mixture to another large saucepan or to a flameproof casserole. Sprinkle the 2 tbsp flour over the onion and mushroom mixture and stir well, then add the stock, browned chicken pieces, and reduced wine. Bring to the boil, stirring. Reduce the heat to low and simmer gently, uncovered, for 15–20 minutes or until the chicken is tender and cooked through. Make sure the sauce does not boil or the chicken will toughen.

Remove and discard the thyme sprig and bay leaves, then use a slotted spoon to transfer the chicken pieces to a serving platter. Return the pan with the sauce to a moderately high heat and whisk until the sauce combines and thickens. Taste and adjust the seasoning with more salt and pepper, if necessary. Ladle the sauce over the chicken pieces and garnish with the parsley. Serve at once.

1 bottle (750 ml) fruity red wine

8 chicken drumsticks and thighs, with the skin

Fine sea salt and pepper

75 g (2½ oz) flour, plus 2 scant tbsp

60 g (2 oz) butter

1 large onion, thinly sliced

4 thick rashers streaky bacon, cut into 2.5 cm (1 inch) pieces

3 cloves garlic, crushed

500 g (1 lb 2 oz) button mushrooms, stalks removed, brushed clean, and quartered

1 sprig fresh thyme

2 bay leaves

4 tbsp brandy

500 ml (16 fl oz) chicken stock (page 216)

1 tbsp chopped fresh parsley

Spiced Roast Turkey

seasoning **4** hours | preparation **15** minutes | cooking **2½–3** hours | resting **30** minutes |
12 servings

*Once you serve this turkey to your family for Christmas lunch, you'll never need to travel
anywhere again. Instead, everyone will want to come to your house. For the best results,
season the turkey the day before roasting it. While the turkey rests in the fridge, lightly
curing, you'll have plenty of time to get other things done. For suggestions on creating an
entire Christmas feast, see page 243.*

tools | small frying pan | large roasting tin | roasting rack | chef's knife | bulb baster or brush |
instant-read thermometer

1 turkey, 6.5–8 kg (14–18 lb)

6 tbsp olive oil

FOR THE SPICE RUB

1 tbsp fennel seeds

¾ tsp dried chilli flakes

3 tbsp Madras or other curry
powder

2 tbsp caster sugar

1 tbsp sweet paprika

1½ tsp fine sea salt

To make the spice rub, toast the fennel seeds in a small dry frying pan over a
moderate heat for about 1 minute or until lightly browned and fragrant. Transfer
to a blender or mortar, add the chilli flakes, and pulse or grind with a pestle until
the mixture is finely ground. Place the mixture in a small bowl and stir in the
curry powder, sugar, paprika, and salt.

Pull off and discard any lumps of fat from the cavity of the turkey and remove
the giblets and neck. (Save the giblets for the gravy, if you like.) Rinse the turkey
inside and out and pat dry with kitchen paper.

In a small bowl, stir together the spice rub and olive oil. Cover the whole turkey
with the spice mixture, massaging it thoroughly all over the skin and inside both
the neck and body cavities. Refrigerate for at least 4 hours or up to 12 hours.

Remove the turkey from the refrigerator about 2 hours before you want to roast
it, to allow the bird to lose its chill, which helps it cook more evenly. Preheat the
oven to 170°C (350°F).

Place the turkey breast side up on a rack in a large roasting tin and place in the
oven. Roast the turkey, basting every 20 minutes with the pan drippings, for about
2½ hours or until an instant-read thermometer inserted in the thickest part of
the breast registers 71°C (160°F).

Transfer the turkey to a platter and leave to rest for 30 minutes in a warm place.
This allows the juices within the bird to be redistributed, which results in moist and
tender meat. Reserve the drippings in the roasting tin to make gravy (right).

When the gravy is ready, carve the turkey and serve.

Gravy

preparation **10** minutes | cooking **15** minutes | **12** servings

Good gravy is essential with roast turkey, and this recipe uses the simpler method of thickening with cornflour instead of a roux. Prepare it while the turkey rests.

tools | medium saucepan | gravy strainer or glass measuring jug | wooden spatula

Place the turkey roasting tin with the drippings over a moderately high heat. Add all but 4 tbsp of the stock to the roasting tin and bring to a brisk simmer. Deglaze the tin by stirring and scraping with a wooden spatula to loosen the caramelized bits from the bottom, cooking for about 5 minutes.

Remove from the heat and pour the liquid into a gravy strainer, in batches as needed. Leave for a minute to allow the fat to rise, then pour off the gravy from the bottom; discard the fat. (If you don't have a gravy strainer, pour the liquid into a glass measuring jug and allow to settle for a minute, then carefully spoon off as much fat as possible from the top of the gravy.) Transfer the gravy to a medium saucepan. Place over a moderately high heat and simmer briskly for 5 minutes.

In a small bowl, stir the reserved 4 tbsp chicken stock into the cornflour until evenly mixed. Gradually stir this "slaked" cornflour into the gravy. Cook for 3–4 minutes or until the gravy thickens. Season to taste with salt and pepper.

Pour the gravy into a warmed gravy boat or jug and serve.

1.7 litres (3 pints) chicken stock (page 216)

30 g (1 oz) cornflour

Fine sea salt and freshly ground pepper

Puff-topped Chicken Pie

preparation **20** minutes | cooking **45** minutes | Makes **two** 23 cm (9 inch) pies

There are countless versions of chicken pie, such as with courgettes, sweetcorn, or leeks in the filling and a shortcrust top. Our recipe uses a mixture of vegetables and a creamy herb sauce. This recipe will make two 23 cm (9 inch) pies, so you can feed a crowd or freeze the second pie to have for supper another time.

tools | medium saucepan | small saucepan | 2 baking sheets | 2 pie dishes | chef's knife | paring knife | large metal spoon | wooden spoon

2 skinless, boneless chicken breasts (fillets)

2 skinless, boneless chicken thighs

2 tbsp olive oil

250 g (9 oz) diced onions

125 g (4½ oz) sliced carrots

150 g (5½ oz) diced celery

300 g (10 oz) peeled, diced boiling potatoes, such as Maris Piper

125 g (4½ oz) button mushrooms, quartered

750 ml (1¼ pints) chicken stock (page 216)

1 tsp finely chopped fresh sage

2 tsp finely chopped fresh thyme

2 tsp finely chopped celery leaf

Fine sea salt and pepper

30 g (1 oz) butter

3 tbsp flour

6 tbsp double cream

2 sheets frozen puff pastry

Preheat the oven to 200°C (400°F). Cut the chicken breasts and thighs into 2 cm (¾ inch) dice. Set aside.

Heat the olive oil in a medium saucepan over a moderate heat. Add the onion, carrots, and celery and sauté the vegetables for 4–5 minutes or until slightly softened. Add the potatoes and mushrooms and sauté, stirring often, for 3–4 minutes. Add the stock and bring to the boil. Reduce the heat to moderately low and add the chicken pieces. Bring to a gentle simmer. Using a large metal spoon, skim off any fat or scum that rises to the surface. Add the sage, thyme, celery leaf, 1 tsp salt, and several grindings of pepper. Simmer for 10 minutes.

Meanwhile, make a roux by melting the butter in a small saucepan over a low heat. Add the flour and stir with a wooden spoon to mix thoroughly. Cook, stirring constantly, for 5 minutes. Do not allow the roux to brown. Add the cream and stir vigorously until the mixture thickens. Season to taste with salt and pepper. Stir the roux into the chicken and vegetable mixture and simmer gently for 5 minutes. The chicken mixture should thicken slightly. Check the potatoes to see if they are cooked through. Taste and adjust the seasoning with salt, pepper, sage, thyme, and celery leaf. Remove from the heat. The dish can be prepared to this point up to a day in advance; keep in the fridge. Bring back to room temperature before baking.

Divide the chicken and vegetable mixture evenly between two 23 cm (9 inch) pie dishes, filling to within 1 cm (½ inch) of the rim. Allow to cool slightly.

Remove the puff pastry from the freezer 10 minutes before using, so it can thaw. Cut a 23 cm (9 inch) round from each sheet of pastry. Cover each pie with a pastry round, pinching the edges of the pastry over the rim of the dish with your thumb and forefinger to secure the pastry to the dish. Make several slits in the centre of the pastry lid with a paring knife, to allow steam to escape during baking.

Place the pies on baking sheets and bake for 15 minutes or until the pastry is puffed and golden brown. Leave to cool for 5 minutes before serving.

Duck with Tart Cherry and Port Sauce

preparation **10** minutes | cooking **25** minutes | resting **10** minutes | **4** servings

Tart cherries deliciously complement the smoky flavour of duck breast and add fruity notes to a port wine sauce. For a stress-free dinner party, make the sauce a day in advance and keep it, covered, in the refrigerator, until ready to reheat for serving.

tools | cast-iron frying pan | saucepan | baking sheet | chef's knife

If using the hazelnuts, preheat the oven to 180°C (350°F). Spread the hazelnuts on a baking sheet and toast for 10–12 minutes or until golden and fragrant. Allow to cool slightly, then wrap in a clean tea towel and rub gently to remove the skins. Chop the nuts coarsely and set aside.

Meanwhile, to make the cherry and port sauce, combine the cherries, vinegar, port, and stock in a saucepan. Simmer over a moderate heat for 10–12 minutes or until reduced by half. Remove from the heat and set aside.

Trim any extra skin hanging over the edges of the duck breasts. Turn the breasts skin side up and make 4 shallow slashes diagonally across the breasts, cutting into the skin and fat; take care not to cut into the meat. Create a crosshatch pattern by making a second set of 4 diagonal slashes in the opposite direction. Season the duck breasts liberally with salt and pepper on both sides.

Heat a cast-iron frying pan over a moderately high heat. Add the olive oil. When the oil is very hot, add the duck breasts, skin side down. Reduce the heat to moderately low. Cook for 10–12 minutes, without turning, until the skin is nicely browned and plenty of fat is rendered. Reduce the heat to low, turn the duck breasts over, and cook for a further 4–5 minutes for medium-rare; an instant-read thermometer inserted into the centre of a duck breast should register 60°C (140°F). For medium to well-done, cook the breast for 5–10 minutes; the thermometer should register 71–74°C (160–165°F). Transfer the duck breasts to a platter and leave to rest, loosely covered with foil, for 10 minutes.

While the duck rests, reheat the cherry and port sauce. Cut each duck breast into thin slices and arrange the slices on 4 warmed plates. Spoon the sauce over the duck slices and sprinkle with the hazelnuts, if using. Serve at once.

Note: For even better flavour, season the duck breasts 1 or 2 days in advance and keep them, covered, in the refrigerator. In early summer, substitute 2 handfuls of fresh dark, sweet cherries for the dried tart cherries. Roast the cherries for 10 minutes in a 180°C (350°F) oven, stone them if you like, and serve warm with the duck.

30 g (1 oz) hazelnuts (optional)

4 boneless duck breasts with skin, about 175 g (6 oz) each

Fine sea salt and pepper

1 tbsp olive oil

FOR THE CHERRY AND PORT SAUCE

2 tbsp dried tart cherries or cranberries

1 tbsp sherry vinegar or red wine vinegar

120 ml (4 fl oz) ruby port

600 ml (1 pint) veal or chicken stock (page 216)

Plaice with Brown Butter and Capers

preparation **10** minutes │ cooking **15** minutes │ **2** servings

Plaice has a sweet and mild flavour that pairs well with tart lemon, briny capers, and sweet butter. Seek out the freshest fish you can find, since its quality will shine through in a simple dish such as this. Because it's ready in a flash, this is another good weeknight recipe. Serve with sautéed spinach (page 163) and mashed potatoes (page 178).

tools │ large and small sauté pans │ small frying pan │ chef's knife │ slotted spoon or skimmer │ slotted metal turner

2 lemons

75 g (2½ oz) flour

2 tbsp polenta flour

¼ tsp cayenne pepper

2 plaice fillets, about 175 g (6 oz) each

Fine sea salt and freshly ground black pepper

1 tbsp olive oil

60 g (2 oz) butter

½ shallot, finely diced

1 tbsp chopped fresh chives

1 tbsp capers, rinsed and patted dry, and fried if liked (*see right*)

Peel and segment the lemons using a chef's knife (page 233).

On a plate, stir together the flour, polenta, and cayenne. Season each fish fillet on both sides with salt and pepper, then dredge the fish in the flour mixture to coat, shaking off any excess. Heat the olive oil in a large sauté pan over a moderate heat. Add the fish fillets and cook, turning once, for 3–4 minutes on each side or until golden brown. Transfer to individual plates and keep warm in a low oven.

In a small sauté pan over a moderate heat, melt the butter. Add the shallot with a pinch of salt and sauté until the butter foams. Reduce the heat slightly and continue to cook for 2–3 minutes or until the butter browns. Add the lemon segments to the butter and swirl the pan to mix and heat them through.

Remove the pan from the heat and spoon an equal amount of the lemon segments and brown butter sauce over each fish fillet. Sprinkle the fish with the chives and capers and serve at once.

> **fried capers** Heat 2 tbsp olive oil in a small frying pan over a moderate heat. When the oil is hot, add a few of the capers. As they cook, they will open, lighten in colour, and float to the top of the oil. After 2 minutes, remove the capers from the oil with a slotted spoon or skimmer and drain on kitchen paper. Repeat until all the capers are fried. The fried capers will keep for up to 2 days, tightly covered. Before using, re-crisp them in a 150°C (300°F) oven for 3 minutes.

Sea Bass with Fennel and Bacon

preparation **10** minutes | cooking **25** minutes | **4–6** servings

Roasting a whole large fish fillet is a clever way to entertain: presenting the fillet at the table in the dish it was roasted in always brings on oohs and aahs.

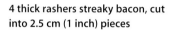

tools | baking dish | small sauté pan | chef's knife

Preheat the oven to 180°C (350°F). In a small sauté pan over a moderate heat, fry the bacon for about 3 minutes or until browned but not crisp. Transfer to kitchen paper to drain.

Arrange half of the fennel in a single layer in a shallow baking dish. Season the fish with salt and pepper on both sides. Place the fish on top of the fennel and place the remaining fennel on top of the fish. Sprinkle with the bacon and olive oil. Roast the fish for 18–25 minutes or until the surface is slightly firm to the touch and the centre is just opaque. Leave the fish to rest for a few minutes before serving directly from the baking dish.

4 thick rashers streaky bacon, cut into 2.5 cm (1 inch) pieces

5 or 6 wild fennel tops, or 1 trimmed fennel bulb, cut into thick slices

1 whole sea bass or halibut fillet, about 1 kg (2¼ lb)

Fine sea salt and pepper

2 tbsp extra virgin olive oil

Halibut with a Breadcrumb Crust

preparation **10** minutes | cooking **20** minutes | **6** servings

Slow roasting may take a little longer, but it results in extremely moist and tender fish. Serve with spicy Italian-style cauliflower (page 158) or braised red cabbage (page 158).

tools | large baking dish | baking sheet | chef's knife

Preheat the oven to 200°C (400°F). In a bowl, toss the breadcrumbs with 1 tbsp olive oil, 1 tsp of the garlic, and the wine. Spread the crumbs on a baking sheet and toast in the oven for about 8 minutes or until lightly browned. Reduce the oven temperature to 170°C (350°F).

Meanwhile, in a bowl, combine 120 ml (4 fl oz) olive oil with the rocket, parsley, oregano, marjoram, vinegar, and the remaining 1 tsp garlic. Season the herb sauce with salt and pepper.

Lightly oil a large baking dish. Arrange the halibut fillets in the dish side by side, season with salt and pepper, and roast for 8 minutes. Sprinkle the fish with the toasted breadcrumbs and continue roasting for 12–15 minutes or until the fish is just opaque in the centre and the crumbs are crisp and golden. Transfer the fish to individual plates, drizzle with the herb sauce, and serve at once.

60 g (2 oz) coarse fresh breadcrumbs (page 215)

Extra virgin olive oil

2 tsp finely chopped garlic

1 tbsp dry white wine

1 bunch rocket

4 tbsp finely chopped parsley

1 tbsp *each* finely chopped fresh oregano and marjoram

2 tsp red wine vinegar

Fine sea salt and pepper

6 skinless halibut fillets

Salmon with Puy Lentils

preparation **20** minutes | cooking **30** minutes | **4** servings

The combination of lentils and salmon is a classic French brasserie dish. Serve this with a dry but fruity white wine such as a Viognier, Pinot Blanc, or Riesling. When the weather disappoints, you can cook the fish under the grill instead of outdoors.

tools | medium saucepan | sauté pan | chef's knife | barbecue

4 salmon fillets, about 175 g (6 oz) each

Extra virgin olive oil

Fine sea salt and pepper

FOR THE LENTILS

200 g (7 oz) Puy lentils

4 sprigs fresh thyme

30 g (1 oz) butter

½ onion, finely diced

1 carrot, peeled and finely diced

1 stick celery, finely diced

½ tsp fine sea salt, or to taste

1 tsp red wine vinegar

1 tbsp extra virgin olive oil

Prepare a charcoal fire in the barbecue.

Meanwhile, to prepare the lentils, rinse them in cold water and place in a medium saucepan. Add 750 ml (1¼ pints) water and the thyme and bring to a simmer over a moderate heat. Cook for 15 minutes.

While the lentils are cooking, melt the butter in a sauté pan and sauté the onion, carrot, and celery over a moderately low heat for about 5 minutes or until slightly softened. Season with the salt. Add the vegetables to the lentils, stir, and continue to simmer for 10 minutes or until the lentils are tender. Add the vinegar and olive oil. Stir once more, then taste and adjust the seasoning. Remove from the heat, cover, and keep warm.

When the coals have burned down to glowing embers covered with grey ash, spread them out. Rub the salmon fillets with olive oil and season with salt and pepper. Place the fish on the hot barbecue grill and cook on one side for 3–4 minutes, depending on the thickness. Turn and cook on the other side for 2–3 minutes longer for medium-rare (the centre will still be slightly translucent). Remove the salmon from the grill. Spoon a small mound of lentils onto each serving plate and top with a salmon fillet. Drizzle with olive oil and serve at once.

lentils Lentils come in a wide range of colours, including brown, green, yellow, red, pink, and ochre. The town of Le Puy in eastern France is famous for its tiny, olive green lentils, known as lentilles du Puy, or simply Puy lentils. The prized lentils are harvested in summer and traditionally dried under the hot sun. Unlike the more common brown lentils, which can become very soft and lose their shape when cooked, Puy lentils keep their lens-like profile and subtle flavour, making them a favourite for lentil side dishes and salads.

Mussels with Wine and Tomato

preparation **20** minutes | cooking **35** minutes | **4** main-course servings or
8 first-course servings

This dish of mussels quickly steamed in stock and wine is a twist on the French classic moules marinière. *You need to allow 500 g (1 lb 2 oz) of mussels per person. Pair the shellfish with a crisp Italian white wine such as Pinot Grigio or Sauvignon Blanc and serve with bread – warm, buttery garlic bread is particularly delicious.*

tools | large saucepan | chef's knife | ladle

In a large saucepan, heat the olive oil over a moderately low heat. Add the onions and garlic and sauté gently for 10–15 minutes or until slightly softened. Do not allow the onions to brown. Add the tomatoes, thyme, and bay leaf and season with salt. Reduce the heat to low and simmer, stirring occasionally, for 10 minutes or until the mixture becomes saucelike. Stir in the white wine, increase the heat to moderately high, and bring to the boil. Reduce the heat to a simmer and cook until the wine is reduced by half. Add the chicken stock and clam juice and bring to a vigorous simmer.

Meanwhile, rinse the mussels thoroughly under cold water, pulling off any "beards" (see below) with your fingers. Discard any mussels that do not close to the touch. Add the mussels to the simmering tomato broth, cover, and steam for 4–6 minutes or until the shells open. Stir the mussels once or twice while they are cooking to ensure that they cook evenly.

Use a large ladle to transfer the mussels to 4 large serving bowls, discarding any that failed to open. Distribute the broth evenly among the bowls. Drizzle the extra virgin olive oil over the mussels, sprinkle with the parsley, and serve at once.

2 tbsp olive oil

2 small onions, cut into
1 cm (½ inch) wedges

1 clove garlic, very thinly sliced

175 g (6 oz) canned chopped
tomatoes, drained

1 sprig fresh thyme

1 bay leaf

Fine sea salt

250 ml (8 fl oz) dry white wine

750 ml (1¼ pints) chicken
stock (page 216)

250 ml (8 fl oz) bottled
clam juice or fish stock

2 kg (4½ lb) mussels

3 tbsp extra virgin olive oil

2 tbsp chopped fresh parsley

mussels For this dish, you can use small blue mussels; larger, more tender Mediterranean mussels; or green-lipped mussels from New Zealand or China. When choosing mussels, select those with tightly closed shells (open shells can mean the mussel inside is dead). To store, place the mussels in a deep bowl, cover with a damp tea towel, and keep in the fridge for up to 1 day. Before cooking, scrub the shells with a stiff-bristled brush under cold running water. Using a small knife or scissors, cut off any beard, which is a fibrous tuft at the edge of the shell. Cultivated mussels, the variety you find today in most fishmongers and supermarkets, have little or no beards and are easier to clean.

Wok-glazed Scallops

preparation **10** minutes | cooking **5** minutes | **2** servings

This bold and saucy stir-fry is quick to prepare and utterly delicious. Serve over steamed jasmine rice and accompany with pak choy (page 168).

tools | wok or large sauté pan | chef's knife

1 tbsp cornflour

2 tbsp Chinese black beans

1 tbsp chopped fresh ginger

2 tbsp *each* chopped garlic, Chinese rice wine, and groundnut oil

300 g (10 oz) shelled large scallops without corals

250 ml (8 fl oz) chicken stock

4 tbsp light soy sauce

pinch of dried chilli flakes

2 tbsp chopped fresh coriander

Mix the cornflour with 3 tbsp water; set aside. Coarsely chop the black beans. In a small bowl, stir together the black beans, ginger, garlic, and wine. Set aside.

Heat a wok or large sauté pan over a high heat. Add the oil and heat for 1 minute. Add the scallops and stir-fry for 1 minute to brown them on both sides. Remove the scallops from the wok and set aside.

Add the black bean mixture to the wok and stir for 1 minute or until fragrant. Return the scallops to the wok and add the stock, soy sauce, chilli flakes, coriander, and cornflour mixture. Stir to mix, then cook for about 2 minutes or until the sauce is nicely thickened. Serve at once.

Fried Rice with Prawns

preparation **10** minutes | cooking **7** minutes | **4** servings

This is the perfect dish to make when you have leftovers. Shredded roast chicken or pork, diced ham, or your favourite vegetables could all be substituted for the prawns.

tools | wok or large frying pan | chef's knife | paring knife

600 g (1 lb 5 oz) cooked rice

1 spring onion

2 tbsp groundnut oil

200 g (7 oz) cooked peeled prawns

2 tbsp soy sauce

1 tsp chilli oil

½ tsp toasted sesame oil

Freshly ground pepper

2 eggs, lightly beaten

If the rice has been in the fridge, allow the rice to come to room temperature. Thinly slice the spring onion on the diagonal.

Heat the groundnut oil in a wok or large frying pan over a moderate heat and add the rice, spring onion, prawns, soy sauce, chilli oil, sesame oil, and pepper to taste. Sauté, stirring often, for about 5 minutes or until the onion is softened. Add the eggs and stir quickly to mix them into the rice and cook evenly. As soon as the eggs are set, remove the rice from the heat and serve at once.

Roast Crab with Garlic and Fennel

preparation **15** minutes | cooking **30** minutes | **2** servings

As you'll be using your fingers to deal with the crab, be sure to set out paper napkins plus finger bowls and lemon wedges. A lobster pick is a very useful tool for getting the white meat out of the claws and legs, or you can use wooden toothpicks or skewers. Take care to pick over all the crab meat to remove any pieces of shell or cartilage before eating.

tools | large roasting tin | small saucepan | medium sauté pan | chef's knife | tongs

Prepare the crabs (see below) and set aside.

Preheat the oven to 220°C (425°F). Cut all the stalks from the fennel bulbs, reserving a handful of the green fronds. If the fronds do not look fresh, discard them, but otherwise finely chop enough of the best-looking ones to measure about 2 tbsp and set aside. Cut the fennel bulbs into quarters.

Toss the fennel with some olive oil and a pinch of salt. Heat a medium sauté pan over a moderate heat and lightly sauté the fennel quarters for about 5 minutes on each side or until they begin to turn golden brown. Transfer the fennel quarters to a large roasting tin and stir in the potatoes and the crab claws, legs, and pieces of body section.

Melt the butter in a small saucepan, add the garlic, and sauté gently for 5 minutes. Pour the garlicky butter over the crab, potatoes, and fennel. Roast for 3–5 minutes or until the edges of the crab shells are just beginning to turn golden brown.

Arrange the crab and vegetables on a serving platter and keep warm. To create a fragrant crab sauce, set the roasting tin with its juices over a very low heat. Pour the Pernod into the tin and stir for about 1 minute to combine with the pan juices and garlic. If you like, stir in some of the brown crab meat.

Pour the crab sauce over the crab and vegetables, garnish with the finely chopped fennel fronds, if using, and the lemon wedges, and serve at once.

2 freshly cooked crabs, about 1 kg (2¼ lb) each

2 fennel bulbs, with stalks and fronds still attached, if possible

Olive oil for tossing

Pinch of fine sea salt

4 or 5 small new potatoes, boiled until tender and cut in half

125 g (4½ oz) butter

Cloves from 1 head garlic, finely chopped

4 tbsp Pernod

1 lemon, cut into wedges

> **preparing cooked crab** Place the crab on its back and pull and twist off the claws and all legs; set aside. Lift off the apron (triangular tail flap) on the underside of the body shell and twist it off; discard. Prise the central section from the body shell. Pull off the gills (dead man's fingers), which are the greyish-white feather-shaped pieces on each side of the central section; discard. Also pull out and discard the firm, crooked white intestine along the centre or on either side. Crack or cut the central section into several large pieces; set aside. Spoon out the soft brown meat from the body shell, as well as any roe (these can be added to a dish for extra crab flavour). Use the flat side of a chef's knife, a lobster cracker, or small hammer to gently crack the shells on the claws.

Pasta, Pizza, and Risotto

We know that this chapter will get a lot of use. These brilliant Italian dishes are staples we rely on again and again in our own dinnertime repertoire. Take, for example, pasta carbonara or spaghetti with tomato sauce: where would we be without them on nights when we haven't planned our dinner? The ingredients are bound to be on hand, so a delicious hot meal is only minutes way. We hope you delight in the several pizza ideas we give here and invent some of your own topping combinations. Similarly, once you master making risotto, flavour possibilities are as limitless as your imagination.

Pasta Puttanesca

preparation **10** minutes | cooking **25** minutes | **4–6** servings

A fiery chilli punch is the hallmark of this classic pasta dish from Naples. It's a good recipe to have in your repertoire – quick and easy, and packed with flavour.

tools | medium saucepan | pasta pan | chef's knife | colander

4 tbsp olive oil

2 tbsp finely chopped garlic

2 cans (about 400 g each) chopped tomatoes, drained

60 g (2 oz) stoned black olives, coarsely chopped

3 tbsp coarsely chopped anchovies

2 tbsp capers, rinsed and chopped

¾ tsp fine sea salt, or to taste

¼ tsp dried chilli flakes, or to taste

4 tbsp chopped fresh parsley

500 g (1 lb 2 oz) linguine, fedelini, spaghettini, or other long pasta

Parmesan cheese to serve (optional)

Heat the olive oil over a low heat in a medium saucepan. Add the garlic and sauté for about 5 minutes or until softened and just starting to turn golden. Add the tomatoes, olives, anchovies, capers, salt, and chilli flakes. Simmer gently over a moderately low heat for about 15 minutes or until the sauce is reduced by about one-third. Taste and add more salt, if needed. Add the parsley.

Meanwhile, bring a large pan of water to the boil. Add the pasta and cook until al dente, according to the packet instructions.

Drain the pasta thoroughly and add to the warm sauce. Toss the pasta vigorously until it is evenly coated with sauce. Check the seasoning, then serve the pasta in warmed bowls, with Parmesan for grating over, if you like.

capers Caper bushes grow wild throughout southern France and around the Mediterranean. Before they can flower, the small, olive-green buds are harvested and preserved in salt or a vinegar brine. Pleasantly tangy, capers add a piquant bite to dishes. Salt-packed capers have a slightly more pungent flavour and are worth seeking out. They should be rinsed and drained before using. Capers labeled "nonpareils", from the south of France, are the smallest and considered to be the best.

Spaghetti with Quick Tomato Sauce

preparation **10** minutes | cooking **20** minutes | **2** servings

Here is a basic tomato sauce to enjoy with pasta for a simple lunch or supper. Use perfectly ripe tomatoes in midsummer when they are in season. For variations, add rinsed chopped capers, chopped olives, or ricotta cheese, or garnish the dish with warm toasted breadcrumbs (page 215).

tools | medium sauté pan | pasta pan | chef's knife | grater or vegetable peeler | colander

Heat the olive oil in a medium sauté pan over a moderately low heat. Add the garlic, basil, and marjoram and sauté gently for about 1 minute or until fragrant. Add the tomatoes, stir well, and season with salt and pepper. Add the sugar and chilli flakes. Reduce the heat and cook for 10–15 minutes or until the mixture has a nice saucelike consistency and you like the way it tastes.

Meanwhile, bring a large pan of water to the boil. Add the spaghetti and cook until al dente, according to the packet instructions. Drain thoroughly, reserving a few tablespoons of the pasta cooking water.

Return the pasta to the pan, season with salt, and add the tomato sauce. Add the reserved pasta cooking water as needed to loosen the sauce, then add the rocket. Mix well and drizzle over the extra virgin olive oil. Transfer the pasta to warmed pasta bowls and serve with the cheese.

3 tbsp olive oil

1 tbsp finely chopped garlic

2 tbsp chopped fresh basil

1 tbsp chopped fresh marjoram or parsley

1 can (about 400 g) chopped tomatoes

Fine sea salt and pepper

Pinch of sugar

Pinch of dried chilli flakes

250 g (9 oz) spaghetti

1 small bunch of rocket, coarsely chopped

2 tbsp extra virgin olive oil

Freshly shaved or grated pecorino or Parmesan cheese to serve

Pasta Carbonara

preparation **10** minutes | cooking **20** minutes | **2** servings

When you need a good supper for the two of you and haven't planned ahead, you can make this pasta in a pinch, as we often do. It requires just a few storecupboard staples.

tools | sauté pan | pasta pan | chef's knife | box grater | colander | wooden spatula | tongs

250 g (9 oz) spaghettini, fedelini, or other long pasta

2 tbsp olive oil

3 thick rashers streaky bacon, diced

2 eggs

¼ tsp freshly grated nutmeg (optional)

Fine sea salt

Chopped fresh parsley to garnish (optional)

Pecorino or Parmesan cheese to serve

Coarsely ground pepper

Bring a large pan of water to the boil. Add the pasta and cook until al dente, according to the packet instructions. While the pasta cooks, heat the olive oil in a medium sauté pan over a moderate heat and add the bacon. Sauté for 3–5 minutes or until browned and slightly crisp. Pour off all but 1½ tbsp of the fat. Set aside the pan with the bacon and reserved fat.

In a small bowl, beat the eggs with a fork to loosen them. Add the nutmeg, if using, and season with a little salt.

Drain the pasta, reserving 4 tbsp of the pasta cooking water for use later. If the bacon pan has cooled down, warm it up again and add the pasta to the warm bacon in the pan. Using tongs, thoroughly toss the pasta with the bacon and its fat. Taste and season with salt, if needed. Remove from the heat and, working quickly, add the egg mixture to the pasta, tossing thoroughly. (The heat of the pasta and the pan will cook the eggs just enough to thicken them; the pan should be off the heat to avoid scrambling the eggs.) If the pasta seems too dry, add 1 or 2 tbsp of the reserved pasta cooking water and toss again.

Divide the pasta among warmed shallow bowls and sprinkle with parsley, if using. Grate cheese and coarsely grind pepper over each serving. Serve at once.

Note: This recipe includes semi-cooked egg. For more information, see page 226.

Orecchiette with Cime di Rapa

preparation **10** minutes | cooking **15** minutes | **4** servings

We use the pasta called orecchiette, or "little ears", for this dish because the shape holds the braised greens and fruity olive oil well. Other chunky shapes of pasta such as penne or fusilli will also work well in this recipe.

tools | medium sauté pan | pasta pan | chef's knife | colander | wooden spatula

Bring a large pan of water to the boil. Trim off the ends of the cime di rapa stalks, then chop the rest – the leaves, tender stalks, and flowering buds – into 2.5 cm (1 inch) pieces. Heat 2 tbsp of the olive oil in a medium sauté pan over a moderate heat. Add the cime di rapa, salt and chilli flakes to taste, garlic, and a few splashes of water to help the greens cook. Reduce the heat to low and cook, stirring frequently, for 6–10 minutes or until the greens are tender. Remove from the heat.

Add the pasta to the boiling water and cook until al dente, according to the packet instructions. Drain well, reserving 2 tbsp of the pasta cooking water. Return the pasta and the reserved pasta cooking water to the pan. Season the pasta with salt and the remaining 1 tbsp olive oil, or more to taste.

Stir in the braised greens and mix thoroughly. Taste again and adjust the seasoning with salt, then transfer the pasta to a warmed serving bowl. Sprinkle with the breadcrumbs and serve at once.

750 g (1 lb 10 oz) cime di rapa (*see below*)

3 tbsp extra virgin olive oil, or to taste

Fine sea salt

Pinch of dried chilli flakes

1 tbsp chopped garlic

500 g (1 lb 2 oz) orecchiette pasta

60 g (2 oz) toasted breadcrumbs (page 215)

cime di rapa Delicious on its own or tossed with your favourite pasta, cime di rapa is a versatile Italian green that has nutty, sweet, and bitter notes. It is a leafy green with long, thin stalks topped with tiny broccoli-like florets. Despite this similarity, and its other name of broccoli rabe, it is not related to broccoli but is in fact a variety of turnip. If cime di rapa is not available, you can substitute young turnips tops. Or, for an equally good dish, you can use sprouting broccoli, with its leaves. This will not take as long to cook as it is more tender, so adjust the time accordingly.

Fettuccine with Peas and Asparagus

preparation **20** minutes | cooking **10** minutes | **4** servings

Sweet peas and asparagus are abundant in the spring. For this pasta dish, these two flavourful vegetables are paired with fragrant basil and zesty lemon. The peas are cooked with the pasta, to make preparation – and washing-up – easier.

tools | small sauté pan | pasta pan | paring knife | box grater or citrus zester | citrus reamer | colander | vegetable peeler

8 thick asparagus spears

15 g (¹/₂ oz) butter or 1 tbsp olive oil

150 ml (5 fl oz) double cream

Grated zest and juice of 1 lemon

Fine sea salt and pepper

125 g (4¹/₂ oz) freshly podded peas

500 g (1 lb 2 oz) fresh fettuccine (page 143)

Leaves from several sprigs fresh basil

Shaved or grated Parmesan or pecorino cheese to garnish

To prepare the asparagus, snap off the tough woody ends of the stalks and, if the skin is fibrous, peel them starting from just below the tips. With a sharp paring knife, cut the asparagus on the diagonal into pieces about 3 mm (¹/₈ inch) thick. In a small sauté pan, melt the butter over a moderate heat. Add the asparagus and sauté for 2 minutes. Reduce the heat to low, add the cream, and heat until warm. Add the lemon zest and salt and pepper to taste. Keep warm.

Bring a large pan of water to the boil. Add the peas and cook for 30 seconds. Add the pasta and cook until it is tender and rises to the surface, which will take from 30 seconds to 5 minutes, depending on freshness. Stir occasionally so that the pasta cooks evenly. Drain the pasta and peas, reserving 2–3 tbsp of the cooking water.

Return the pasta and peas to the pan and season with salt. Pour the asparagus cream mixture over the pasta and toss to coat thoroughly. Add the reserved pasta cooking water as needed to loosen the sauce. Tear up some of the basil leaves and add together with lemon juice to taste and more salt if needed. Serve at once in warmed pasta bowls sprinkled with additional torn basil leaves, pepper, and cheese.

Linguine with Clams

preparation **15** minutes | cooking **10** minutes | **2** servings

Once you've measured out the ingredients, this satisfying pasta dish is very quick to put together and gorgeous to look at. We find that thin noodles glistening with the parsley-infused broth and trapping a mosaic of tiny clam shells pleases the eye as much as the palate. Choose baby clams if they are available, for their sweet, flavourful, and tender meat. Provide extra plates for discarding the shells as you devour the clams.

tools | sauté pan | pasta pan | box grater | colander | ladle | tongs

Rinse the clams under cold water and rub away any dirt with your fingers. The clams should glisten and feel clean. Discard any clams that do not close to the touch.

Bring a large pan of water to the boil. Add the linguine and cook until al dente, according to the packet instructions.

While the pasta cooks, heat the olive oil in a sauté pan over a moderate heat. Add the clams, garlic, and wine, if using. Cover and steam for 3–5 minutes or until the clams begin to open. For clams that do not open, try to open them by inserting the flat end of a pair of tongs between the shells. If they open easily, return them to the pan. Discard any clams that do not open easily.

Drain the linguine thoroughly and add to the pan containing the clams. Season the linguine liberally with salt, add a generous drizzle of olive oil, and toss. Divide the linguine between warmed bowls. Ladle the clams over the pasta, neatly tucking the clam shells into the pasta. Moisten each bowl of pasta with the clam juices. Drizzle with more olive oil and sprinkle the lemon zest and parsley on top. Serve at once.

500 g (1 lb 2 oz) fresh clams

250 g (9 oz) dried linguine

1 tbsp olive oil

1 large clove garlic, peeled

4 tbsp dry white wine (optional)

Fine sea salt

Extra virgin olive oil

1 tsp grated lemon zest

1 tbsp chopped fresh parsley

clams The best clams for this classic pasta dish are the smallest ones you can find, because they will be the most tender. Always buy clams from a reputable fishmonger and look for even-coloured, firm, tightly closed shells (like mussels, clams are sold live in their shells). If a shell has opened slightly, tap it; it should immediately close tightly. If it does not, the clam is dead and should be discarded. Scrub the shells under cold running water to clean them thoroughly before cooking.

Fettuccine with Roquefort and Lemon

preparation **10** minutes | cooking **20** minutes | **4** servings

Even though the pasta sauce is made with cream and blue cheese, this dish is light and fragrant. Reserving a little of the pasta cooking water to add to the pasta and sauce at the end keeps the sauce from becoming heavy and claggy.

tools | saucepan | pasta pan | box grater | colander | wooden spoon

250 ml (8 fl oz) double cream

45 g (1½ oz) Roquefort cheese, crumbled

500 g (1 lb 2 oz) fresh or dried fettuccine

Fine sea salt

Grated zest of 1 lemon

Freshly grated nutmeg

Freshly ground pepper

Bring a large pan of water to the boil. Meanwhile, warm the cream in a saucepan over a moderately low heat and add the Roquefort. Mash the cheese with a wooden spoon until it is fully incorporated into the cream. When the mixture is warm and well blended, remove it from the heat and set aside. Keep warm.

Add the pasta to the boiling water and stir it to prevent sticking, then cook until al dente, from 30 seconds to 5 minutes for fresh pasta, depending on freshness, or according to the packet instructions for dried pasta. Drain well, reserving 120 ml (4 fl oz) of the pasta cooking water.

Return the pasta to the pan and season liberally with salt. Pour the cream mixture over the pasta and toss to coat thoroughly, adding a little of the reserved pasta cooking water as needed to loosen the sauce. Add the lemon zest and season to taste with nutmeg and pepper. Taste to check the seasoning. Serve at once in warmed pasta bowls.

Bolognese Sauce with Tagliatelle

preparation **20** minutes | cooking **2** hours **45** minutes | **6–8** servings

Bolognese, the classic meat sauce from Bologna, benefits from being prepared a day ahead to give the flavours a chance to blend. This shouldn't keep you from eating it the same day it's made, though, and any leftovers will be especially good! Fresh fettuccine can be used in place of the tagliatelle as can dried spaghetti.

tools | large saucepan | pasta pan | chef's knife | box grater | colander | wooden spatula

Heat the olive oil in a large saucepan over a moderate heat. Add the onion and sauté, stirring often, for 5 minutes. Reduce the heat to low, cover, and cook, stirring occasionally, for a further 20 minutes.

Add the carrot, celery, and bacon and cook for 10–15 minutes. The bacon should be starting to brown. Add the garlic, 2 tsp salt, and pepper to taste and cook for 1 more minute or until the garlic is fragrant.

Increase the heat to moderate, add the beef, veal, and pork, and stir vigorously with a wooden spatula to break up the meat. Cook, stirring occasionally, for about 10 minutes or until the meat is lightly browned. Add the mushrooms, tomatoes, chicken and beef stocks, wine, and chilli flakes. Stir well, then reduce the heat to low. Simmer, uncovered, for 2 hours, stirring occasionally. When ready, the sauce should look glistening and deep in colour, and taste rich.

Bring a large pan of water to the boil. When the sauce is just about ready, add the tagliatelle to the boiling water and cook until it is tender and rises to the surface, which can take 30 seconds to 5 minutes, depending on freshness. Drain, reserving a few tablespoons of the pasta cooking water.

Return the tagliatelle to the pan, season with salt, and ladle in the Bolognese sauce. Add the reserved pasta cooking water as needed to loosen the sauce. Stir in the cream. Taste for salt and adjust the seasoning, if necessary. Divide the pasta among warmed pasta bowls, sprinkle with the parsley and Parmesan, and serve at once.

> **fresh pasta** Bolognese sauce is often served over spaghetti, but tagliatelle is more traditional in Italy. If you prefer, you can use dried tagliatelle instead of fresh. While dried pastas can take more than 10 minutes to cook (following timings suggested on the packet), fresh pastas are usually ready in less than 5 minutes, and really fresh home-made pasta cooks in less than 1 minute. Cooked fresh pastas won't have the same al dente (firm "to the tooth") texture as dried pastas, but instead are cooked until tender. Take care, though, not to overcook them until they are mushy.

4 tbsp olive oil

1 large onion, finely diced

1 carrot, peeled and finely diced

1 small stick celery, finely diced

3 rashers streaky bacon, finely chopped

1 tbsp finely chopped garlic

Fine sea salt and pepper

500 g (1 lb 2 oz) minced steak or other lean beef

250 g (9 oz) minced veal

250 g (9 oz) minced pork

85 g (3 oz) button mushrooms, chopped

500 ml (16 fl oz) basic tomato sauce (page 213)

250 ml (8 fl oz) chicken stock

250 ml (8 fl oz) beef stock

500 ml (16 fl oz) dry red wine

Pinch of dried chilli flakes

1 kg (2¼ lb) fresh tagliatelle *(see left)*

150 ml (5 fl oz) double cream, warmed

4 tbsp chopped fresh parsley

Freshly grated Parmesan cheese

Penne with Sausage and Greens

preparation **20** minutes | cooking **20** minutes | **4** servings

The addition of potatoes and greens gives this classic sausage and tomato sauce a satisfying heartiness. You can use any greens that are available and in season, or you can substitute fresh flat-leaf parsley leaves.

tools | large sauté pan | pasta pan | small saucepan | chef's knife | box grater | colander | vegetable peeler

150 g (5½ oz) peeled and finely diced new potatoes

Fine sea salt

500 g (1 lb 2 oz) penne, ziti, or small conchiglie (shells)

2 tbsp olive oil

1 small onion, finely diced

2 sweet or spicy Italian sausages, about 200 g (7 oz) total weight, casings removed and meat crumbled

2 small cloves garlic, chopped

250 ml (8 fl oz) basic tomato sauce (page 213)

Pinch of dried chilli flakes

Handful of rocket or red mustard greens, patted dry

Freshly grated Parmesan cheese to serve

Bring a small saucepan of water to the boil. Add the potatoes and a pinch of salt, reduce the heat to moderate, and simmer for 6–9 minutes or just until tender. The potatoes should retain their shape without falling apart. Drain and set aside to cool.

Meanwhile, bring a large pan of water to the boil. Add the pasta and cook until al dente, according to the packet instructions.

While the pasta is cooking, heat the olive oil in a large sauté pan over a moderate heat. Add the onion and sauté for 5–7 minutes or until golden. Add the sausage, stir well, and cook for 3 minutes. Add the garlic, tomato sauce, chilli flakes, and cooked potatoes. Taste and adjust the seasoning with salt and chilli flakes.

Drain the pasta thoroughly, reserving a few tablespoons of the pasta cooking water. Add the pasta and the reserved pasta cooking water to the sauce. Toss well. Taste and adjust the seasoning with more salt or chilli flakes, if needed. Immediately before serving, fold in the rocket. Serve in warmed bowls, with Parmesan for sprinkling over.

Pizza Four Ways

preparation **20** minutes | cooking **10** minutes | each pizza serves **1**

Instead of presenting traditional courses at a dinner party, surprise your guests with a series of delicious home-made pizzas. Provide an array of toppings from the choices below, or invent your own. Each recipe below will top one 20 cm (8 inch) pizza base; on page 219 you'll find a recipe for 6 bases.

tools | chef's knife | box grater | pizza peel | pizza stone | citrus zester

Pizza Bianca This is a modern version of a winter classic. *Pizza bianca* means "white pizza"; the name refers to the lack of tomato sauce. *Pizza bianca* is graced with three cheeses: ricotta, fresh mozzarella, and Fontina. We like to add a chiffonade of sweet escarole leaves, lemon zest, and garlic to decorate the rich canvas of cheese. Add chilli flakes in place of the pepper, if you like a little more heat. If escarole is not available, use radicchio or chicory.

Place a pizza stone in the oven and preheat to its highest temperature. Lightly flour a wooden pizza peel and place the dough round on it. Scatter the cheeses evenly over the dough. Avoid placing too much cheese in the centre of the pizza; the cheese will flow towards the centre during baking. Scatter the escarole in an even layer on top of the cheese. It will shrink during baking. Sprinkle over the lemon zest, garlic, salt to taste, and olive oil. Slide the pizza from the wooden peel onto the stone in the oven and bake for about 10 minutes or until the base is crisp and the toppings are cooked. Use the peel to transfer the pizza to a wooden board, grind over some pepper, if using, and serve at once.

Flour for dusting

20 cm (8 inch) pizza base (page 219)

30 g (1 oz) fresh mozzarella cheese, torn into small pieces

30 g (1 oz) Fontina cheese, grated

2 tablespoons fresh ricotta

Handful of inner escarole leaves, thinly sliced

Grated zest of $\frac{1}{2}$ lemon

1 small clove garlic, finely chopped

Fine sea salt

1 tbsp fruity extra virgin olive oil

Freshly ground pepper (optional)

Pizza Margherita This simple classic can be served year-round. Our secret is to use high-quality canned tomatoes, chopped and mixed with olive oil, salt, and a pinch of sugar. If possible, use buffalo mozzarella (*mozzarella di bufala*) and the best extra virgin olive oil you have.

Place a pizza stone in the oven and preheat to its highest setting. Drain the tomatoes, reserving 1–2 tbsp of the juices, and coarsely chop them, leaving a few large chunks. Toss the tomatoes and the reserved juice together with the sugar, olive oil, and a good pinch of salt. Lightly flour a wooden pizza peel and place the dough round on it. Scatter the mozzarella evenly over the dough. Scatter the chopped tomatoes liberally over the mozzarella, trying to avoid putting too many in the centre of the pizza. Sprinkle with more salt. Slide the pizza from the wooden peel onto the stone in the oven and bake for about 10 minutes or until the base is crisp and the toppings are cooked. Use the peel to transfer the pizza to a wooden board. Scatter some basil leaves over the pizza and serve at once.

250 g (9 oz) canned whole plum tomatoes

Pinch of caster sugar

2 tbsp extra virgin olive oil

Fine sea salt

Flour for dusting

20 cm (8 inch) pizza base (page 219)

45–60 g (1$\frac{1}{2}$–2 oz) fresh mozzarella cheese

Fresh basil leaves

continued >

Grilled Aubergine Pizza Fresh herby breadcrumbs give this summertime pizza a fabulous crunchy texture. The lacy layer of breadcrumbs will absorb flavours from the tomatoes, garlic, herbs, and Parmesan. For a salty kick, sprinkle with chopped rinsed capers before baking.

1 aubergine

1 tbsp olive oil

Fine sea salt and pepper

Flour for dusting

20 cm (8 inch) pizza base (page 219)

60 g (2 oz) fresh mozzarella cheese

1 ripe red tomato, cut into 3 mm (⅛ inch) slices

3 tbsp fresh breadcrumbs (page 215)

2 tsp chopped fresh oregano

2 tsp chopped fresh parsley

1 small clove garlic, crushed

1 tbsp freshly grated Parmesan cheese

1 tbsp extra virgin olive oil

Place a pizza stone in the oven and preheat to its highest setting. Preheat the grill. Trim off the stalk end of the aubergine and cut the aubergine into slices 5 mm (¼ inch) thick. Brush both sides of each slice with olive oil and lightly season with salt. Place the aubergine on the grill pan and grill for 2 minutes. Turn the slices over and grill for another 2 minutes. Allow to cool slightly, then cut on the diagonal into strips 4 cm (1½ inches) wide. Season with pepper.

Lightly flour a wooden pizza peel and place the dough round on it. Tear the mozzarella into bite-sized pieces. Scatter the mozzarella evenly over the dough. Arrange the tomato slices evenly on top of the mozzarella. (If the tomato is large you may have too much.) Layer and intersperse the aubergine with the tomato and mozzarella. In a bowl, stir together the breadcrumbs, oregano, parsley, and garlic. Sprinkle the breadcrumb mixture liberally over the pizza. Sprinkle the pizza with the Parmesan, season with a good pinch of salt, and drizzle over the extra virgin olive oil. Slide the pizza from the wooden peel onto the stone in the oven and bake for about 10 minutes or until the base is crisp and the toppings are cooked. Use the peel to transfer the pizza to a wooden board and serve at once.

Pizza Quattro Stagione Each quadrant of this pizza, available at nearly every pizzeria in Rome, is topped with a different ingredient: artichoke hearts, Parma ham, button mushrooms, and capers. And although it's debatable whether these four staples accurately represent the "four seasons" suggested by the name, we still think it's a charming idea. You can vary this recipe with your own favourite ingredients. We like to sprinkle fresh rocket leaves over the entire pizza to bring "the seasons" together.

Flour for dusting

20 cm (8 inch) pizza base (page 219)

30 g (1 oz) fresh mozzarella cheese, torn into 1 cm (½ inch) pieces

4 button mushrooms, brushed clean and thinly sliced

Good pinch of fine sea salt

1 tbsp capers, rinsed and coarsely chopped

3 marinated artichoke hearts, quartered

2 slices Parma ham

Handful of rocket leaves

1 tbsp extra virgin olive oil

Place a pizza stone in the oven and preheat to its highest setting. Lightly flour a wooden pizza peel and place the dough round on it. Scatter the cheese evenly over the dough. Arrange the mushroom slices evenly over one-quarter of the pizza. Season with the salt. Scatter the capers evenly over a second quarter and arrange the artichoke hearts on the third quarter. Leave one-quarter empty – that one is for the Parma ham.

Slide the pizza from the wooden peel onto the stone in the oven and bake for about 10 minutes or until the base is crisp and the toppings are cooked. Use the peel to transfer the pizza to a wooden board. Drape the slices of Parma ham on the final quarter. Scatter the rocket leaves over the entire pizza, and drizzle over the olive oil. Serve at once.

Risotto Milanese

preparation **10** minutes | cooking **40** minutes | **4–6** servings

This dish, the classic accompaniment to osso buco (page 100), relies on the best ingredients: deep orange-red saffron, good home-made stock, and well-aged Parmesan cheese.

tools | small baking dish | 2 large saucepans | chef's knife | box grater | ladle

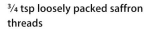

Preheat the oven to 190°C (375°F).

Put the saffron in a small baking dish and toast for 3 minutes; this will deepen its colour and awaken its flavour.

Melt 60 g (2 oz) of the butter in a large saucepan over a low heat. Add the onion, cover, and cook for 10–12 minutes or until the onion is soft but not browned.

Meanwhile, crumble half the saffron into the stock in a large saucepan. Bring to the boil over a high heat, then remove from the heat.

Add the rice and remaining saffron to the onion and stir to coat. Stirring constantly, add 250 ml (8 fl oz) of the stock. Season with the salt and continue stirring over a moderately low heat until the stock is absorbed. Add another ladleful of stock and stir until it is absorbed. Repeat this process, adding the rest of the stock gradually, ladle by ladle, until the rice is creamy but al dente. If the rice seems dry or sticky, add a splash of extra stock. Total cooking time will be about 20 minutes.

Stir in the remaining butter and taste and adjust the seasoning. Sprinkle over the Parmesan and serve at once on warmed plates or bowls.

¾ tsp loosely packed saffron threads

75 g (2½ oz) butter

1 small onion, finely diced

2 litres (3½ pints) chicken stock (page 216)

350 g (12 oz) Arborio rice

½ tsp fine sea salt

45 g (1½ oz) Parmesan cheese, freshly grated

---

risotto with peas and Parma ham Follow the instructions above but omit the saffron. After 10 minutes of stirring stock into the risotto, add 300 g (10 oz) podded fresh peas. Continue adding stock until the risotto is creamy but al dente and the peas are tender. To serve, stir in 1 tsp finely chopped fresh parsley and 1 tsp finely chopped fresh mint, and garnish liberally with strips of Parma ham or Serrano ham.

risotto with pumpkin and sage Follow the instructions above but omit the saffron. Just before cooking the risotto, sauté 300 g (10 oz) diced peeled pumpkin in olive oil until almost tender. After 15 minutes of stirring stock into the risotto, add the sautéed pumpkin and 2 tsp finely chopped fresh sage. Continue adding stock until the risotto is creamy but al dente and the pumpkin is completely tender.

Vegetables

Here is a group of recipes we gathered to help you through the year of changing seasons and to celebrate the availability of so much wonderful fresh produce. When we were growing up, it seemed that carrots, peas, and spinach were the only choices. Now, thanks to a green-market revolution, we truly have a wealth of options. This chapter contains some of our absolute favourites, including fragrant braised fennel and nutty caramelized Brussels sprouts. Some of these recipes can make a main course – try summery ratatouille with a garden salad and crisp warm bread.

Asparagus Mimosa

preparation **15** minutes | cooking **15** minutes | **4–6** servings

Chopped hard-boiled egg resembles the fluffy yellow and white mimosa flower, hence the name of this recipe. The mimosa flower blooms in springtime, which is also the best season for asparagus. Serve this dish for an al fresco brunch to celebrate the return of longer days and milder weather.

tools | large saucepan | baking sheet | chef's knife | tongs | vegetable peeler | whisk

2 hard-boiled eggs (page 214)

30 g (1 oz) coarse fresh breadcrumbs (page 215)

5 tbsp extra virgin olive oil

Fine sea salt and pepper

1 shallot, finely chopped

2 tsp champagne vinegar

750 g (1 lb 10 oz) thick asparagus spears

Preheat the oven to 190°C (375°F). Peel the eggs, chop finely, and set aside.

Toss the breadcrumbs with 1 tbsp of the olive oil and salt to taste. Spread on a baking sheet and toast for 10–12 minutes or until golden.

In a bowl, combine the shallot with the vinegar and salt and pepper to taste. Leave the shallot to macerate in the vinegar for 5 minutes. Whisk in the remaining 4 tbsp olive oil. Taste and adjust the seasoning. Set this vinaigrette aside.

To prepare the asparagus, snap off the tough woody ends of the stalks and trim the ends neatly. Using a vegetable peeler, peel the stalks lengthways, starting from beneath the tip, to expose the tender, light green flesh and remove the fibrous exterior. Bring a large saucepan of salted water to the boil. Blanch half of the asparagus for about 1 minute or until just tender but still firm. Remove the asparagus from the water with tongs and spread on a baking sheet to cool. Repeat to blanch the remaining asparagus.

Toss the asparagus spears with the vinaigrette to coat. Check the seasoning. Arrange the spears on a serving platter. Sprinkle the chopped egg over the asparagus, followed by the breadcrumbs. Pour over any remaining vinaigrette and serve.

Ginger Carrot Salad

preparation **10** minutes | cooking **10** minutes | marinating **1** hour | **6** servings

These carrots can accompany a main dish or be served as part of an antipasto platter with thin slices of your favourite salami, a hard cheese such as pecorino, cucumber salad (page 156), and warm marinated olives (page 58). For the best flavour, look for small, slender young carrots with green leaves still attached to indicate freshness (remove the tops as soon as you get the carrots home).

tools | large sauté pan | small sauté pan | baking sheet | chef's knife | citrus reamer | mortar and pestle (optional) | vegetable peeler

Trim the carrots, leaving 5 mm (¼ inch) of the green stalk intact, then peel. Heat 5 cm (2 inches) of water in a large sauté pan. Add 2 tsp of the vinegar and the salt and bring to a simmer. Taste the water: it should have a mildly acidic, salted flavour. This gives a sparkle to the carrots as they cook. Add the carrots and simmer for 7–8 minutes or until tender but still firm. Drain the carrots and leave to cool in a single layer on a baking sheet.

Place the cumin and caraway seeds in a small sauté pan over a moderate heat and toast, shaking the pan so that they heat evenly, for 20 seconds or until fragrant. Coarsely grind the seeds with a mortar and pestle, or chop firmly using a sharp chef's knife.

In a shallow serving bowl, toss the carrots with the lemon juice, ginger, cayenne, the remaining 2 tsp vinegar, the ground cumin and caraway, and the olive oil until well coated. Taste and adjust the seasoning with additional salt, ginger, or lemon juice. Sprinkle with the chopped coriander. Allow the carrots to marinate at room temperature for 1 hour before serving.

Note: The carrots will keep in the fridge for 1–2 days.

2 bunches of slender, young carrots

4 tsp champagne vinegar or sherry vinegar

½ tsp fine sea salt

¼ tsp cumin seeds

¼ tsp caraway seeds

1 tsp fresh lemon juice

¾ tsp peeled and finely chopped fresh ginger

¼ tsp cayenne pepper

2 tbsp extra virgin olive oil

2 tbsp chopped fresh coriander

Cucumber Salad

preparation **10** minutes | **2–4** servings

Serve this refreshing salad as part of a summertime supper, with toasted bagels and slices of smoked salmon for brunch, or with ginger carrot salad (page 155) and sautéed spinach (page 163) for a colourful antipasto course. For a touch of heat, add a pinch of cayenne pepper with the curry powder.

tools | chef's knife | vegetable peeler

2 cucumbers

Fine sea salt

2 tbsp crème fraîche

4 tbsp plain yogurt

¼ tsp curry powder

Leaves from 6 sprigs fresh coriander, chopped

Peel the cucumbers, cut in half lengthways, and scrape out the seeds with a spoon. Cut across into uniform slices about 3 mm (⅛ inch) thick. Season the cucumbers with salt and mix with the crème fraîche, yogurt, and curry powder. Transfer to a serving bowl, garnish with the coriander, and serve.

Peas with Lemon, Tarragon, and Shallots

preparation **15** minutes | cooking **10** minutes | **4** servings

If tiny fresh, sweet peas are available, by all means use them. The spring season for fresh peas is short and their sweetness is fleeting. Luckily, frozen petit pois are a good substitute here, making this a year-round dish.

tools | sauté pan | chef's knife | citrus reamer | citrus zester

15 g (½ oz) butter

1 tbsp olive oil

2 shallots, finely chopped

300 g (10 oz) frozen petit pois

2 tsp finely chopped fresh parsley

1 tbsp chopped fresh tarragon

1 tsp finely chopped lemon zest

1½–2 tsp fresh lemon juice

Fine sea salt

Heat the butter with the olive oil in a sauté pan over a moderate heat. When the butter has melted, sauté the shallots for about 5 minutes or until softened but not browned. Add the petit pois, 2 tbsp water, the parsley, tarragon, lemon zest, lemon juice, and salt to taste. Cook, stirring occasionally, for 3–5 minutes or until the peas are heated through. Serve at once.

Stuffed Courgettes

preparation **15** minutes | cooking **20** minutes | **6–8** servings

Serve stuffed courgettes as a side dish, as a starter before a pasta main dish, or with a mixed salad for a light lunch on a sunny day.

tools | large baking tin | large saucepan | chef's knife | box grater | colander

Bring a large saucepan of salted water to the boil. Add the whole courgettes and reduce the heat to a simmer. Simmer the courgettes for 10–15 minutes or just until tender. Drain and leave to cool.

Preheat the grill. Lightly oil a large baking tin. In a bowl, stir together the ricotta, Parmesan, flour, salt and black pepper to taste, the cayenne, and the lemon zest.

Slice the courgettes in half lengthways and scoop out the seeds with a small spoon. Place the courgette halves in the prepared baking tin. Season with salt and pepper, then fill with the cheese mixture, mounding it slightly. Sprinkle with the pecorino. Place the baking tin under the grill and cook for 5–7 minutes or until the cheese filling is warm and starts to brown slightly. Scatter the shredded basil over the courgettes and serve warm.

> **seeding courgettes** The method of removing seeds from courgettes is the same as for cucumber. Cut the vegetable in half lengthways, then draw the tip of a small spoon (or a melon baller) down the length of the vegetable, scooping out the seeds.

4 courgettes, each 10–12.5 cm (4–5 inches) long

Olive oil for greasing

250 g (9 oz) fresh ricotta

30 g (1 oz) Parmesan cheese, freshly grated

1 tbsp flour

Fine sea salt and black pepper

Pinch of cayenne pepper

Pinch of grated lemon zest

2 tbsp freshly grated pecorino or Parmesan cheese

Leaves from 1 large sprig fresh basil, shredded

Spicy Italian-style Cauliflower

preparation **15** minutes | cooking **25** minutes | **4–6** servings

This caramelized cauliflower has an appealing texture and spiciness that can convert even those who swear they don't like cauliflower. Try this technique with broccoli too.

tools | large sauté pan | chef's knife | citrus zester

1 cauliflower, about 1 kg (2¼ lb)

3 tbsp olive oil, or as needed

¼ tsp fine sea salt

3 tbsp capers, rinsed and chopped, or to taste

2 tsp finely chopped lemon zest

3 cloves garlic, crushed

¼ tsp dried chilli flakes, or to taste

3 tbsp finely chopped black or green olives

Remove the outer leaves of the cauliflower and trim off the stalk end. Cut the cauliflower into 1 cm (½ inch) slices from the top to bottom, using the entire head, florets and stalks. The cauliflower will break up as you slice it, leaving you with pieces of varying sizes and shapes. Heat the olive oil in a large sauté pan over a moderate heat. (You may need to cook the cauliflower in batches.) When the oil is hot, add the cauliflower. Allow it to sizzle and begin to brown, stirring often so it does not scorch. When the cauliflower begins to soften slightly, after 3–4 minutes, add the salt, capers, lemon zest, garlic, chilli flakes, and olives. Continue cooking, stirring often, for 10–15 minutes or until the cauliflower is golden brown and the other ingredients have caramelized. As you stir, scrape the pan with your spoon to loosen the caramelized bits that have stuck to the bottom. Taste and adjust the seasoning with chilli flakes, capers, and salt, then serve at once.

Braised Red Cabbage

preparation **10** minutes | cooking **35** minutes | **4** servings

Braised cabbage is an essential comfort food for autumn, winter, and even a chilly early spring. Serve with roast turkey (page 116) or duck (page 121).

tools | large saucepan | chef's knife | paring knife or vegetable peeler | wooden spatula

1 red cabbage

45 g (1½ oz) butter or 3 tbsp olive oil

4 shallots, thinly sliced

2 tsp sugar

2 tbsp cider vinegar

120 ml (4 fl oz) dry red wine

Fine sea salt and pepper

1 large, firm but ripe pear

Cut the cabbage in half lengthways. Cut out the core and slice the cabbage thinly.

Melt the butter in a large saucepan over a moderate heat. Add the shallots and sauté, stirring constantly, for 3–5 minutes or until they are soft but not browned.

Add the cabbage, sugar, vinegar, and wine and season to taste with salt and pepper. Cover, reduce the heat to low, and braise slowly for about 25 minutes. The cabbage should deepen in colour and become tender, but with a slightly firm texture.

Peel the pear and cut in half lengthways, removing the stalk. Scoop out the core and dice the pear. Add to the cabbage and cook for a further 5 minutes. Taste and adjust the seasoning with salt and pepper. Serve warm.

Celeriac Rémoulade

preparation **15** minutes | **4** servings

This dish can wear a lot of hats. Serve it with a combination of salad greens or sliced apples at a picnic or brunch, or as an accompaniment to Parma ham and salami, cured or smoked fish, or roast chicken (page 112). One of our favourite ways to eat celeriac rémoulade is as a late-night supper with marinated beetroot (see page 90) or perfectly ripe avocado wedges. The flavour of the dish improves as it sits, so it can be made a day or two in advance. Just be sure to keep it tightly covered to prevent discoloration.

tools | chef's knife or mandolin | citrus reamer | vegetable peeler or paring knife | whisk

To make the dressing, combine the vinegar, lemon juice, salt, and olive oil in a small bowl. Whisk in the mustard, mustard seeds, and cream until well blended.

Carefully peel the outer skin of the celeriac with a vegetable peeler or sharp paring knife. Cut the bulb lengthways into thin slices, then stack the slices and cut again to make julienne (thin matchstick shapes). Put the celeriac in a serving bowl.

Pour the dressing over the celeriac and toss with your hands to coat thoroughly. Taste and adjust the seasoning. Cover and chill for 1–2 hours, or until ready to serve. Serve chilled or at room temperature.

> **celeriac** This knobbly, round winter vegetable contributes a subtle celery flavour to purées when cooked and a crisp crunch to salads when used raw. It discolours quickly once cut, so if not using immediately drop it into water with a squeeze of lemon juice.

1 medium celeriac, about 500 g (1 lb 2 oz)

FOR THE DRESSING

2 tbsp champagne vinegar

2 tsp fresh lemon juice

¼ tsp fine sea salt

120 ml (4 fl oz) olive oil

1 tbsp Dijon mustard, or to taste

2 tsp yellow or black mustard seeds

6 tbsp double cream

Ratatouille

resting **45** minutes | preparation **20** minutes | cooking **65** minutes | **8** servings

Ratatouille is Provence's velvety mélange of colourful summer vegetables. Some think that it's better served the day after it is made, once the flavours have had a chance to marry. We think it's great hot or cold, and it's delicious when folded into scrambled eggs. Choose smaller aubergines for better flavour.

tools | large baking dish | large frying pan | chef's knife | colander | vegetable peeler

500 g (1 lb 2 oz) aubergines

Fine sea salt

5 small courgettes

1 red pepper

1 yellow pepper

1 large onion

4 large, ripe tomatoes, peeled

6–8 tbsp extra virgin olive oil

1 bay leaf

1 tsp finely chopped garlic

4 sprigs fresh thyme

Freshly ground black pepper

Cayenne pepper

Fresh basil leaves to garnish

Preheat the oven to 190°C (375°F). Peel the aubergines and cut the flesh into 2.5 cm (1 inch) chunks. Lightly season with salt, place in a colander, and weight down with a plate and a can of food or something similar. Leave the aubergine to drain for 45 minutes. Cut the courgettes into 2.5 cm (1 inch) chunks. Remove seeds and ribs from the red and yellow peppers and cut into 2.5 cm (1 inch) squares. Cut the onion and tomatoes into large dice.

Pat the aubergine dry with kitchen paper. Heat 4 tbsp of the olive oil in a large frying pan over a moderate heat and sauté the aubergine for 10–15 minutes or until lightly browned. Transfer the aubergine to a large baking dish. Add the courgettes and peppers to the same frying pan, with additional oil if necessary to prevent the vegetables from sticking. Season with salt and sauté for about 2 minutes or until the vegetables are slightly softened. Transfer to the baking dish. Add the onion and tomatoes to the baking dish. Add the bay leaf, garlic, and thyme and season generously with salt, black pepper, and cayenne. Stir all the vegetables together.

Cover the dish with foil and bake for 30 minutes (the foil will cause the vegetables to cook in their own steam). Remove the foil and continue to bake for about 20 minutes or until the ratatouille has thickened and you like the way it tastes. Serve warm or cold, sprinkled with freshly torn basil leaves.

Sautéed Kale with Sultanas

preparation **15** minutes | cooking **25** minutes | **4** servings

Kale is a delicious leafy green available in the autumn, winter, and early spring. Cooking time can depend on the age and tenderness of the plant. Cook these greens a little longer if they are mature; if using tender, young kale, cook it a little less.

tools | small saucepan | large sauté pan | chef's knife | salad spinner

In a small saucepan, combine the sultanas with water to cover and add the red wine vinegar. Warm gently over a low heat for about 5 minutes or until the sultanas are plump. Remove from the heat, drain, and set aside.

Meanwhile, remove the stalks from the kale. Rinse and lightly dry the leaves, leaving a little water clinging to them. Chop the leaves into bite-sized pieces. Heat a large sauté pan over a moderately low heat. Add the olive oil and a handful of kale to cover the bottom of the pan. Cook gently, adding more kale as it wilts and cooks down, until all of the kale has been added. Season with salt, reduce the heat to low, cover, and cook for 10 minutes. Uncover, add the sultanas, and continue to cook for about 10 minutes or until the excess moisture has evaporated and the kale is tender. Stir in the cider vinegar and serve warm or at room temperature.

45 g (1½ oz) sultanas or raisins

1 tsp red wine vinegar

1 kg (2¼ lb) kale

3 tbsp olive oil

Fine sea salt

1½ tbsp cider vinegar

Spinach with Chilli and Garlic

preparation **10** minutes | cooking **4** minutes | **2** servings

Here's a quick-cooking vegetable side dish that makes a classic accompaniment for fish. Try it with plaice with lemon, brown butter, and capers (page 122), or with salmon with Puy lentils (page 124).

tools | large sauté pan | chef's knife | salad spinner | tongs

Warm the olive oil in a large sauté pan over a low heat. Add the pancetta and sauté gently for 2–3 minutes or until lightly golden but not crispy. Add the garlic and sauté for 30 seconds, then add the spinach. Use tongs to lift and turn the spinach gently in the pan just until it is wilted. Don't overcook, or the spinach will become wet and soggy. Add the chilli flakes and season with salt. Serve at once.

1 tbsp olive oil

2 slices pancetta, or 1 rasher streaky bacon, finely chopped

½ tsp finely chopped garlic

250 g (9 oz) spinach leaves, patted dry

Pinch of dried chilli flakes

Fine sea salt

Caramelized Brussels Sprouts

preparation **10** minutes | cooking **5** minutes | **2** servings

This oft-maligned vegetable is meltingly delicious when cooked right. For an autumn and winter treat, we like to separate Brussels sprouts into leaves and quickly sauté them until lightly caramelized. Sautéing in fruity olive oil brings out a sweet, nutty flavour.

tools | sauté pan | paring knife | wooden spatula

16 Brussels sprouts

2 tbsp fruity olive oil

Fine sea salt and pepper

Remove any loose fibrous outer leaves from the Brussels sprouts. Trim the bottom ends and remove the tiny cores with a sharp paring knife. Use your fingers to separate the individual leaves. If the inner core of leaves is too compact to separate, slice it into thin sections.

Heat the olive oil in a sauté pan over a moderate heat. When the oil is hot, add the Brussels sprout leaves. Season with salt and pepper. Sauté vigorously, stirring and tossing, for about 5 minutes or until the leaves have softened and are beginning to crisp and brown slightly. Serve at once.

Roast Onion Squash Crescents

preparation **10** minutes | cooking **30** minutes | **4–6** servings

Bright orange onion squashes, so-called because of their onion-like shape, are usually available in the autumn. Serve these roasted crescents with roast turkey (page 116) or duck (page 121), alongside sautéed kale (page 163).

tools | baking sheet | chef's knife

3 medium onion squashes

4 tbsp olive oil

1 tbsp soft light brown sugar

½ tsp fine sea salt

Freshly ground pepper

Preheat the oven to 180°C (350°F). Rinse the squashes under cold water and pat them dry. Cut each squash in half lengthways. Using a spoon, scrape out the seeds and discard. Trim off the ends of the squash, then cut each squash half into slices 1 cm (½ inch) thick, making crescent shapes.

Combine all the squash crescents in a large bowl with the olive oil, brown sugar, salt, and pepper to taste and toss until well coated. Arrange the squash crescents on 1 or 2 baking sheets in a single layer. Roast for 15 minutes, then turn the pieces over and roast for another 15 minutes or until the flesh is golden and tender. You should be able to pierce the flesh easily with a fork; if there is still slight resistance, roast for a further 5–10 minutes. Serve warm.

Braised Fennel

preparation **15** minutes | cooking **50** minutes | **4** servings

As fennel cooks, its flavour deepening and its texture becoming velvety, its heady anise aroma fills your kitchen. This versatile autumn side dish complements a number of main courses, including brined pork chops (page 105), roast sea bass with bacon (page 123), and roast chicken (page 112).

tools | small sauté pan | small baking dish | chef's knife | mortar and pestle (optional)

Preheat the oven to 200°C (400°F). Put the fennel seeds in a small sauté pan and toast over a low heat, shaking the pan frequently so that the seeds toast evenly, for 2–3 minutes or until fragrant. Crush and grind the seeds with a mortar and pestle, or chop firmly using a sharp chef's knife.

Cut all the stalks from the fennel bulbs, reserving a handful of the green fronds. If the fronds do not look fresh, discard them, but otherwise lightly chop enough of the best-looking ones to give about 4 tbsp. Remove any bruised outer layer from the fennel bulbs, then cut the bulbs into 4 cm (1½ inch) wedges and arrange them in a small, shallow baking dish. Drizzle the olive oil and wine over the fennel and sprinkle with salt and the ground fennel. Add the stock and sprinkle over the chopped fennel fronds, if using. Toss to coat evenly.

Cover the dish with foil and braise in the oven for 30 minutes. Remove the foil and continue cooking for 15–20 minutes or until the fennel is golden. The fennel should be tender when pierced with the tip of a knife. Serve warm.

> **fennel gratin** About 10 minutes before the fennel has finished cooking, brush the top of the fennel wedges with 1 tbsp melted butter and sprinkle with 3 tbsp freshly grated Parmesan cheese, to achieve a gratinéed effect.

1 tsp fennel seeds

3 medium fennel bulbs, with stalks and fronds still attached, if possible

2 tbsp olive oil

120 ml (4 fl oz) dry white wine

Fine sea salt

4 tbsp vegetable stock (page 216) or water

Honey-Balsamic Sweet Potato Mash

preparation **10** minutes | cooking **50** minutes | **4** servings

Honey and balsamic vinegar give these sweet potatoes an alluring sweet-sour flavour. Serve with roast turkey (page 116), chicken (page 112), or pork (page 106).

tools | chef's knife | food mill, ricer, potato masher, or fork

1.5 kg (3 lb 3 oz) sweet potatoes

60 g (2 oz) butter

4 tbsp double cream

1 tbsp wildflower, lavender, or your favourite honey

2 tsp balsamic vinegar

¼ tsp fine sea salt

Freshly ground pepper

Preheat the oven to 200°C (400°F). Line a baking sheet with foil. Prick the sweet potatoes in a few places with a fork. Place on the prepared sheet and bake for 50–60 minutes or until very tender. Set the sweet potatoes aside to cool slightly.

When cool enough to handle, halve the sweet potatoes lengthways and scoop out the flesh into a large bowl. Discard the skins. For a velvety texture, pass the flesh through a ricer or food mill. For a more rustic texture, mash them with a potato masher or fork. Mix in the butter, cream, honey, vinegar, salt, and pepper to taste. Serve at once.

Stir-fried Pak Choy

preparation **10** minutes | cooking **7** minutes | **4** servings

Pak choy, or Chinese white cabbage, is a cousin of broccoli and has a nutty, spinach-like flavour – only mildly reminiscent of typical cabbage. To trim, just cut away the tough core. This dish is particularly delicious served with wok-glazed scallops (page 128).

tools | chef's knife | wok or large frying pan

1–2 tbsp groundnut or olive oil

2 cloves garlic, peeled and lightly crushed

¼ tsp fine sea salt

1 kg (2¼ lb) pak choy, trimmed and cut into 5 mm (¼ inch) slices

1 tbsp toasted sesame oil

Heat a wok or large frying pan over a moderately high heat until hot. Add the oil and garlic and stir-fry for about 30 seconds or until the oil is perfumed. Add the salt and pak choy, increase the heat to high, and stir-fry for 2 minutes. Add 2 tbsp water and continue to stir-fry for 4–5 minutes or until the pak choy is wilted and tender. Serve at once, drizzled with the sesame oil.

Celeriac Purée

preparation **10** minutes | cooking **30** minutes | **4** servings

Because it turns creamy when puréed, celeriac makes a nice alternative to mashed potatoes. Serve with roast beef (page 98), roast pork loin (page 106), or chops (page 105).

tools | large saucepan | chef's knife | vegetable peeler | whisk

Peel the celeriac and potato and cut into 2.5 cm (1 inch) chunks. Put them in a large saucepan with the butter and add water just to cover. Bring to a simmer over a low heat, then cover and simmer for about 30 minutes or until the celeriac and potato are tender. Stir from time to time, adding more water, if necessary, to keep the celeriac and potato from sticking to the bottom of the pan.

Drain the vegetables and return to the saucepan. Whisk until smooth. Whisk in the cream and season to taste with salt and pepper. Sprinkle with nutmeg and serve.

2 medium celeriac

1 medium boiling potato such as Maris Piper

30 g (1 oz) butter

175 ml (6 fl oz) double cream

Fine sea salt and pepper

Freshly grated nutmeg to garnish

Field Mushroom Salad

preparation **15** minutes | **4** servings

In this simple but elegant dish, raw mushrooms are sliced paper-thin and adorned with olive oil, lemon juice, and very fresh mint. We like to use Parmesan as the finishing touch, but you could use a well-aged pecorino or goat's cheese instead. Serve the salad immediately or its delicacy will be lost.

tools | chef's knife | paring knife | lemon juicer | vegetable peeler

Right before you intend to serve the salad, use a dry cloth to brush any dirt off the mushrooms. Trim off the stalks with a sharp paring knife. Place the mushrooms flat side down and thinly slice each cap. Spread the mushroom slices in a single layer on a large serving platter. Crush ½ tsp salt between your fingers to create a fine dust and sprinkle it evenly over the mushrooms. Drizzle most of the olive oil evenly over the mushrooms, reserving a little more for later, and do the same with the lemon juice. Pick the leaves from the mint sprigs, stack and roll them, and finely slice them across to make a chiffonade. Sprinkle the mint over the mushrooms. Use a vegetable peeler to shave thin curls of Parmesan on top. Drizzle the remaining olive oil over the mushrooms, sprinkle with more lemon juice to taste, and grind over some fresh pepper. Serve at once.

500 g (1 lb 2 oz) portabellini or chestnut mushrooms

Coarse sea salt and pepper

3 tbsp fruity extra virgin olive oil

2 tsp fresh lemon juice, or more to taste

Sprigs fresh mint

Parmesan cheese for shaving

Roast Radicchio with Pancetta

preparation **10** minutes | cooking **15** minutes | **4** servings

In this recipe, crisp radicchio is roasted until tender, while the pancetta wrapped around it turns crisp. It's an out of the ordinary side dish or starter for a hearty autumn or winter supper. Smoked streaky bacon rashers can be substituted for the milder pancetta as long as they are stretched with the back of a knife until very thin. If you have a fine aged balsamic vinegar, this is the time to use it – sparingly – as a condiment.

tools | baking tray | chef's knife

1 head of radicchio
(350–450 g/12–16 oz)

2 tbsp extra virgin olive oil

Fine sea salt and freshly
ground pepper

100 g (3½ oz) very thinly sliced
pancetta

2–3 tsp aged balsamic vinegar

Preheat the oven to 180°C (350°F). Slice the radicchio into wedges about 2.5 cm (1 inch) thick at the widest point. The core at the bottom of the radicchio should help keep each of the wedges intact. Place the wedges on a baking tray, drizzle over the olive oil, and sprinkle with salt and pepper.

Loosely wrap each radicchio wedge with a slice or two of pancetta (don't worry if the pancetta slices tear). Leave some of the radicchio exposed to encourage even cooking. Use all of the the pancetta slices. Rub the wrapped wedges in any olive oil that remains on the baking tray, then arrange them flat on the tray.

Roast for 15–20 minutes or until the pancetta has rendered its fat and is crisp and the radicchio is a dark mauve and completely soft. The edges of some of the radicchio wedges may be crisp. Drizzle over the balsamic vinegar and serve at once.

radicchio A variety of chicory native to Italy, radicchio is characterized by its variegated purplish or deep ruby red leaves and pleasantly bitter, peppery taste. It grows in round or elongated heads, and the leaves may be red and white or red, green, and white. The sturdy raw leaves hold up well to cooking, and their assertive flavour is nicely matched with strong cheeses, cured meats, anchovies, olives, and capers.

Sides

Don't let the name of this chapter mislead you. We have been known to crave one of these "sides" and create an entire meal around it. Side dishes can be as inspiring as main courses – it's all in how you think about them. For example, you could make courgette and potato cakes the centrepiece of a quick meal with olives, cheese, and Parma ham. Each recipe offers its own delights of texture and flavour: tarragon-spiked twice-baked potatoes, earthy mushroom pilaf, and comforting soft polenta will each inspire a different mood.

Mushroom Pilaf

preparation **10** minutes | cooking **45** minutes | resting **10** minutes | **4** servings

In this recipe, fresh golden chanterelles give a rich, earthy flavour to a simple pilaf.
If chanterelles are not available, you can use chestnut mushrooms instead.

tools | saucepan | chef's knife | muslin | kitchen string

1 sprig fresh lavender or thyme

115 g (4 oz) butter

1 onion, finely chopped

1 clove garlic, crushed

85 g (3 oz) fresh chanterelles, chopped

300 g (10 oz) long-grain rice

360 ml (12 fl oz) *each* vegetable stock (page 216) and beef stock (page 217)

½ tsp fine sea salt and pepper

Wrap the lavender tightly in muslin and tie with kitchen string. Melt 85 g (3 oz) of the butter in a saucepan over a moderate heat. Add the onion and garlic and sauté for about 10 minutes or until tender but not browned. Add the remaining 30 g (1 oz) butter, then add the mushrooms and stir well. Cook, stirring often, for about 10 minutes or until the mushrooms release their liquid and it is reabsorbed.

Add the rice to the saucepan and reduce the heat to low. Stir for 2 minutes to toast the rice lightly and ensure that each grain is thoroughly coated with butter and turns slightly opaque. Add the vegetable and beef stocks, the salt, and the lavender bundle. Cover and simmer for 25 minutes.

Remove from the heat. Remove the lavender and allow the rice to stand, covered, for 10 minutes. Transfer to a warmed serving dish. Have a pepper mill on the table.

Potato Gratin

preparation **20** minutes | cooking **25** minutes | **4–6** servings

Thinly sliced potatoes are cooked gently in cream on the hob, then finished in the oven for a golden gratinéed top. Warm up leftovers and serve for breakfast with fried eggs.

tools | baking dish | large saucepan | chef's knife or mandolin | paring knife | vegetable peeler

knob of butter, at room temperature

1 kg (2¼ lb) boiling potatoes such as Maris Piper

2 small cloves garlic

250 ml (8 fl oz) double cream

360 ml (12 fl oz) single or half cream

½ tsp fine sea salt

Freshly ground pepper

Preheat the oven to 200°C (400°F). Grease a 2 litre (3½ pint) baking or gratin dish with the butter. Peel the potatoes and, with a chef's knife or mandolin, cut them across into slices about 3 mm (⅛ inch) thick. Place the potatoes in a large, heavy saucepan. Lightly crush the garlic cloves and add to the pan together with the creams, salt, and 10 or more grinds of the pepper mill. Bring the mixture just to the boil over a moderate heat, then lower the heat and simmer, stirring occasionally, for 10–12 minutes. (The dish can be prepared up to this point in advance.) Transfer the potatoes and cream to the prepared baking dish, arranging the potatoes in layers. Bake for about 15 minutes or until the potatoes are tender. Serve hot.

Crisp Rosemary Potatoes Two Ways

preparation **10** minutes | cooking **25–35** minutes | **4** servings

Boiling potatoes in salted water imbues them with seasoning and brings out their flavour, then roasting in a hot oven or frying in olive oil gives them crisp texture. Choose between these two cooking methods based on the other dishes you want to cook at the same time.

tools | large saucepan | baking tray | cast-iron frying pan (optional) | chef's knife | colander | slotted metal turner

If you will be roasting the potatoes, preheat the oven to 200°C (400°F). Wash the potatoes and trim away any blemishes, then cut the unpeeled potatoes into irregularly shaped pieces about 2.5 cm (1 inch) thick. Bring a large saucepan of water to the boil and add the salt. Stir the water and add the potatoes. Lower the heat to a simmer. Cook the potatoes for about 10 minutes or until they are tender and a bit "frayed" at the edges but still retain their shape. Don't worry if the skins start to peel away and a few bits of potato break off. Drain the potatoes well.

To roast the potatoes, toss them with the olive oil to coat. Arrange the potatoes in a single layer in a baking tray, with space in between. Pick the leaves from the rosemary sprigs, coarsely chop, and sprinkle evenly over the potatoes. Roast for 10 minutes, then start turning the potatoes individually as they brown. Continue roasting for 15 minutes, occasionally flipping the potatoes so that they brown evenly on all sides. If the potatoes stick to the tray, loosen them with a metal turner.

To pan-fry the potatoes, spread them out on a baking sheet to cool. Heat the olive oil in a cast-iron frying pan over a moderate heat. In batches as needed, add a layer of potatoes and cook for 8 minutes, flipping the potatoes individually so that they brown evenly. Scatter over the chopped rosemary, then continue cooking for 6–8 minutes or until the potatoes are golden on all sides.

Whichever method you choose, the potatoes can be served at once or kept warm in a low oven for up to 20 minutes.

1 kg (2¼ lb) boiling or baking potatoes

2 tsp coarse sea salt

4 tbsp olive oil

1 sprig fresh rosemary

Best Mashed Potatoes

preparation **10** minutes | cooking **20** minutes | **4** servings

There's no comfort food quite as comforting as mashed potatoes. All good cooks have a secret for their mashed potatoes, and here's ours: use an electric mixer to beat your mashed potatoes into a feathery lightness that your children and grandchildren (or nieces and nephews) will remember fondly. A balloon whisk also works well. Use half cream for the richest results and the greatest future nostalgia.

tools | large saucepan | chef's knife | paring knife | colander | vegetable peeler | electric mixer, whisk, or potato masher

1 kg (2¼ lb) floury baking potatoes, peeled and cut into chunks 4 cm (1½ inches) thick

Fine sea salt and pepper

60 g (2 oz) butter

120 ml (4 fl oz) half cream, or whole, semi-skimmed, or skimmed milk

Put the potatoes in a large saucepan of cold water and season with salt. Bring the water to the boil, then lower the heat slightly to maintain a vigorous simmer and cook the potatoes for about 20 minutes or until tender when pierced with a small knife. Drain the potatoes and return them to the pan. Cover with a tea towel and steam until dry. With an electric mixer, or by hand with a whisk or potato masher, beat in the butter. Beat in the half cream. Continue to beat or whisk vigorously until the potatoes are fluffy. Season to taste with salt and pepper and serve at once.

mashed potatoes with rocket and garlic   In this variation, peppery rocket and fragrant garlic imbue the mashed potatoes with a sweet and nutty flavour. Omit the half cream or milk. Cook the potatoes in boiling salted water as instructed above. While the potatoes cook, heat 1 tbsp olive oil or 15 g (½ oz) butter in a frying pan over a low heat and add 1 finely chopped garlic clove. Cook the garlic slowly, stirring constantly so that it doesn't burn, for about 10 minutes. Add 125 g (4½ oz) rocket leaves to the garlic and cook for about 2 minutes or until the rocket has wilted slightly. After draining the potatoes and beating in the butter, coarsely chop the garlicky greens and stir them into the potatoes with any pan juices. Season to taste and serve at once.

mashed potatoes with mascarpone   Mashed potatoes take on an ethereal quality with the addition of creamy Italian cheese. Follow the recipe for mashed potatoes, but use only 2 tbsp half cream and add 4 tbsp mascarpone cheese.

Warm Potato Salad Dijon

preparation **10** minutes | cooking **12** minutes | **4** servings

For this delicious salad, hot, freshly boiled potatoes are tossed with a mustardy vinaigrette, so that the potatoes soak up its flavours. It makes a nice change from the usual baked or mashed potatoes, but it's still easy enough to prepare for an everyday supper. The best potatoes to use are waxy salad potatoes, which hold their shape after cooking better than floury baking potatoes or all-purpose potatoes. To dress the salad up a bit for entertaining, you could garnish it with deep-fried sage leaves.

tools | small sauté pan | large saucepan | chef's knife | colander | slotted spoon | whisk

Cut the unpeeled potatoes into irregularly shaped pieces about 2.5 cm (1 inch) thick. Bring a large saucepan of water, lightly seasoned with salt, to the boil over a high heat. Add the potatoes and lower the heat to maintain a simmer. Cook for 12–15 minutes or until the potatoes are just tender but still retain their shape. Drain the potatoes, then transfer to a large bowl and, while they are still warm, toss them with the wine and mustard seeds. Season with salt.

While the potatoes are cooking, combine the shallots, vinegar, and 1 tbsp salt in a bowl and leave to stand for 5–10 minutes to soften the shallots. Whisk in the Dijon mustard, then drizzle in the olive oil while whisking to make a vinaigrette.

Toss the potatoes with the vinaigrette to mix thoroughly (don't worry if the potatoes break apart a bit during the tossing). Season with pepper and serve warm, with fried sage leaves arranged on top, if you like.

2 kg (4½ lb) waxy salad potatoes

Fine sea salt and pepper

120 ml (4 fl oz) dry white wine

2 tbsp mustard seeds, lightly toasted (page 61)

60 g (2 oz) shallots, finely chopped

4 tbsp red wine vinegar

3 tbsp Dijon mustard

175 ml (6 fl oz) olive oil

Deep-fried sage to garnish (*see left;* optional)

deep-fried sage leaves Sturdy, pungent fresh sage leaves become delightfully crisp when deep-fried. They pair very well with potatoes in any form. Pour groundnut oil to a depth of about 1 cm (½ inch) into a small sauté pan and heat over a moderate heat until hot but not smoking. Pick the leaves from 1 bunch of fresh sage and pat dry. Place the sage leaves, a few at a time, in the oil and fry for 5–10 seconds or until they just begin to crisp but have not begun to brown. Remove with a slotted spoon and drain on kitchen paper. Repeat with the remaining sage leaves. The leaves will crisp as they cool.

Crispy Onion Rings

preparation **15** minutes | cooking **15–20** minutes | **2–4** servings

A buttermilk and flour batter creates a lacy, fragile coating that seals in the sweet onion flavour. These require close attention, so while one of you cooks the onion rings, the other can grill some burgers or steak. Now that's teamwork.

tools | cast-iron frying pan | baking sheet | chef's knife | deep-frying thermometer | tongs

500 ml (16 fl oz) buttermilk

1 tbsp finely chopped fresh parsley

½ tsp chopped fresh thyme

210 g (7½ oz) flour

1 tsp fine sea salt

2 sweet onions, cut into 5 mm (¼ inch) slices and separated into rings

750 ml (1¼ pints) groundnut oil

Pour the buttermilk into a small bowl and add the parsley and thyme. Combine the flour and salt on a plate. Dip the onions into the buttermilk mixture, then dredge in the flour and place on a baking sheet.

Pour the oil into a deep, cast-iron frying pan and heat over a moderate heat to 150–165°C (300–330°F) on a deep-frying thermometer. Add the onion rings to the hot oil in small batches, being careful not to crowd the pan. Fry for about 3 minutes, turning so that they cook and brown evenly. Adjust the heat as needed to maintain the temperature. Using tongs, transfer the onion rings to kitchen paper to drain and keep warm on a warm corner of the hob while you fry the next batch. Serve immediately.

Twice-baked Potatoes with Tarragon

preparation **15** minutes | cooking **1** hour **15** minutes | **6–8** servings

These irresistible potatoes make a good side dish to serve with a main course that needs last-minute attention. You can prepare them in advance and set aside until you're ready, then put them back in the oven for 15 minutes to heat.

tools | saucepan | baking sheet | chef's knife | potato masher or large fork

4 medium, floury baking potatoes

2 tsp olive oil

60 g (2 oz) butter

120 ml (4 fl oz) milk

Fine sea salt and ground pepper

3 tbsp crème fraîche or soured cream

15 g (½ oz) fresh tarragon, chopped

Preheat the oven to 200°C (400°F). Prick the potatoes with a fork, rub with the olive oil, and sprinkle with 1 tbsp water. Wrap each potato in foil and bake for 1 hour. Remove the potatoes from the oven and unwrap. Leave the oven on.

When the potatoes are cool enough to handle, halve them lengthways. Scoop the flesh into a saucepan and set the skins aside. Mash the flesh with the butter, milk, and salt and pepper to taste. Reheat over a low heat, stirring in the crème fraîche. Remove from the heat, adjust the seasoning, and stir in the tarragon.

Use a spoon to fill the potato skins with the mashed potato mixture, filling them evenly to the top. Place on a baking sheet and bake for about 15 minutes or until golden on top. Serve at once.

Courgette and Potato Cakes

preparation **10** minutes | cooking **30** minutes | **10** small cakes

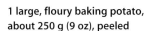

These green-flecked griddle cakes can be served for brunch, lunch, supper, or a late-night snack. Cook them slowly so that they crisp on the outside and stay creamy inside. Serve with soured cream or plain yogurt, Parma ham, and a watercress salad.

tools | cast-iron frying pan | chef's knife | box grater | ladle | vegetable peeler

Grate the potato and courgette using the large holes of a box grater and place in a bowl. Add the onion and egg, season with the salt and pepper to taste, and mix well. The mixture will oxidize and brown slightly, so work quickly.

Heat 2 tbsp of the oil in a large cast-iron frying pan over a low heat. When the oil is hot enough to create a small sizzle, ladle enough mixture into the pan to form several 7.5 cm (3 inch) cakes, leaving some space around each one. Cook for 7–10 minutes or until golden on the base. Using a slotted metal turner, turn the cakes over and cook for 6 minutes or until browned on the second side. Transfer to a plate and keep warm in a low oven. Repeat with the remaining mixture, adding more oil to the pan if needed. Serve hot.

1 large, floury baking potato, about 250 g (9 oz), peeled

1 large courgette, about 250 g (9 oz), ends trimmed

45 g (1½ oz) diced onion

1 egg

½ tsp fine sea salt

Freshly ground pepper

2–4 tbsp groundnut or olive oil

Flaky Buttermilk Rolls

preparation **15** minutes | cooking **15** minutes | **16** rolls

Our favourite recipe for buttermilk rolls comes from our friend Marion Cunningham, author of the Fanny Farmer Cookbook. *We bake these tender, flaky rolls every time we make our grandmother's chicken (page 111) as they are perfect with it.*

tools | baking sheet | chef's knife | whisk or fork

Preheat the oven to 220°C (450°F). Combine the flour, salt, baking powder, and bicarbonate of soda in a bowl and stir to combine with a whisk or fork. Drop the shortening or margarine into the dry ingredients, then use your fingers to rub the fat into the dry ingredients until the mixture forms fine, irregular crumbs that resemble soft breadcrumbs. Add the buttermilk all at once and stir with a fork just until the dough comes together into a mass.

Place the dough on a lightly floured work surface and knead with your hands 12–14 times. Pat into a 20 cm (8 inch) square about 1 cm (½ inch) thick. Use a sharp knife to cut the dough into 5 cm (2 inch) squares. Arrange the rolls with their edges touching on a large ungreased baking sheet. Bake for 15–20 minutes or until risen and golden. Serve at once.

300 g (10 oz) flour

¼ tsp fine sea salt

2 tsp baking powder

½ tsp bicarbonate of soda

115 g (4 oz) solid vegetable shortening or hard margarine, cut into dice

150 ml (5 fl oz) buttermilk

Cheese Soufflé

preparation **10** minutes | cooking **1** hour | **2–4** servings

Here is a classic recipe that always impresses guests when served at a dinner party, either as an unusual side dish or a starter. It also makes a satisfying supper for two, accompanied by a green salad and a glass of white wine.

tools | 2 saucepans | soufflé dish | box grater | fine-mesh sieve | rubber spatula | stainless steel or copper bowl (optional) | whisk | balloon whisk or electric mixer

75 g (2½ oz) butter, plus butter for greasing

50 g (1¾ oz) flour, plus flour for dusting

360 ml (12 fl oz) milk

250 ml (8 fl oz) double cream

5 eggs, separated

175 g (6 oz) Gruyère cheese, grated

Good pinch of cream of tartar

Preheat the oven to 180°C (350°F). Butter and flour a 20 cm (8 inch) diameter soufflé dish. In a large, heavy saucepan melt the butter over a moderately low heat. Stir in the flour and cook for 6–8 minutes or until the flour loses its raw taste, making a roux. Do not allow the roux to get too brown; it should be just a light beige colour. Remove the saucepan from the heat. Combine the milk and cream and slowly pour into the roux, whisking constantly until the mixture is smooth. Return the saucepan to a very low heat and simmer, stirring occasionally, for about 10 minutes or until the mixture thickens.

Put a saucepan with 5 cm (2 inches) of water over a very low heat and bring to a bare simmer. Put the egg yolks in a stainless steel bowl. Slowly strain the hot milk mixture through a fine-mesh sieve into the bowl with the yolks, whisking constantly until well blended. Add the cheese, then place the bowl on top of the saucepan of barely simmering water. Heat the mixture gently, stirring until the cheese is melted.

Place the egg whites in another stainless steel or copper bowl. Add the cream of tartar (omit this if you are using a copper bowl). Whisk until stiff peaks form (page 234). With a wide rubber spatula, fold the whites gently into the yolk mixture, being careful not to deflate the whites by stirring too much.

Pour the mixture into the prepared dish (the dish will be about three-quarters full) and place in the oven. Bake for 40–45 minutes or until the soufflé doubles in height and the top is a deep golden colour. Serve at once.

Almond and Currant Stuffing

preparation **20** minutes | cooking **60** minutes | **6–8** servings

When it comes to stuffing for the Christmas turkey, there are no rules. Use this recipe as a starting point and invent a tradition for your own new family. This basic stuffing includes plumped currants and toasted almonds, with cumin seeds for a savoury depth. Chopped turkey giblets, browned and caramelized sausagemeat, and gently cooked greens are just a few of the ingredients you could add to create your own signature stuffing.

tools | small and medium saucepans | baking sheet | chef's knife | large baking dish

If the bread you are using is fresh, preheat the oven to 170°C (325°F). Place the bread cubes on a baking sheet and place in the oven to dry out for 10–15 minutes. Set aside. Raise the oven temperature to 190°C (375°F). Spread the almonds on a baking sheet and toast for 10–12 minutes or until golden and fragrant. Coarsely chop and set aside. Leave the oven on.

While the almonds are toasting, put the currants in a small saucepan, cover with water, and add the vinegar. Place over a low heat and simmer for 10 minutes or until the currants are plump. Set aside.

Melt the butter in a medium saucepan over a low heat. Add the onion, carrot, and celery and sauté for about 5 minutes or until slightly softened. Add the sage, thyme, cumin seeds, and stock and bring to the boil. Remove from the heat and leave the mixture to cool for 3 minutes.

Place the bread cubes in a large bowl. Pour over the stock mixture. Add the almonds and currants, plus a little of their soaking liquid, and season with salt and pepper. Mix well. Loosely fill the cavity of a 4–5 kg (8–10 lb) turkey with the stuffing and roast immediately (see page 116).

Alternatively, spread the stuffing in a large baking dish and cover with foil. Bake for 30 minutes. Remove the foil and continue to bake for about 20 minutes or until the stuffing is golden. Serve hot with the roast turkey.

500 g (1 lb) sourdough bread, day-old if possible, cut into 1 cm (½ inch) cubes

85 g (3 oz) shelled almonds

60 g (2 oz) dried currants

1 tsp red wine vinegar

45 g (1½ oz) butter

1 small onion, finely diced

1 small carrot, peeled and finely diced

1 stick celery, finely diced

1 tsp chopped fresh sage

½ tsp chopped fresh thyme

½ tsp toasted cumin seeds

360 ml (12 fl oz) chicken or vegetable stock (page 216)

Fine sea salt and pepper

Polenta Two Ways

preparation **10** minutes | cooking **50** minutes | **4** servings

We have been making polenta for years – it's a staple in our house, and we hope it will become one in yours too. You'll find it makes a nice change from the usual potatoes or rice. There are two methods for making polenta, one for "soft" polenta and the other for "set". One of our favourite ways to serve soft polenta is with Bolognese sauce (page 143). Set polenta is delightful grilled or fried, with a simple warm tomato sauce (page 213) and a grating of your favourite cheese. The key to making good polenta is using fresh stone-ground polenta flour with an intense yellow hue and distinct flavour.

tools | baking dish or baking tray | saucepan | whisk

FOR SOFT POLENTA

115 g (4 oz) polenta flour

1 tsp fine sea salt

45 g (1½ oz) butter

A hunk of Parmesan cheese to serve

FOR SET POLENTA

210 g (7½ oz) polenta flour

1 tsp fine sea salt

45 g (1½ oz) butter

To make soft polenta, bring 1.1 litres (2 pt) water to the boil in a heavy saucepan over a high heat. Reduce the heat slightly and gradually add the polenta, whisking constantly. Cook for 5 minutes, whisking often to disperse any lumps that appear. Lower the heat to a simmer and continue cooking, whisking every 5–10 minutes, for 20 minutes. Season the polenta with the salt, stir in the butter, and cook, whisking occasionally, for a further 25 minutes or until thick, smooth, and no longer grainy on the tongue. Taste and adjust the seasoning with salt. Serve at once, with Parmesan for grating on top.

To make set polenta, bring 1.1 litres (2 pt) water to the boil in a heavy saucepan over a high heat. Reduce the heat slightly and gradually add the polenta, whisking constantly. Cook for 5 minutes, whisking often to disperse any lumps that appear. (Note that the larger amount of polenta used may require more whisking than soft polenta in order to eliminate lumps, and you may have to use a wooden spoon rather than a whisk.) Lower the heat to a simmer and continue cooking, whisking every 5–10 minutes, for 20 minutes. Season the polenta with salt, stir in the butter, and cook for a further 20 minutes, whisking occasionally. Taste and adjust the seasoning with salt.

Pour the polenta into a baking dish or a baking tray and leave to cool completely. When cold and set, the polenta can be cut into pieces and grilled, char-grilled, or pan-fried in olive oil or butter. Set polenta will keep for several days, tightly wrapped, in the fridge.

> **polenta additions** To vary the texture and flavour, add 75 g (2½ oz) diced onions and an extra pinch of salt during the second half of cooking. Also, cooked and chopped greens, such as kale or chard, turn polenta green and add flavour, vitamins, and interest to soft polenta. Stir the greens into the polenta during the last 10 minutes of cooking.

White Beans and Sage

preparation **10** minutes | cooking **1¾–2¼** hours | **8–10** servings

White beans and sage go together like love and marriage. Serve this rustic Tuscan dish with grilled sausages, roast chicken (page 112), or a simple green salad and a chunk of your favourite cheese. Use leftovers to make bruschetta (page 64).

tools | deep sauté pan | chef's knife | large metal spoon

Rinse and pick over the beans, discarding any misshapen or discoloured beans. Place in a bowl, add water to cover by 7.5 cm (3 inches), and leave to soak for at least 4 hours or up to overnight.

Drain the beans, rinse them with cold water, and place them in a deep sauté pan. Add cold water to cover by 5 cm (2 inches) and bring to a gentle simmer over a moderate heat, skimming off any particles that rise to the top with a large spoon.

Add the olive oil, onion, garlic, bay leaf, and sage. Simmer for 20 minutes, stirring often so that the beans cook evenly. Add the tomato sauce and season with salt. Cook for a further 30 minutes, stirring occasionally and adding more water if necessary to keep the beans submerged.

Reduce the heat to low and continue to simmer gently, stirring occasionally, for 45 minutes to 1¼ hours or until the beans are tender but not falling apart. Top up the water if needed to keep the beans moist while they cook.

Remove from the heat and allow to cool slightly. Remove the bay leaf and serve.

Note: The timing of bean cooking can vary greatly depending on the age of your dried beans. They may have been on a shelf or in a bin for 2 weeks or for 6 months, and there's no way to tell until you start to cook them. Be patient and taste-test the beans from time to time as they simmer until they are to your liking.

400 g (14 oz) dried white beans such as cannellini, haricot, or butter beans

2 tbsp extra virgin olive oil

1 onion, finely diced

2 cloves garlic, finely chopped

1 bay leaf

4 or 5 fresh sage leaves

250 ml (8 fl oz) basic tomato sauce (page 213)

Fine sea salt

Tuscan Farro

preparation **10** minutes | cooking **20** minutes | **4–6** servings

Farro, an ancient variety of wheat with a nutty flavour similar to that of wild rice, has a distinguished history in ancient Roman cuisine and has recently been enjoying a modern renaissance. Here, we combine the versatile grain with char-grilled cime di rapa and shaved pecorino cheese. Using char-grilled sprouting broccoli, tomatoes, or diced roasted butternut squash instead of the cime di rapa will result in distinct and delicious variations.

tools | large saucepan | baking sheet | chef's knife | colander | vegetable peeler | grill pan

Coarse sea salt

300 g (10 oz) whole-grain farro

500 g (1 lb 2 oz) cime di rapa (see page 137), tough ends trimmed

2 tbsp olive oil

6 tbsp extra virgin olive oil

1 tbsp red wine vinegar or sherry vinegar

A hunk of pecorino cheese to shave

Bring 1 litre (1¾ pints) water and 1 tsp sea salt to the boil in a large saucepan over a high heat. Add the farro and stir once or twice, then cook for 12–14 minutes or until tender but with a little resistance to the bite – neither too firm nor too soft. Drain the farro in a colander and immediately spread on a baking sheet to cool.

Meanwhile, heat a ridged cast-iron grill pan. Toss the cime di rapa with 1 tbsp water, a pinch of salt, and the olive oil. Char-grill on one side for 2 minutes, then turn over and continue cooking for 1–2 minutes or until slightly charred and some of the leaves are crisp. Remove from the pan, coarsely chop, and toss with the farro. Sprinkle with the extra virgin olive oil and the vinegar. Season with salt. Arrange on a warmed platter and, using a vegetable peeler, shave pecorino over the top to garnish. Serve warm or at room temperature.

Spoon Bread with Sweetcorn

preparation **15** minutes | cooking **55** minutes | **4–6** servings

Spoon bread is a wonderful old-fashioned American dish that can be served with just about anything, including pork chops (page 105), roast chicken (page 112), lamb (page 104), or barbecued steak (page 97). You can replace the sweetcorn with sautéed sweet onions or wild mushrooms like morels or chanterelles. Buttermilk gives the dish a pleasant tang.

tools | large saucepan | baking dish | chef's knife | whisk

Preheat the oven to 220°C (450°F). Grease a square baking dish with butter.

Strip off the husks and the silk from the sweetcorn. Holding one of the cobs by its tip, stand it on its end in a large bowl and use a sharp knife to slice off the kernels into the bowl. Repeat with the other cob.

In a large saucepan, bring 600 ml (1 pint) water and the salt to the boil over a moderate heat. Slowly pour the cornmeal or polenta into the water, whisking constantly to dissolve any lumps. Reduce the heat to moderately low and cook for 5–8 minutes or until the mixture becomes very thick and begins to pull away from the sides of the pan. Stir in the butter. Remove from the heat and leave to cool slightly for about 5 minutes.

Meanwhile, in a bowl, whisk together the eggs, buttermilk, and cream until well blended. Add the egg mixture and sweetcorn kernels to the cornmeal mixture and stir until blended. Pour the mixture into the prepared dish.

Bake for 35–40 minutes or until the top is golden brown and a skewer inserted in the centre comes out clean. The spoon bread will have risen much like a soufflé. Serve at once.

Butter for greasing

1 or 2 cobs sweetcorn

1½ tsp fine sea salt

125 g (4½ oz) cornmeal or instant polenta flour

30 g (1 oz) butter

4 eggs

250 ml (8 fl oz) buttermilk

6 tbsp double cream

Tabbouleh

preparation **45** minutes | **6–8** servings

Bright-flavoured ingredients like lemon juice, mint, and tomatoes make this bulghur wheat salad particularly appealing. It is ideal picnic fare, as it is best at room temperature and it travels well. Serve with pitta bread and hummus.

tools | chef's knife | lemon juicer | fine-mesh sieve

175 g (6 oz) bulghur wheat
60 g (2 oz) fresh parsley leaves
30 g (1 oz) fresh mint leaves
6 spring onions
3 medium tomatoes
Juice of 1 lemon
6 tbsp olive oil
Fine sea salt and pepper

Put the bulghur wheat in a large bowl and add cold water to cover generously (you want the bulghur to remain covered after it absorbs some of the water). Allow the bulgur to swell and soften for 30–40 minutes.

Finely chop the parsley and mint. Slice the spring onions, including the tender green tops. Core and coarsely chop the tomatoes.

Drain the bulghur in a fine-mesh sieve, pressing out all the excess moisture with the back of a large spoon. If the bulghur still seems moist, wrap it in a clean tea towel and squeeze out the excess water.

In a serving bowl, toss the bulghur with the parsley, mint, spring onions, tomatoes, and lemon juice. Stir in the olive oil and season with salt and pepper. Serve.

Sautéed Apples

preparation **10** minutes | cooking **10** minutes | **4** servings

Choose sweet yet tart, firm apples, such as Braeburn, Fuji, Gala, or Cox's. Sautéed apples accompany pork or turkey especially well, or try them with duck breasts (page 121) and use the duck fat in place of the butter to cook the apples.

tools | medium sauté pan | paring knife or vegetable peeler | wooden spatula

3 or 4 medium apples
15 g (½ oz) butter
Good pinch of fine sea salt
Pinch of sugar

Peel the apples and cut into wedges 1–2.5 cm (½–1 inch) thick, depending on the size of the apples. Trim away the seeds and cores.

Melt the butter in a medium sauté pan over a low heat. Add the apple wedges and cook for 5 minutes, then sprinkle with the salt and sugar. Arrange and adjust the apples as they begin to soften to ensure that each wedge is cooking evenly, and continue to cook for 2–3 minutes. Turn the apples over as they begin to colour slightly. Raise the heat to moderate to start browning the apples and sauté briskly for a further 2 minutes or until evenly golden. Keep the apples on the firmer side of tender for a toothy yet soft texture. Serve at once, or set aside and reheat when ready to serve.

Desserts

We think of dessert not so much as a sweet afterthought, but as the crowning touch – balancing, complementing, and, in a sense, honouring the meal it follows. These varied dessert recipes represent some of our favourites, from lighter-than-light lemon angel cake that melts in your mouth to little chocolate pots de crème in all their glorious silkiness. We often find perfectly ripe fresh fruit makes the best ending to a meal, and that instinct inspired both the irresistible nectarine and blackberry crumble with its rich almond topping and the chilled and creamy blueberry fool.

Blueberry Fool

preparation **10** minutes | cooking **10** minutes | chilling **1** hour | **4** servings

The combination of sweet-tart berries and smooth cream is a memorable match for a warm summer night. A splash of crème de cassis, a liqueur made from blackcurrants, brings out the flavour of the blueberries perfectly.

tools | medium saucepan | electric mixer or whisk | box grater or zester | rubber spatula

125 g (4½ oz) blueberries

3 tbsp caster sugar

1 tbsp crème de cassis

250 ml (8 fl oz) double cream

½ tsp pure vanilla extract

¼ tsp grated lemon zest

Combine the blueberries with 5 tbsp water in a saucepan and simmer over a moderate heat for about 10 minutes or until the berries are very soft. Add 2 tbsp of the sugar and the liqueur and stir. Pour into a bowl and allow to cool, then cover and chill for 1–2 hours.

With an electric mixer or a whisk, whip the cream in a large bowl with the remaining 1 tbsp sugar and the vanilla extract until soft peaks form. Gently fold and swirl in the blueberry mixture and lemon zest using a rubber spatula.

Divide the mixture evenly among chilled dessert glasses or bowls (or, if preferred, you can pipe the fool, using a piping bag without a nozzle). The fool should be served quite cold, so keep briefly in the fridge, if necessary.

Mascarpone-stuffed Figs

preparation **10** minutes | cooking **15** minutes | **2–4** servings

On a late-summer evening, the garden or terrace is the natural place to savour these luscious figs. If you have cause to celebrate, enjoy them with Champagne.

tools | baking dish | baking sheet | chef's knife | citrus zester | whisk

60 g (2 oz) shelled almonds

8 very ripe figs

125 g (4½ oz) mascarpone, at room temperature

1 tsp fine orange zest strips

1 tbsp lavender or wildflower honey

Preheat the oven to 180°C (350°F). Spread the almonds on a baking sheet and toast for about 10 minutes or until fragrant. Coarsely chop and set aside.

Trim the stalks from the figs and cut the figs in half lengthways. Place cut side up in a shallow baking dish large enough to hold the fig halves in a single layer. Bake for 15 minutes or until the figs are swollen and heated through. Remove from the oven and arrange the figs on individual plates. Keep hot. Reserve any fig drippings in the baking dish to garnish the figs.

In a medium bowl, whisk the mascarpone with the strips of orange zest. Place a small dollop of the mascarpone mixture on each fig. Drizzle the figs with the honey and any reserved fig juices. Sprinkle over the toasted almonds and serve.

Almond Biscuits

preparation **30** minutes | chilling **3** hours | cooking **8** minutes per batch | about **96** biscuits

Delicate almond biscuits are a nice treat for the cold months, when nuts are newly harvested. Serve these with mulled cider at Christmastime.

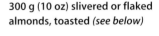

tools | baking sheets | chef's knife | stand electric mixer | baking parchment | wire racks

In a bowl, stir together the almonds and both flours; set aside.

In the bowl of an electric mixer fitted with the paddle attachment, beat the butter on medium speed until soft and creamy. Add the salt and icing sugar and mix on medium-low speed for about 5 minutes or until thoroughly combined, scraping down the bowl as necessary. Reduce the speed to low and add the egg; mix until blended. Add the flour and almond mixture. As soon as the dough comes together, turn off the mixer.

Scrape the dough onto a large sheet of cling film. Using another piece of cling film to help, gently press the dough into a rectangle about 12 x 20 cm (4½ x 8 inches) and about 4 cm (1½ inches) thick. Wrap the dough in the cling film and chill for at least 3 hours or until it is firm enough to slice. (The dough can be kept in the fridge for several days.)

Preheat the oven to 200°C (400°F). Line 2 baking sheets with baking parchment.

Unwrap the dough. Trim the edges to neaten them, then slice the dough length-ways into 3 logs each 4 cm (1½ inches) wide. Slice each log across into squares 5 mm (¼ inch) thick. Arrange the squares 1 cm (½ inch) apart on the lined baking sheets. (You will have to bake the biscuits in batches.)

Bake for about 8 minutes or until lightly browned around the edges, swapping round the baking sheets and rotating them halfway through for even baking. Allow to cool on the baking sheets until slightly set, then transfer the biscuits to wire racks to crisp and cool completely.

300 g (10 oz) slivered or flaked almonds, toasted *(see below)*

225 g (8 oz) plain flour

75 g (2½ oz) bread flour

225 g (8 oz) butter, slightly softened

½ tsp fine sea salt

325 g (11 oz) icing sugar, sifted

1 egg, at room temperature

> **toasting nuts** To toast nuts, spread them out in a baking tray and toast in a 180°C (350°F) oven for 7–15 minutes, depending on size. Shake the tray occasionally.

Nectarine and Blackberry Crumble

preparation **30** minutes | cooking **20** minutes | **4–6** servings

Nectarines and blackberries both enjoy a brief but glorious midsummer season. When they are available, you have to make the most of them. A crumble is a very simple dessert that allows the delicious ripe fruit to play the starring role. Serve with vanilla ice cream, whipped cream, or crème fraîche, if you like.

tools | large saucepan | baking sheet | baking dish | paring knife | slotted spoon | whisk

FOR THE TOPPING

200 g (7 oz) flour

75 g (2½ oz) soft light brown sugar

85 g (3 oz) caster sugar

Good pinch of fine sea salt

¼ tsp ground cinnamon

150 g (5½ oz) shelled almonds, toasted and coarsely chopped (page 199)

175 g (6 oz) cold butter

FOR THE FRUIT

5 or 6 ripe nectarines

125 g (4½ oz) fresh blackberries

Pinch of fine sea salt

2 tbsp caster sugar

1 tsp balsamic vinegar

To make the topping, whisk together the flour, both sugars, the salt, and the cinnamon. Stir in the almonds. Cut the butter into small pieces and rub into the flour mixture with your fingertips until the mixture comes together and has a crumbly texture. Set aside.

Preheat the oven to 180°C (350°F).

To prepare the fruit, bring a large saucepan of water to the boil. Have a large bowl of iced water ready nearby. Immerse each nectarine in the boiling water for 4–5 seconds, depending on its ripeness, then remove it from the water with a slotted spoon and plunge into the iced water for several seconds. Pull the skin off the nectarines; it should peel right off. Remove any stubborn bits of peel with a paring knife. Halve each nectarine and discard the stone. Slice each half into 3 wedges and place in a bowl. Add the blackberries, salt, and sugar. Drizzle the vinegar over the fruit and toss to mix.

Spoon the fruit mixture into a baking dish; the fruit should come nearly up to the top. Sprinkle an even layer of the topping mixture over the fruit. Set the dish on a baking sheet to catch any drips and place the baking sheet in the oven. Bake for 20–25 minutes or until the crumble topping is golden brown and the fruit juices have begun to bubble up the sides of the dish. Remove from the oven and allow to cool slightly before serving.

Note: This recipe makes more crumble topping than you will need, but is best made in larger quantities. The excess can be kept, tightly covered, in the fridge or freezer for next time.

Strawberry Shortcakes

preparation **20** minutes | cooking **20** minutes | **6** servings

Fragrant berries paired with sweet cream and tender shortcakes remind us that simplicity never falls out of favour. You can make the shortcake dough ahead of time, roll it out, and keep it in the fridge until you are ready to bake. Cut up the berries and macerate them before serving for the best flavour. The berries can be replaced with other summer fruits that appeal to you, such as peaches or nectarines or a combination of fruits.

tools | baking sheet | paring knife | brush | citrus reamer | fine-mesh sieve (optional) | wooden spoon | balloon whisk or electric mixer | rolling pin | wire rack

To prepare the strawberries, roll them on kitchen paper to blot off any excess moisture. Remove the core and trim away any unripe white areas or blemishes from each berry, then cut lengthways into quarters. Sprinkle with the sugar and add the orange juice and orange flower water. Toss well. Leave to macerate for 30 minutes, stirring occasionally.

While the berries are macerating, make the shortcakes. Preheat the oven to 190°C (375°F). Combine the flour, sugar, baking powder, and salt in a mixing bowl and stir with a fork. Rub in the butter until it is broken down into unevenly sized pieces, the largest as big as a pea. Pour over the 250 ml (8 fl oz) cream and mix quickly with a wooden spoon or an electric mixer on low speed just until the dough starts to come together. The dough should look and feel sticky in spots.

Turn the dough out onto a lightly floured, cool work surface. Dust the top lightly with flour and, using a rolling pin, roll out into a rectangle about 12 x 18 cm (5 x 7½ inches) and 2.5 cm (1 inch) thick. Using a sharp knife, cut into six 6 cm (2½ inch) squares. Arrange the squares on a baking sheet about 5 cm (2 inches) apart and brush the tops with the 1 tbsp cream. Bake for 20–25 minutes or until risen and golden. Transfer to a wire rack and allow to cool briefly.

Meanwhile, make the Chantilly cream. Gently whip the cream in a large bowl with the vanilla extract and icing sugar until soft peaks form.

To serve, split each shortcake in half horizontally and place the bottom half on a dessert plate or in a shallow bowl. Spoon the strawberries and their juices on top. Place a dollop of Chantilly cream on the berries and set the shortcake tops in place. Dust with icing sugar, if liked, and serve.

FOR THE STRAWBERRIES

350 g (12 oz) very ripe strawberries

60 g (2 oz) caster sugar

175 ml (6 fl oz) fresh orange juice

2 tsp orange flower water (optional)

FOR THE SHORTCAKES

300 g (10 oz) flour

3 tbsp caster sugar

1 tbsp baking powder

¼ tsp fine sea salt

75 g (2½ oz) cold salted butter, cut into 5 mm (¼ inch) pieces

250 ml (8 fl oz) plus 1 tbsp double cream

FOR THE CHANTILLY CREAM

360 ml (12 fl oz) cold double cream

½ tsp pure vanilla extract

1 tbsp icing sugar, sifted, plus sugar to dust (optional)

Ginger Cake with Rum Butter

preparation **20** minutes | cooking **25** minutes | cooling **20** minutes | **8** servings

The unmistakable taste of fresh ginger shines through in this cake, which is extremely tender and stays moist stored at room temperature if well wrapped. If you prefer, serve with a fruit compote or ice cream instead of the rum butter.

tools | 23 cm (9 inch) round cake tin | chef's knife | blender or box grater | fine-mesh sieve | skewer | whisk

1 large knob fresh ginger (enough to make 3 tbsp purée)

325 g (11 oz) dark molasses or treacle

225 g (8 oz) sugar

250 ml (8 fl oz) groundnut oil

350 g (12 oz) flour

1 tsp ground cloves

1 tsp ground cinnamon

1 tbsp baking powder

¼ tsp fine sea salt

Rum butter to serve (*see right*)

Preheat the oven to 170°C (350°F). Use the edge of a spoon to scrape the skin from the ginger. Cut the ginger across the grain into 1 cm (½ inch) slices, then pulse the ginger in a blender to purée. Alternatively, finely grate the ginger. Measure out 3 tbsp of puréed or grated ginger and put in a medium mixing bowl. Add 250 ml (8 fl oz) cool water, the molasses, sugar, and oil. Mix vigorously with a whisk until the sugar is dissolved and the mixture is glossy. Sift the flour, cloves, cinnamon, baking powder, and salt into a separate bowl. Add the flour mixture to the ginger mixture and mix thoroughly until smooth.

Pour into an ungreased 23 cm (9 inch) round cake tin. Bake for 25–35 minutes or until a skewer inserted in the centre comes out clean. Leave the cake cool in the tin for 20 minutes, then turn out onto a serving plate. Serve at room temperature or still slightly warm, with rum butter.

rum butter This traditional accompaniment to Christmas pudding also works well with other hearty autumn or winter desserts and puddings. Beat 125 g (4½ oz) butter at room temperature with 75 g (2½ oz) sifted icing sugar. Beat in 1 tbsp dark rum (or brandy or 1 tsp pure vanilla essence) and a good pinch of freshly grated nutmeg. Pile into a serving bowl, cover, and put into the fridge to firm and mellow.

Raspberry and Lemon Tart

preparation **30** minutes | cooking **10** minutes | chilling **2** hours | **8** servings

This tart is elegant enough to serve for a special occasion, and both the tart case and the lemon curd can be made ahead of time. When choosing raspberries, look for ones that are pretty, plump, and firm. Most important, smell the berries and choose the ones with the deepest perfume. To make the tart in winter, replace the berries with sliced mango.

tools | large saucepan | small saucepan | 23 cm (9 inch) tart tin | chef's knife | box grater | brush | citrus reamer | fine-mesh sieve | small spatula | stainless steel bowl | whisk

Follow the directions on page 218 to make the tart case.

To make the lemon curd filling, whisk together the whole eggs, egg yolks, and sugar in a large stainless steel bowl. Whisk in the lemon zest, lemon juice, and salt. Put 5 cm (2 inches) of water in a saucepan over a low heat to create steam and set the bowl with the egg mixture on top of the pan; the base of the bowl should not touch the water. Heat the egg mixture, whisking constantly, for about 10 minutes or until the mixture is thick enough to coat the back of a spoon. Remove the bowl from the heat and whisk in the butter. Strain the mixture through a fine-mesh sieve into a clean bowl and set this in a larger bowl filled with iced water. Leave the lemon curd to cool, whisking occasionally. Transfer the curd to a smaller container, cover, and chill for 2 hours or until completely cold.

Combine the raspberry jam and kirsch in a small saucepan and stir over a moderate heat for 3–4 minutes or until warm and liquid. Pour the jam mixture into a fine-mesh sieve held over a bowl and press through with the back of a spoon; discard the pips left in the sieve.

Brush a very thin layer of the jam glaze over the bottom of the tart case. Fill the case with the chilled lemon curd, spreading it evenly. Check the raspberries and discard (or eat) the imperfect ones. Place the perfect raspberries on top of the curd in one snug layer. Keep the tart in the fridge until ready to serve.

Tart case (page 218)

85 g (3 oz) raspberry jam

½ tsp kirsch

250 g (9 oz) raspberries

FOR THE LEMON CURD

3 eggs

3 egg yolks

115 g (4 oz) caster sugar

4 tbsp grated lemon zest

120 ml (4 fl oz) fresh lemon juice

Good pinch of fine sea salt

60 g (2 oz) butter, cubed and slightly softened

Sabayon with Peaches

preparation **10** minutes | cooking **5** minutes | **4** servings

Sabayon, a frothy golden foam made with wine, seduces all who taste it. Halve the recipe to serve two – what could be more perfect for an anniversary dinner or Valentine's Day dessert? Silky fresh peaches are the perfect accompaniment and should be eaten immediately after slicing, before the flesh has a chance to oxidize and darken. Choose the ripest peaches you can find and serve the dessert in old-fashioned champagne saucers.

tools | saucepan | whisk

8 egg yolks

85 g (3 oz) caster sugar

175 ml (6 fl oz) Champagne or sparkling wine

3 or 4 large, perfectly ripe peaches, unpeeled, sliced into wedges

Combine the egg yolks and sugar in a large stainless steel bowl. Whisk in the Champagne. Set the bowl over a saucepan with 2.5–5 cm (1–2 inches) of gently simmering water. The base of the bowl should not touch the water. Reduce the heat to low – you don't want to cook the egg, but simply create a light mist of steam below the bowl that will gently warm and thicken the egg. Whisk the egg mixture constantly for 2–3 minutes or until it thickens. There should be no liquid left at the bottom of the bowl. Remove from the heat.

Arrange the peach slices in individual shallow bowls or Champagne saucers and spoon the warm sabayon on top.

> **a bain marie pan** A bain marie pan is a set of two pans, one nested atop the other, with room for water to simmer in the bottom pan. Delicate foods such as chocolate and custards are placed in the top pan to heat them gently, or to melt them in the case of chocolate. The top pan should not touch the water beneath it, and the water should not be allowed to boil. A tight fit between the pans ensures that no water or steam can escape and mix with the ingredients in the top, which can cause melting chocolate to seize or stiffen. You can create your own bain marie pan by setting a heatproof mixing bowl or a slightly smaller saucepan over a larger pan.

Chocolate Cake

preparation **50** minutes | cooking **45** minutes | **8** servings

This chocolate cake is perfect for birthdays. Soured cream makes it particularly luscious and tender. Serve the cake with your favourite ice cream or pouring cream.

tools | two 20 cm (8 inch) cake tins | electric mixer | cake comb (optional) | palette knife | skewer | wire rack | wooden spoon

Preheat the oven to 180°C (350°F). Butter and flour two 20 cm (8 inch) round cake tins. Melt the chocolate in the top of a bain marie pan (see note on opposite page) or in the microwave, then set aside to cool.

Sift the flour, sugar, bicarbonate of soda, and salt together into a large bowl. Add the butter and soured cream and beat for 1 minute. Stir in the melted chocolate, then add the eggs, vanilla extract, and hot water and beat for another minute.

Divide the mixture between the prepared tins and jiggle the tins to even out the mixture. Bake for 30–35 minutes or until a skewer inserted into the centre comes out clean. Remove from the oven and cool in the tins on a wire rack for about 5 minutes, then turn out the cakes onto the rack and leave to cool completely.

Place one of the cakes flat side up on a serving plate. Tuck 4 strips of greaseproof paper under the sides to keep the plate clean. Using an icing spatula, put a large dollop of buttercream in the centre of the cake and spread it over the surface. Place the second cake on top, flat side down. Brush off any loose crumbs, then apply a thin coating of buttercream to the top and sides of the cake. To ice the sides, sweep more buttercream upwards, creating a raised edge at the top of the cake. Drop the rest of the buttercream at 3 or 4 points on the top of the cake and spread it in a circular motion outwards from the centre, meeting the raised edge of buttercream at a right angle. Smooth the top and any excess buttercream that may have fallen down the sides. If you like, use a cake comb to create a pattern in the buttercream. Remove the greaseproof paper and serve.

Butter for greasing

125 g (4 oz) dark chocolate with 70% cocoa solids

250 g (9 oz) flour

350 g (12 oz) caster sugar

1 tsp bicarbonate of soda

½ tsp fine sea salt

85 g (3 oz) butter, slightly softened

225 g (8 oz) soured cream

2 eggs

2 tsp pure vanilla extract

2 tbsp hot water

Chocolate buttercream (*see below*)

> **chocolate buttercream** Heat 175 ml (6 fl oz) milk in a saucepan over a moderate heat until small bubbles form around the edge. Meanwhile, combine 3 egg yolks, 125 g (4½ oz) sifted icing sugar, and a good pinch of fine sea salt in a mixing bowl. Beat with an electric mixer until blended and smooth. Slowly pour the hot milk over the yolk mixture, stirring constantly with a spoon. Pour the mixture into the saucepan, add 85 g (3 oz) chopped dark chocolate (with 70% cocoa solids), and cook over a moderately low heat, stirring constantly, until slightly thickened. Do not allow to boil. Remove from the heat. Add 1 tbsp pure vanilla essence and beat until the mixture is cool. When it is cool, beat in 350 g (12 oz) slightly softened butter, a knob at a time, beating until smooth after each addition. If the buttercream begins to separate, beat it well. Use immediately.

Lemon Angel Cake

preparation **20** minutes | cooking **30** minutes | cooling **1** hour | **8** servings

Light and airy angel cake is baked in a special tin – a tall, straight-sided tube tin – which enables the delicate mixture to cook from the centre as well as the outside and helps the cake rise high. Separating the eggs requires care. Be sure not to let a speck of yolk get mixed in with the egg whites, or they will not whisk up and "mount" properly to a stiff foam. Also, make sure the bowl in which you whisk the whites is spotlessly clean, without a trace of grease, for the same reason.

tools | angel cake tin | small serrated knife | electric mixer | citrus reamer | fine-mesh sieve | rubber spatula | skewer

125 g (4½ oz) flour

350 g (12 oz) caster sugar

¼ tsp fine sea salt

500 ml (16 fl oz) egg whites, from 12–13 eggs, at room temperature (page 233)

½ tsp pure vanilla extract

2 tsp fresh lemon juice

1½ tsp cream of tartar

Icing sugar to dust

Fresh fruit to serve (optional)

Whipped cream to serve (optional)

Position a rack in the lower third of the oven and preheat to 180°C (350°F). Have ready an ungreased 25 cm (10 inch) angel cake tin. Sift the flour, 125 g (4½ oz) of the caster sugar, and the salt together into a bowl. Set aside. In a large, spotlessly clean bowl, combine the egg whites, vanilla extract, and lemon juice. Using an electric mixer, whisk the egg whites on low speed for 1 minute. Add the cream of tartar and continue mixing on low speed for 30 seconds, then increase the speed to medium. Gradually sprinkle the remaining caster sugar into the egg whites and continue whisking on medium speed until soft, drooping peaks form when the beater is lifted. The whites should be voluminous but still moist.

Sift one-third of the flour mixture on top of the egg whites and fold in with a rubber spatula. Scrape down the sides of the bowl to ensure thorough blending. Add the remaining flour mixture and quickly fold in, scraping the sides and bottom of the bowl.

Fill the tin with the mixture (the mixture will begin deflating almost immediately, so work quickly). Gently smooth the surface of the mixture with the spatula, then bake for 30 minutes. To test if the cake is cooked, insert a long wooden skewer in the centre; it should come out clean. If any cake mixture clings to the skewer, bake for a few more minutes, or until a skewer comes out clean.

Remove the cake from the oven and immediately invert the tin to cool upside down. If your tin does not have feet, invert it onto the neck of a full wine or similar bottle. Allow the cake to cool completely, then carefully run a long, thin knife around the inside of the tin to free the cake. Gently tap the tin to turn out the cake, using the knife if necessary to coax the cake out of the tin. Place the cake upright on your favourite serving platter. To slice the cake, use a serrated knife dipped in water. Dust with sifted icing sugar and serve with fresh fruit and whipped cream, if you like.

Chocolate Pots de Crème

preparation **20** minutes | cooking **30** minutes | chilling **2** hours | **6** servings

We use small ramekins for this recipe so these creams cook evenly and quickly. This makes the perfect amount of rich custard to complete a meal. if you like, finish these rich little chocolate puddings with a dollop of whipped cream on top.

tools | deep roasting tin | medium saucepan | ramekins or other pots | chef's knife | large glass measuring jug | fine-mesh sieve | wooden spoon

Preheat the oven to 150°C (300°F). Heat the milk and cream in a medium saucepan over a moderate heat until you see small bubbles form around the sides of the pan. Add the chocolate and stir just to melt it (do not cook the chocolate). Remove from the heat and set aside to cool slightly.

In a bowl, gently combine the egg yolks and sugar with a wooden spoon until the sugar is dissolved. Do not create too many bubbles as you mix; they will be hard to settle. Slowly pour the chocolate mixture into the egg yolk mixture, stirring constantly. Pour through a fine-mesh sieve into a large glass measuring jug. Spoon off any foam from the surface.

Arrange 6 ramekins or other little pots in a deep roasting tin. Divide the chocolate mixture evenly among the ramekins. Fill the tin with enough water to come about halfway up the sides of the ramekins. Cover loosely with foil to prevent a skin from forming on the creams. Bake for about 30 minutes or until the creams are just firm at the edges but still tremble in the centre when gently shaken.

Remove the tin from the oven and carefully lift the ramekins out of the water. Allow to cool completely, then cover and chill for at least 2 hours or overnight to set. Serve chilled, dolloped with whipped cream, if you like.

120 ml (4 fl oz) whole milk

175 ml (6 fl oz) double cream

85 g (3 oz) best-quality dark chocolate (70% cocoa solids), finely chopped

3 egg yolks

85 g (3 oz) caster sugar

Whipped cream to serve (optional)

Basic Recipes

The recipes that follow serve as building blocks for the other recipes in this book, as well as other cookery books. Although some of these items can be bought for convenience, you'll find that your home-made dishes taste even better if you make these elements yourself. Some can be made ahead, perhaps on a quiet day at the weekend when you have some free time to devote to cooking, and kept on hand until needed.

Crème Fraîche

preparation **5** minutes | cooking **5** minutes | standing **8** hours | **250 ml** (8 fl oz)

Crème fraîche is a popular French version of soured cream. It's very simple to make your own, and you can decide how thick you want it to be and how mild or tart.

tools | small saucepan

250 ml (8 fl oz) double cream

1 tbsp buttermilk

Combine the cream and buttermilk in a small saucepan and warm over a moderately low heat. Do not allow to simmer. Remove from the heat, cover loosely, and leave to thicken and sour at warm room temperature for 8–48 hours or until it is to your taste. Once it is as thick and flavourful as you want it, chill well before using.

Basic Vinaigrette

preparation **15** minutes | about **120 ml** (4 fl oz)

Far superior in flavour to any shop-bought vinaigrette, this will keep well in the fridge for up to 1 week. Shake well before using.

tools | chef's knife

2 tbsp red wine vinegar

Fine sea salt and pepper

1 small clove garlic (optional)

120 ml (4 fl oz) extra virgin olive oil

1 tsp Dijon mustard (optional)

Combine the vinegar and salt in a small screwtop jar. If using the garlic clove, crush it lightly with the palm of your hand or the flat side of a chef's knife to release its flavour. Add to the vinegar and allow to stand for 10 minutes.

Remove and discard the garlic. Add the olive oil and mustard, if using, then put the lid on the jar and shake vigorously until blended. Season to taste with pepper.

Basic Mayonnaise

preparation **15** minutes | **400 ml** (14 fl oz)

Mayonnaise is not difficult to make, as long as you remember to drizzle the oil into the egg very slowly at first to help it combine, or emulsify. The flavour is wonderful.

tools | blender or food processor

Warm the uncracked egg in a bowl of hot water for 3 minutes, then break the egg into a blender or food processor. Add the mustard, lemon juice, salt, and pepper. Combine the vegetable and olive oils. With the motor running, slowly drizzle the combined oils into the blender (this should take several minutes) to make a thick mayonnaise. Stir in 1 tbsp hot water.

Note: This recipe contains uncooked egg. For more details, see page 226.

> **spicy mayonnaise** Combine 120 ml (4 fl oz) basic mayonnaise with the juice of ½ lemon, 1 tsp chilli oil, ¼ tsp Tabasco sauce, and ¼ tsp cayenne pepper. Blend well.

1 egg

1 tsp Dijon mustard

1 tsp lemon juice or white wine vinegar

½ tsp fine sea salt

¼ tsp pepper

175 ml (6 fl oz) vegetable oil

175 ml (6 fl oz) olive oil

Basic Tomato Sauce

preparation **15** minutes | cooking **45** minutes | **600 ml** (1 pint)

This all-purpose sauce made with good-quality canned tomatoes, perferably organic, can be used winter or summer in a wide variety of dishes.

tools | large saucepan | chef's knife | kitchen string

Tie the basil sprigs together with kitchen string. Heat the olive oil in a large, heavy saucepan over a moderate heat. Add the onions and garlic and sauté for about 15 minutes or until the onions are soft and translucent. Add the tomatoes, sugar, bay leaf, basil, and salt. Reduce the heat to low and simmer, stirring occasionally, for about 30 minutes or until you have a good sauce consistency. Taste and add more salt, if necessary. Remove the bay leaf and basil. The sauce will keep for up to 1 week, covered, in the fridge, or frozen for up to 1 month.

Notes: As a finishing touch, stir in 1–2 tbsp fruity extra virgin olive oil. In the height of summer, when flavourful fresh tomatoes are available, substitute 1 kg (2¼ lb) ripe fresh tomatoes, skinned, seeded, and chopped (page 234), for the canned tomatoes.

3 sprigs fresh basil

3 tbsp olive oil

2 onions, finely chopped

3 cloves garlic, crushed

2 cans (400 g each) chopped plum tomatoes

1 tsp caster sugar

½ bay leaf

½ tsp fine sea salt, or more to taste

Hard-boiled Eggs Perfected

preparation **5** minutes | cooking **8** minutes

Smooth, creamy yolks and tender whites are the hallmarks of perfect hard-boiled eggs. We feel strongly that everyone should know how to cook these eggs, and we hope that once you learn how, you'll be inspired to use these perfect eggs to garnish foods such as asparagus, green beans, crostini, and salads.

tools | saucepan | slotted spoon

3 or 4 fresh eggs

Fine sea salt

Prepare an ice bath by filling a large bowl with cold water and ice cubes.

Bring a saucepan of salted water to the boil over a high heat. Lower the eggs gently into the water with a slotted spoon and reduce the heat slightly to a gentle simmer; if cooked in boiling water, the eggs might crack against the pan. Exactly 8 minutes after adding the eggs to the water, remove them with the slotted spoon and plunge them into the ice bath to stop the cooking.

When cool, after 30 seconds to 1 minute, crack the shells and peel the eggs. The shells will peel off more easily after the ice bath.

Poached Eggs

preparation **5** minutes | cooking **5** minutes | **2** servings

Like hard-boiled eggs, poached eggs are an item that you'll find many uses for once you master the simple technique of preparing them.

tools | shallow pan or sauté pan | paring knife | ramekin | slotted spoon

Fine sea salt

4 eggs

Put 5–7.5 cm (2–3 inches) of water in a shallow pan or large sauté pan. Season the water with salt and bring to a simmer over a moderate heat. One at a time, and working quickly, break each egg into a small ramekin and carefully slip it into the water. Leave space around the eggs. Adjust the heat so that the water barely simmers. Poach the eggs gently for 3–5 minutes, depending on how well you want them to be cooked. Remove each egg from the water with a slotted spoon, and while the egg is still in the spoon, blot the base dry with kitchen paper and trim off the ragged edges with a paring knife.

Fresh Breadcrumbs

preparation **10** minutes

There is really no substitute for freshly made breadcrumbs. They lend texture and richness to many dishes such as pasta, sautéed greens, blanched asparagus, and roast fish. Do not substitute fresh breadcrumbs for fine dry crumbs.

tools | food processor

Remove the crust from a baguette. Cut or tear the bread into 5 cm (2 inch) pieces. Put the bread in a food processor and pulse until you have irregular, fluffy, pea-sized pieces. Don't overpulse or the crumbs will become too fine. Freeze freshly made breadcrumbs for up to 2 weeks.

Stale sourdough bread or baguette

Toasted Breadcrumbs

preparation **5** minutes | cooking **12** minutes | **60 g** (2 oz)

Toasted crumbs make a delightful savoury topping for any number of dishes.

tools | baking sheet

Preheat the oven to 170°C (350°F). Toss the crumbs with the olive oil and salt. Spread on a baking sheet and bake for 12–15 minutes or until crisp and golden.

Toasted breadcrumbs can be stored for up to 3 days in a screwtop jar. Reheat them briefly in a 150°C (300°F) oven just before using.

60 g (2 oz) fresh breadcrumbs (*see above*)

1 tbsp olive oil

Pinch of fine sea salt

Crostini

preparation **10** minutes | cooking **12** minutes | **30** crostini

Make crostini to serve with a topping as party nibbles or to garnish a soup.

tools | baking sheets | serrated bread knife | brush

Preheat the oven to 180°C (350°F). Slice the baguette on the bias into 30 slices, each 5 cm (2 inches) in diameter (change the angle of the knife to make the slices wider if needed) and about 5 mm (¼ inch) thick. Place the slices on baking sheets, brush with the olive oil, and sprinkle with salt. Bake for 12–15 minutes or until lightly golden. Let the crostini cool slightly before using.

1 day-old baguette

1 tbsp olive oil

Fine sea salt

Chicken Stock

preparation **15** minutes | cooking **3** hours | about **3 litres** (5 pints)

Using home-made chicken stock in your dishes will make them taste noticeably better. Ask your butcher for chicken backs and necks that he would otherwise discard after jointing birds. These make the best stock.

tools | stockpot | chef's knife | fine-mesh sieve | large metal spoon

2.5 kg (5½ lb) chicken backs and necks, plus wings if available

1 onion, quartered

2 carrots, peeled and cut in half

1 stick celery, cut in half

2 sprigs fresh parsley

1 sprig fresh thyme

½ bay leaf

½ tsp fine sea salt (optional)

Combine the chicken pieces with 4 litres (7 pints) water in a large stockpot and bring to the boil. Reduce the heat to low and use a large spoon to skim off any grey foam that rises to the surface. Do not skim off the fat, however, as this locks in flavour as the stock cooks. Add the onion, carrots, celery, parsley, thyme, bay leaf, and salt (if using). Simmer gently for about 3 hours or until the stock tastes rich and is a light golden colour.

Strain the stock through a fine-mesh sieve and leave to cool completely. Skim off any fat from the surface. If not using immediately, cover and keep in the fridge for up to 3 days (remove the hardened white fat from the surface after chilling) or in the freezer for up to 2 months.

Vegetable Stock

preparation **15** minutes | cooking **1** hour | about **3.5 litres** (6 pints)

For an extra-fragrant vegetable stock, add half a fennel bulb, thickly sliced. Or, for a flavourful summer stock, add fresh tomatoes, cut into quarters.

tools | stockpot | chef's knife | fine-mesh sieve

2 onions, thickly sliced

1 leek, well rinsed and thickly sliced

2 carrots, peeled and coarsely chopped

2 sticks celery, coarsely chopped

3 or 4 sprigs fresh parsley

6 black peppercorns

1 bay leaf

2 sprigs fresh thyme

Combine all the ingredients with 4 litres (7 pints) water in a large stockpot and bring to the boil. Reduce the heat to low and simmer gently for 1 hour. Strain the stock through a fine-mesh sieve, pressing on the vegetables with the back of a spoon to extract as much liquid as possible. Discard the vegetables.

You can use the stock immediately, or keep it in the fridge for up to 3 days or freezer for up to 2 months.

Beef Stock

preparation **15** minutes | cooking **5½** hours | about **3 litres** (5 pints)

This makes a very flavourful stock. Ask the butcher to cut the meaty shin bones (from the foreleg) and leg bones (hind leg) into 5 cm (2 inch) pieces to make them easier to handle.

tools | roasting tin | large stockpot | chef's knife | fine-mesh sieve | wooden spatula | large metal spoon

Preheat the oven to 220°C (425°F). Arrange the beef bones in a single layer in a heavy roasting tin and roast, turning once, for 20–25 minutes or until thoroughly browned. Combine the roasted bones and 5 litres (9 pints) water in a large stockpot and bring to the boil over a high heat.

Meanwhile, place the roasting tin with the drippings over a moderately high heat. Add 5 tbsp water to the roasting tin and bring to a brisk simmer. Deglaze the pan by stirring and scraping with a wooden spatula to loosen the browned bits from the bottom. Add the flavourful pan drippings to the stockpot.

When the stock reaches the boil, use a large metal spoon to skim off any grey foam that rises to the surface. Add the carrots, onions, celery, parsley, thyme, bay leaf, peppercorns, and salt, if using. Reduce the heat to low and simmer gently for about 5 hours or until the stock tastes rich and is a light caramel colour. Strain the stock through a fine-mesh sieve and leave to cool completely. Skim off any fat that has risen to the surface, then cover and keep in the fridge. Season to taste before using.

3 kg (6½ lb) meaty beef shin and leg bones

3 carrots, cut into 5 cm (2 inch) pieces

2 onions, quartered

3 sticks celery, cut into 5 cm (2 inch) pieces

4 sprigs fresh parsley

2 sprigs fresh thyme

½ bay leaf

5 black peppercorns

½ tsp fine sea salt (optional)

Tart Case

preparation **20** minutes | resting **60** minutes | cooking **20** minutes | **1** tart case

This versatile pastry case can be prepared a day or two in advance of filling.

tools | 23 cm (9 inch) tart or flan tin | chef's knife | box grater | wire rack

140 g (5 oz) flour

1 tbsp caster sugar

¼ tsp fine sea salt

¼ tsp grated lemon zest (optional)

115 g (4 oz) cold butter, cut into 1 cm (½ inch) pieces

½ tsp pure vanilla extract

In a medium bowl, stir together the flour, sugar, salt, and lemon zest, if using. Rub the butter into the flour mixture with your fingertips, pressing and blending, until the butter looks granular and the mixture begins to hold together. Combine 1 tbsp water and the vanilla extract and work it into the flour and butter mixture with a fork until the ingredients are well combined and the dough will hold together when pressed. Gather it into a ball and wrap it in cling film. Leave the dough to rest for 30 minutes to allow the flour to absorb the moisture.

Use your fingertips to press the pastry dough into the bottom and sides of a 23 cm (9 inch) tart or flan tin, making sure it is distributed evenly. Cover the tart case and place in the freezer to firm for 30 minutes.

Preheat the oven to 190°C (375°F). Remove the tart case from the freezer, uncover, and prick the pastry all over with a fork. Line the case with foil and weigh down with a thick level layer of baking beans or dried beans. Bake blind for 10 minutes. Remove the foil and beans, then bake for a further 15–20 minutes or until light golden brown. Leave to cool to room temperature on a wire rack before filling.

Pizza Dough

preparation **30** minutes | resting **40** minutes | enough for **6** individual pizzas

A good, crisp home-made base and a choice of interesting toppings raise the pizza to a new level. See page 147 for topping ideas and baking instructions.

tools | baking sheet | instant-read thermometer | pizza peel | pizza stone | stand mixer with dough hook | rolling pin

Combine the water, yeast, vinegar, and 3 tbsp olive oil in the bowl of a stand mixer fitted with the dough hook. Mix on low speed for about 30 seconds or until just blended. Add about one-quarter of the flour and mix on low speed for 30 seconds. In a separate bowl, stir together the remaining flour, the sugar, and salt until well blended. Add the flour mixture to the wet dough mixture in 3 batches, beating on low speed after each addition until thoroughly combined. When all the flour has been added, raise the mixer speed to medium and mix for 2 minutes more. The dough should pull away from the sides of the bowl to come together in a ball, and feel soft to the touch.

Place the ball of dough in a well-oiled bowl and turn it several times to coat the surface lightly with oil. Cover the bowl with a clean tea towel. Leave the dough to rest at room temperature for 30 minutes.

Divide the dough into 6 equal pieces and roll each piece into a smooth ball. Place the balls on a baking sheet and cover with a damp tea towel. Allow the dough to rest for 10 minutes. It is now ready to use, or it can be kept in the fridge for up to 4 hours. (If you have chilled the dough, take it out of the refrigerator about 30 minutes before using it to bring it to room temperature.)

Using your hands and a rolling pin, roll and stretch each ball into a 20 cm (8 inch) round – don't worry if the pizza bases are not perfectly round.

300 ml (10 fl oz) warm water (38–43°C/100–110°F)

5 tsp dried yeast

2 tsp red wine vinegar

3 tbsp olive oil, plus oil for greasing

500 g (1 lb 2 oz) bread flour, plus flour for dusting

2 tsp caster sugar

½ tsp fine sea salt

Pulses and grains

A wide variety of grains and pulses awaits the adventurous cook who ventures beyond the world of white rice and canned beans. And it is a journey every cook should make, as these foods help form the foundation of a healthy diet.

Pulses – beans, peas, and lentils – are nutritious and economical foods. Some people avoid cooking them because the relatively lengthy preparation seems off-putting. Hard as small pebbles, dried beans require rehydrating to soften them. This is done by soaking before cooking. Depending on your schedule, you can choose a long- or quick-soak method *(right)*. Lentils and certain other dried pulses, such as split peas, do not require soaking and cook quickly in comparison to beans. Canned beans can be used in place of soaked beans: simply rinse well and drain before using, and be aware that they may be saltier than home-cooked beans. Or look for beans in jars, which are usually better quality than canned beans.

When buying dried beans, find a shop with good turnover. Organic and healthfood shops and ethnic food shops will often have the widest variety. Although they may seem to keep for ever, old beans will not taste as good as fresh ones. Dried pulses can be stored in an airtight container in a cool, dry place for up to 1 year, but are best used within 2 or 3 months of purchase.

Grains can be used in virtually every course of a meal and at any time of day: as breakfast cereals or savoury side dishes; to add both flavour and texture to salads, soups, stews, casseroles, and stuffings; and as the basis of or embellishment to desserts and breads. When planning a meal, consider making a grain side dish such as barley, bulghur wheat, or wholesome brown rice as a change from the more common potato or white rice. All these grains are packed with fibre as well as nutrients.

Whole grains, and cracked grains made from whole grains, are rich in oil, which goes rancid over time. These grains are therefore perishable so keep whole and cracked grains in airtight containers in the fridge; they can be kept for up to 6 months. Polished grains can be stored in a cupboard for up to a year.

SOAKING DRIED BEANS

To rehydrate beans for cooking, put them in a bowl with water to cover generously. Leave to soak at room temperature for at least 4 hours or up to overnight. The longer they soak, the more quickly they will cook. Add more water if needed to keep the beans covered. Drain and rinse before proceeding with a recipe.

To speed the rehydration process, you can use the quick-soak method. Put the beans in a pan with enough water to cover them by 7.5 cm (3 inches). Bring to a rapid simmer, then adjust the heat to simmer the beans vigorously for 2 minutes. Do not boil. Remove from the heat, cover, and leave to cool in the liquid for 1 hour. Drain and proceed with a recipe.

Some cooks say never to salt beans while they simmer for fear of toughening them, but in fact salt only slows the rate of softening.

Fruits and vegetables

When selecting fruits and vegetables, use all your senses, not just your eyes. Deep, bright colour is one indication that something is ripe, but nowadays many fruits and vegetables are grown to look good, with little regard for flavour, and are picked too early so that they can be shipped long distances without bruising.

Use your nose and fingertips to judge smell and texture, and if possible ask for a taste. Being able to taste before you buy is one of the best reasons to shop at a farmers' market. Don't be shy about asking the greengrocer or farmer for advice about what's ready to eat and what will keep for a few days. Fruits like berries, peaches, and melons and vegetable-fruits like tomatoes should have distinct fragrances. Fruits that are meant to be tender, like mangoes or avocados, should give when gently pressed, rather than feeling rock hard, and crisp vegetables, such as cucumbers or green peppers, should never be soft or wrinkled.

Storing fruits and vegetables

Many – though not all – vegetables and some fruits are best stored in the refrigerator. See the chart on pages 222–23 for details. Keeping these foods cool will extend their life, but don't allow them to get too dry or too cold. The refrigerator's vegetable drawers are designed to create a temperate, humid climate that's ideal for storage of fresh produce, and in newer fridges the drawers can be adjusted specifically for fruits or for vegetables.

In general, store fruits and vegetables unwashed and dry (to discourage mould) in perforated paper or plastic bags to increase their temperature and humidity slightly. Again, see exceptions in the chart. Keep fruits and vegetables away from the back wall of the refrigerator, which is the coldest part and can cause light freezing.

Like cooking times in a recipe, the time frames for storage given in the chart are merely estimates. Fresh produce may last for a shorter or longer time. Use your senses to determine whether an item is still fresh, and when in doubt, discard it.

A GOOD WASH

Always wash fruits and vegetables before cooking or eating them. Many have traces of dirt, dust, bacteria, fungus, or chemicals that can be rinsed off. Even when you don't plan to eat the peel, if you are going to use a knife to cut through a fruit or vegetable, wash the fruit or vegetable first. (Select organic or pesticide-free fruit when you plan to eat the peel.)

Scrub sturdy fruits and vegetables with your hands under slightly warm running water – not hot, but slightly above room temperature. Warm water cleans better and helps bring out the flavours of fruits and vegetables, especially if they've been refrigerated. An exception is salad ingredients that should be crisp; wash these in cold water. Pat fruits and vegetables dry with kitchen paper or a clean tea towel, or spin salad greens dry in a salad spinner so the dressing will not be diluted with excess water.

apples	In fridge for 2–6 weeks. Keep away from other fruits and vegetables, as apples give off ripening gases.
avocado	At cool room temperature, or enclose in paper bag with banana for quicker ripening. After cutting, press cling film onto surface and store in fridge. Keep stone in place to prevent exposure to air and discoloration.
bananas	At cool room temperature, or enclose in paper bag for ripening. Best flavour when speckled brown. Skin will turn black if kept in the fridge (can still eat flesh).
beans in pod	(fresh borlotti, broad, cannellini, flageolets) In perforated plastic bag in fridge for 1 week.
beetroot	In a cool, dark place for 3–4 days. Scrub with a soft brush. Keep green leaves separate, in fridge for 2 days.
peppers	At cool room temperature or in perforated plastic bag in fridge for 5 days.
blackberries	Spread in single layer (not touching), cover with dry kitchen paper and cling film, and store in fridge for 1–2 days. Wash just before using, in colander immersed in warm water.
pak choy	In perforated plastic bag in fridge for 1–2 days.
broccoli	In perforated plastic bag in fridge for 4 days.
cime di rapa	Wrap in damp kitchen paper and cling film and store in fridge for 4 days.
Brussels sprouts	In perforated plastic bag in fridge for 4 days.
butternut squash and pumpkin	(also acorn, kabocha, onion squashes, etc.) In a cool, dark place for a few months. Once cut or cooked, store in fridge for 1 week.

cabbage	Wrap tightly in cling film and store in fridge for 1 week.
carrots	Remove tops and store in perforated plastic bag in fridge for 1 week. Scrub with a soft brush. Soak limp carrots in iced water.
cauliflower	In perforated plastic bag in fridge for 5 days.
celery	Wash and store in plastic bag in fridge for 2 weeks. Soak limp celery in iced water.
celeriac	Wrap in cling film and store in fridge for 1 week.
chicory	(also radicchio) In perforated plastic bag in fridge for 5 days. Brush cut edges with lemon juice.
citrus fruits	At cool room temperature for 1–2 weeks or in fridge for longer storage. Citrus fruits won't ripen after harvest. Scrub with a soft brush if using zest.
sweetcorn	In husks wrapped in damp kitchen paper, or in perforated plastic bag, in fridge for 1–2 days. Best eaten before sugars turn to starch.
cucumber	In vegetable drawer of fridge for 1 week, or for 3 days if cut.
aubergine	At cool room temperature or in perforated plastic bag in fridge for 3–4 days.
fennel bulbs	Wrap in cling film and store in fridge for 3 days. Scrub with soft brush.
figs	Spread in a single layer, not touching, cover with dry kitchen paper and cling film, and store in fridge for 3 days. Wash just before using, in colander immersed in warm water.
grapes	Wash, wrap in kitchen paper and perforated plastic bag, and store in fridge for 1 week.

green beans	Wash and keep in fridge in perforated plastic bag for 4–5 days.	peas	In perforated plastic bag in fridge for 3 days. Best eaten right after purchase, before sugars turn to starch.
spring onions	Remove rubber bands and wilted leaves; store in perforated plastic bag in fridge for 5 days.	potatoes	In a cool, dark place for 2 weeks. The starches in potatoes will turn to sugar in the fridge. Scrub with a soft brush.
herbs	Put stalks in glass of water, cover with cling film, and store in fridge for 3–4 days.	raspberries	Spread in single layer, not touching, cover with dry kitchen paper and cling film, and store in fridge for 1–2 days. Wash just before using, in colander immersed in warm water.
kale	In perforated plastic bag in fridge for 5 days.		
leeks	Remove tops, wrap in damp kitchen paper and plastic bag, and store in fridge for 1 week. Slice in half lengthways and separate layers to wash out grit.	spinach	In perforated plastic bag in fridge for 3 days. Wash by immersing in warm water and lifting out so grit sinks. Repeat with fresh water until water remains clean.
lettuces and salad greens	(butterhead, cos, Iceberg, Little Gem, Oak Leaf, romaine lettuces; dandelion greens, lamb's lettuce, mustard greens, rocket, etc.) In plastic bag in fridge for 2 days to 1 week, depending on sturdiness. Wrap tender leaves like dandelion in damp kitchen paper.	strawberries	Spread in single layer, not touching, cover with dry kitchen paper and cling film, and store in fridge for 1–2 days. Wash just before using, in colander immersed in warm water.
mushrooms	Layer on dry kitchen paper in paper bag and store in fridge for 5–7 days. Wipe delicate wild mushrooms clean with brush or damp cloth, or briefly rinse button mushrooms.	sweet potatoes	In a cool, dark place for 1–2 weeks. Starches in sweet potatoes will turn to sugar in the fridge. Scrub with a soft brush.
onions, shallots, and garlic	In cool, dark place for several weeks or months. Keep away from potatoes, which cause onions to spoil. Green sprouts indicate age and bitterness.	Swiss chard	Wrap in damp kitchen paper, put in a plastic bag, and store in fridge for 3–5 days.
parsnips	Wrap in kitchen paper, put in a plastic bag, and store in fridge for up to 1 month.	tomatoes	Handle gently to avoid bruising. Store at cool room temperature, stalks down and not touching, for 2–3 days if ripe. Place in paper bag with banana for quick ripening. Tomatoes lose their flavour and texture in the fridge.
peaches and nectarines	Handle gently to avoid bruising. Store at cool room temperature, set stalk down and not touching, or place in paper bag for quick ripening. Store in fridge when ripe.	turnips	In perforated plastic bag in fridge for 1 week.
		watercress	Put stalks in glass of water, cover with cling film, and store in fridge for 3–4 days.
pears	Handle gently to avoid bruising. Store at cool room temperature, set stalk up and not touching, or place in paper bag for quick ripening. Store in fridge when ripe.	courgettes	(also pattypan squash, christophene or chayote) In perforated plastic bag in fridge for 2–3 days.

fruits and vegetables | 223

Meat and poultry

The best way to be sure of getting first-rate meat and poultry is to find a good butcher and to become a regular customer. Most butchers are pleased to be asked for advice and can teach you a lot about the food you're buying and how to cook it.

When buying meat and poultry, as with any ingredient, it's worth paying more for better quality. If you care about the food you're putting on your table, it's only logical to care about the animal that has provided it. We love nothing more than a good steak or chop or roast chicken, but we also want to know that the cow or pig or bird was treated well, fed a wholesome and natural diet, not given unneeded hormones, and slaughtered humanely. Seek out meat and poultry that is organic or free range and ask the butcher to tell you about where the meat came from and how it was raised.

A wide array of beef, pork, lamb, and veal cuts are available, and the choice can seem overwheming. One simple way to divide up cuts is into tender and tough. Tender cuts come from the less-exercised part of the animal. Using beef as an example, that means the ribs, sirloin, and rump. Tougher cuts, that is well exercised and with more connective tissue, include chuck and topside. Lamb shanks and pork shoulder are other examples of tougher cuts. Whatever cut you're looking for, check its marbling before you buy it. Marbling refers to the little streaks of fat running through meat that help keep it moist during cooking. The more marbling, the more tender and juicy the meat will be. This streaking is also an indication that the meat is of a superior grade. Look for small flecks or thin "streams" of fat, rather than large deposits or broad white "rivers".

When shopping for chicken, look for plump (but not necessarily big) birds or joints with even colouring, whether pale yellow or ivory. The skin coloration depends on what the bird was fed. Chicken is highly perishable. If poultry ever smells "off", don't buy it or eat it.

When cooking meat and poultry, take it out of the fridge a little ahead of time to allow it to come to room temperature. This will help it cook more evenly. Seasoning well ahead of cooking time will deepen flavours – this is why our recipes sometimes call for

FOOD SAFETY

Meat and poultry are highly perishable foods that carry bacteria. They need to be handled with care in the kitchen to avoid the possibility of food-borne illness. When you bring meat or poultry home from the shop, store it in the wrapper it came in, with additional wrapping if needed, and cook it within 3 days. If you are on the verge of going beyond that time, freeze it for later use. These foods should not sit out for more than 2 hours at most, or less time on a warm day. Always thaw frozen meat in the refrigerator rather than at room temperature (this can take several hours, depending on the size of the joint) and don't freeze it again after thawing (see page 29 for details).

When working in the kitchen, make sure that you prevent chopping boards and utensils used for raw meat and poultry from touching other foods to avoid cross-contamination.

marinating or brining hours ahead when possible. Brining, or soaking meat in a salt solution, adds moisture and flavour to lean cuts.

One of the keys to cooking meat and poultry is browning, which contributes flavour and gives the finished dish eye appeal. Don't rush this stage of cooking, and you'll be richly rewarded. As you cook meat and poultry and turn it in the pan or under the grill, use tongs rather than piercing it with a fork. Piercing will release juices, resulting in a drier finished dish. Overcooking also results in dryness. Use a thermometer or your instincts rather than the recipe timings, as these are just estimates. While chicken and minced meat need to be cooked through for safety reasons, a rare steak is safe from bacteria as long as the surface is seared brown, and even pork chops taste best if there is a touch of rosiness in the centre. Unless you have particular health concerns, we recommend cooking tender, lean cuts of meat only to medium-rare.

CHECKING IF DONE

Using an instant-read thermometer is the most accurate way to judge if meat or chicken is done, using the internal temperatures given below. However, it's useful to learn how to judge doneness by touch. As you cook meat or poultry, prod it with your fingertip at various stages. Uncooked meat and poultry is very soft, while cooked is firm. As you gain experience, you'll learn to distinguish a rare steak from a medium-rare one by touch. This is a much better test than cutting into the meat to look at the centre, which lets out the juices and moisture. (That said, another traditional test for poultry is to pierce the thigh and press, then see if the juices run clear.)

TEMPERATURES FOR MEAT AND POULTRY

TYPE OF MEAT	INTERNAL TEMPERATURE	DESCRIPTION
Minced meat	71°C (160°F) for medium	Centre meat is no longer pink.
Beef and lamb	57°C (135°F) for rare	Interior is red and shiny; meat's texture is soft when pressed.
	63°C (145°F) for medium-rare	Rosy pink interior, juicy; meat has give when pressed.
	71°C (160°F) for medium	Pink only at centre, pale juices; meat has slight give when pressed.
	77°C (170°F) for well done	Evenly brown throughout, no traces of red or pink, moist but no juices; meat feels firm to the touch.
Veal and pork	63°C (145°F) for medium-rare	Rosy pink interior, juicy; meat has give when pressed.
	71°C (160°F) for medium	Pink only at centre, pale pink juices; meat has slight give when pressed.
	77°C (170°F) for well done	Evenly brown throughout, no traces of red or pink, moist but no juices.
Whole chickens	82°C (180°F) in thigh	Legs will move easily in sockets; when thigh is pierced, juices will run clear; juices in cavity are clear, not pink.
Chicken breasts	77°C (170°F)	Meat is opaque and firm throughout.
Chicken drumsticks, thighs, and wings	82°C (180°F)	Meat releases easily from the bone.
Stuffing	74°C (165°F)	Check the temperature of stuffing cooked inside a whole bird.

Note: Since the temperature of larger joints of meat or whole birds continues to rise by 2–7°C (5–15°F) as they rest after cooking and before slicing, plan to remove these foods from the oven a few degrees below ideal internal temperature. The larger the joint, the more the temperature will rise. Allow a resting period before slicing any meat or poultry to let the juices be redistributed.

Eggs and dairy foods

A common kitchen ingredient, the egg is as much a staple as sugar, flour, and salt. But unlike its counterparts, the egg can both be eaten alone and play a role in countless dishes. Eggs are nutritional powerhouses, supplying protein; vitamins A, D, and E; and essential minerals such as iron, calcium, and zinc.

Milk is also highly nutritious and has been a part of the human diet for thousands of years, whether from a cow, a goat, a sheep, or even a yak. Rich in protein, calcium, and B vitamins as well as vitamin A if full-fat, milk sustains us, and also gives us the gifts of yogurt, cheese, butter, and ice cream.

As with all ingredients, it is important to choose and store eggs and milk with care. Buy organic eggs from free-range chickens, which have been allowed access to the outdoors and fed a wholesome diet. Store eggs in the fridge, keeping a close eye on the "best before" date on the box. There is no nutritional difference between brown eggs and white ones, or other colours; the colour of the shell simply depends on the breed of the hen.

Choose organic milk and yogurt. They are more expensive than conventional products, but they taste better and, when used in cooking and baking, will also make your food taste better. Choose whole or semi-skimmed milk for cooking and baking, rather than skimmed, which is thin and lacks flavour. Store milk in the coldest part of the fridge, and observe the "use-by" date. (This is usually conservative, so give older milk a sniff to see if it's still good.)

As a general rule, choose unsalted butter, preferably organic. Salt is added to butter both as a seasoning and as a preservative. If you buy unsalted butter, it is likely to be fresher, since its shelf life is shorter. Using unsalted butter also allows you to season the dishes you use it in to suit your taste. French butters, particularly those from Normandy, are often made with crème fraîche, which gives them a very light and creamy texture and a different, more savoury butter flavor. French butter is a great choice for both eating and cooking. Unsalted Italian butter, which is becoming more widely available, is pale and delicate in flavour with a slight sweetness.

Fish and shellfish

With the growing awareness of the benefits to be derived from eating fish and shellfish, more and more kinds of fish are turning up on menus and fishmonger's slabs. The problems that result from overfishing and pollution are also gaining recognition, so it's important to be an informed fish buyer.

To find the best-quality fish, start with a reliable fishmonger or the fresh fish counter of a well-stocked supermarket. Use your eyes and nose to help you discern quality and freshness. All fish should look moist and bright and have a fresh, clean scent reminiscent of the sea. Steer clear of discoloration, dryness, or an "off" odour. The fishmonger should be able to answer any questions you have about the seafood, including its origin and whether it is fresh or thawed from frozen. (Flash-frozen fish or shellfish – frozen on board the boat soon after being caught, rather than sitting in the hold for a day or two and then in the market for even longer – can in fact be better than some so-called "fresh" fish.)

Fish and shellfish are highly perishable, so whenever possible it's best to buy seafood on the day you plan to cook it. Most bivalves in the shell – clams, mussels, and oysters – as well as crabs and lobsters are still alive at the time of purchase and should be kept alive until you're ready to cook them. You can tell if a bivalve is alive by tapping the shell; the shell should close. At the fishmonger's, reject any that don't. (Shells that don't open after cooking are also a bad sign, although some can just be a little stubborn.) Hurry home with your seafood and keep it fresh nestled in a mound of ice in the fridge before cooking it as soon as you can.

The most important thing to know about cooking fish and shellfish is that it is easy to overcook these delicate foods. The rule of thumb when cooking fish is to allow about 10 minutes per 450 g (1 lb) at 180°C (350°F), but even this timing may be a little long if you are cooking salmon or tuna to a desirable medium-rare, still rosy in the centre. With shellfish such as prawns, a change of colour from grey to pink is a good indication, while the shells of bivalves such as mussels or clams will open when they are cooked.

ENDANGERED FISH

A number of the most popular kinds of fish are now considered endangered because of over-fishing or pollution. These include Chilean sea bass, swordfish, orange roughy, and cod. Lists of endangered fish occasionally change and can be reviewed online with resources such as the Marine Conservation Society website (www.fishonline.org). Because so many kinds of fish are available, there is no need to purchase endangered fish. Ask the fishmonger about types to substitute.

Another current concern is the mercury content in fish. Fish high in mercury include lean fish such as swordfish, tilefish, king mackerel, and shark. These fish should not be eaten by pregnant women, those who may become pregnant, nursing mothers, or young children.

The skilled cook

Among the most important things a novice cook can learn is how to choose the correct cooking method for the ingredients at hand. In other words, knowing the best way to apply heat to any food is as critical to success as choosing the food itself. And usually there is more than one good way to cook most foods. This section will give you an overview of the various cooking methods, to help you understand why a recipe was written the way it was.

Tender, delicate foods like a fish fillet, a chicken breast, or a steak can be cooked quickly over a high heat so that they don't have time to dry out. A tough cut of meat, like the well-exercised leg, needs to cook for a long time to become tender, but you can use liquid and gentle heat to keep it moist in the process. A sturdy vegetable can stand up to boiling. The different ways we apply heat to food can be grouped according to the quality of the heat used.

Quick and hot: grilling and barbecuing

Cooking over an open fire has a long history, reaching back millennia to when our ancestors first discovered that cooked food tasted better than raw. Nowadays, the fire is usually made with charcoal, sometimes with the addition of wood chips, but barbecuing is still appreciated for the excellent flavour it delivers. To start a fire in a charcoal barbecue, pile the coals in a cylindrical metal chimney starter, light them using wadded-up newspaper, and leave them to burn for about 30 minutes or until they have a light coating of grey ash. Then spread out the coals evenly and place the rack over them. For "indirect" grilling in a covered barbecue, when you want the food to cook more slowly, pile all the coals on one side so that you can place the food on the grill rack at the other side.

With indoor grilling, the heat source is above the food, rather than beneath it, but the effect is similar to barbecuing. For most grilling, preheat the grill to high and place the food about 10 cm (4 inches) away from the heat source. Thicker items can be moved further away so that they will cook through, or the heat can be reduced. To brown foods, place them as close to the heat source as possible.

SAUTÉING TIPS

● Preheat the sauté pan on the burner before adding the fat, then heat the fat before you add the food. This ensures that a nice crust will start to form on the food as soon as it is added to the pan. Only when the fat is hot – oil will start to shimmer, butter will foam and the foaming will subside – should you add the food to the pan.

● The pieces of food to be sautéed should fit easily in the pan with a little room on all sides. Packing food too tightly traps the moisture the food releases during cooking, resulting in steaming rather than browning. Too much space causes the fat to burn.

● Resist the urge to move the food in the pan right away, or you could tear the surface and prevent a nice crust from forming. If the food appears to be sticking to the pan at first, do not worry. When it is sufficiently browned, it will release easily. Leave the food undisturbed for 30 seconds or so, depending on its size.

DEEP-FRYING TIPS

● Use a deep-frying thermometer. This way you can check the temperature and adjust the heat under the pan accordingly. A temperature of 180–190°C (350–375°F) is the usual range for deep-fried foods. For the best results, use an electric deep-fat fryer, which will have an inbuilt thermometer.

● Two of the best oils to use are groundnut oil and grapeseed oil. These oils have high smoke points, meaning they can be heated to a higher temperature than some other oils before they begin to smoke and burn.

● Use a skimmer to remove bits of batter or food from the fat during frying and between batches. Burnt bits will make the oil bitter.

● If hot fat or oil catches fire, do not attempt to douse it with water. Extinguish the fire by smothering it with the pan's lid.

Quick and hot: sautéing

Sautéed food is quickly cooked over a moderately high or moderate heat in a small amount of fat such as oil or butter. Small pieces of food, like chopped onion or prawns, are tossed or stirred in the pan; larger items like escalopes are turned rather than tossed. Sautéing gives the outside of a food a richly flavoured brown coating without overcooking the inside. Like grilling, sautéing is considered to be a dry-heat cooking method because it does not involve liquid.

Foods for sautéing should be relatively thin. For thicker pieces of meat or poultry, pound them with a meat mallet to flatten them to a uniform thinness. Pat foods dry before cooking if needed. Moisture will cause hot fat to spatter, and will interfere with browning.

When you first add the food to the pan, put its best-looking side down for larger pieces (like a chicken breast). Leave to brown a little before you start to stir and toss. Larger pieces of food are usually ready to turn when they are golden brown on the underside. For the best appearance, turn large pieces only once; you can turn smaller pieces more often.

Quick and hot: deep-frying

Although deep-frying has been given a bad rap in recent years, the truth is that if you do it right the food will not absorb too much oil and become greasy. And the results of immersing pieces of food in hot oil are incomparably delicious. The key is heating the oil to a high temperature and keeping it constant. At a high temperature, the oil will evaporate the water in the food instantly, turning it into steam that will prevent any oil from seeping into the food. If the oil temperature is too low, there will be no outward push and the food will absorb the oil instead. If the oil gets too hot, it will smoke and impart a bitter flavour. (And if oil is allowed to get extremely hot, it will burst into flame – so watch the temperature carefully.)

Try to keep the temperature as constant as possible. Each time you add food to the oil, the temperature will drop. Cooking food in small batches will prevent big drops in temperature and food from sticking together. Allow the oil to regain its correct temperature between each batch. Having foods at room temperature before frying also prevents a large drop in temperature.

Hot and quick: boiling and blanching

Boiling in water is an intense cooking method best suited to lobsters and crabs, sturdy vegetables, and dried pasta – and not much else. Most other foods need more gentle handling when cooking in a liquid (see simmering, poaching, and steaming, opposite). Partially cooking a food in boiling water is called blanching (when boiled for less than 2 minutes) or parboiling (cooking food halfway). Blanching and parboiling are useful for sturdy vegetables that you want to sauté for colour and flavour, but that wouldn't become tender throughout with just a quick sautéing. Blanching also sets a bright colour in green vegetables, loosens thin skins for easy peeling, and lessens strong flavours that might overpower some dishes.

You can tell that water is at a full rolling boil if you stir it and it doesn't stop bubbling. A moderate boil can be stopped by stirring. When you need to time boiling or blanching carefully, start counting from when the water returns to the boil after you've added the food. This may take a little while, especially when cooking larger items like whole lobsters.

Hot and slow: roasting and baking

Roasting and baking don't demand a lot of attention or effort from the cook, and produce concentrated flavours. The term "baking" is commonly used for breads, cakes, pastries, and the like, but when applied to meats, poultry, seafood, and vegetables, the terms "baking" and "roasting" are nearly interchangeable. Both refer to cooking in the dry heat of an oven. Baking foods are sometimes covered; roasting foods are always uncovered and typically cook at relatively high temperatures. This high heat releases the natural sugars in vegetables and fruits, leaving them tender on the inside and caramelized and sometimes even crisp on the outside. All meats, but especially lean meats, need a more watchful eye when roasting, as they will dry out if cooked for too long. Brining lean cuts, or soaking them in a salt or salt and sugar solution, can also counteract the drying effects of roasting and add good flavour.

Some recipes call for tying or trussing whole poultry or joints into a compact shape, to hold in stuffing or make an attractive presentation when carving at the table. Trussing is not strictly necessary, and poultry thighs cook more evenly when the bird is not trussed.

● When boiling pasta or potatoes, use a large pan and plenty of water. This helps the food to cook evenly, preventing sticking in the case of pasta. (Stirring also prevents sticking.)

● You can salt boiling water before adding the food, but for the best control over seasoning, do it after draining. If you want to salt cooking water, do it after the water has come to the boil. Adding salt raises the boiling temperature of water, so salted water takes longer to come to a full boil.

● Recipes will often instruct you to "boil to reduce" a liquid. This means to let the liquid evaporate away, which results in a thicker consistency and more concentrated flavour.

● When blanching, have ready a large bowl of iced water. Plunge the food into it to halt the cooking. Move the food quickly from the hot water to the iced water with tongs or a slotted spoon so that it does not continue cooking longer than you want.

ROASTING AND BAKING TIPS

● Use an oven thermometer to make sure the oven has reached the correct temperature before you put the food in. This will ensure good browning and better flavour.

● There should be room in the tin for the food to fit comfortably and air to circulate.

● Foods from the fridge should be allowed to stand at room temperature to take the chill off before roasting. This encourages even cooking.

● Foods to be roasted should be patted dry and, in general, lightly oiled before they go into the oven. This helps encourage browning.

● Allow roast meat and poultry to rest before carving so the juices are redistributed evenly. Depending on its size, the food's temperature will rise 3–9°C (5–15°F) as it rests.

● When a recipe instructs you to simmer, keep an eye on the pan. You may need to stir and adjust the heat from time to time to keep the liquid from coming to the boil.

● Poaching is ideal for cooking eggs, chicken, fish, fruits such as pears, and other delicate foods that need careful treatment to prevent them from breaking apart or overcooking.

● Because it is a gentle cooking method, steaming is well suited to delicate foods like seafood and tender vegetables. It helps a food to retain its shape, colour, flavour, and texture better than boiling, simmering, or even poaching.

● If food must steam for a long time, check periodically to make sure that the water has not boiled away completely, and top up with more boiling water as needed.

● Steam can scald you like boiling water, so take care when uncovering a pan.

BRAISING AND STEWING TIPS

● When braising, the food isn't covered with liquid. The pot will be covered, creating a moist and steamy cooking environment. For stewing, the liquid should just cover the food.

● Stews and braises should simmer very gently, never boil, which would toughen meat or poultry. The easiest way to keep the heat gentle and even is to do the cooking in the oven at about 170°C (350°F).

● In a braise, the liquid should reduce to a saucelike consistency. To help it along, remove the food from the liquid when tender and simmer the liquid to reduce and thicken it.

● A final step in a stew or braise is to use a large spoon to skim the clear fat from the surface of the liquid. If you plan to serve the dish in a day or so, you can simply cool and chill it. The fat will solidify, making it easier to scrape off.

Gentle and slow: simmering, poaching, and steaming

These three "moist" cooking methods have a lot in common. All involve water, and each is gentler than the last. Simmering is boiling slowed down, with smaller bubbles around the pan edges that disappear when you stir. Where boiling might cause a food to toughen, simmering firms it nicely (in the case of meat) or makes it tender (in the case of vegetables). Poaching is simmering in slow-motion: big bubbles occasionally break the surface of the liquid. Steaming lets food gently cook in a steamy vapour.

These moist-heat cooking methods, unlike dry-heat grilling and roasting, do not involve browning. Foods remain pale in colour and more delicate in flavour, which is desirable for some dishes.

The term "steaming" is sometimes used to describe cooking some foods, such as mussels and clams, in a small amount of simmering liquid in a covered pan. But generally it means to cook food over boiling or simmering water in a covered pan. You can use a steamer insert or basket, which will turn almost any saucepan into a steamer. In a pinch, you can also use a metal colander. In all cases, the steaming water in the pan must not touch the base of the rack or basket.

Gentle and slow: braising and stewing

These long, slow cooking methods give the cook plenty of time to do other things while the food cooks, and result in some of the world's most tender and meltingly delicious dishes. Braising is used for some sturdy leafy greens, but is especially suitable for tough cuts of meat. In the case of meat, it is usually first seared to brown it and add flavour, then it is immersed partway in liquid, covered, and cooked very gently on the hob or in the oven. The flavours have plenty of time to blend together, even more so if the braised dish is allowed to sit until the next day. Stewing is similar to braising but uses more liquid and smaller pieces of food, and it may cook gently uncovered or partly covered.

When browning foods before braising and stewing, the goal is to add attractive colour and good flavour without cooking the foods through. Since they will cook in liquid for a good deal of time, you don't want to toughen them up. Brown over a moderately high to high heat and use tongs to turn the food so it can colour on all sides.

Other techniques

Chopping and dicing

Even a task as simple as chopping has some basic rules to it. Keep the fingers of the hand holding the food tucked under so that you don't cut them. When cutting up food in order to cook it, try to cut the pieces into roughly the same size, so that they will cook at an even rate. To finely chop, which is how herbs and garlic are often prepared, first chop the item roughly, then gather it into a pile. Holding down the knife tip with your free hand, use the knife in a rocking motion to firmly and quickly cut the food to size. The term dice refers to neat cubes ranging in size from 5 mm (¼ inch) to 1 cm (½ inch). To dice an item, first slice it lengthways as thick as you want the dice to be. Turn the slices 90 degrees and slice them lengthways again. Now cut the strips across into dice.

Dicing onion

Here's a trick that will make your life easier whenever you cook. Cut the onion lengthways through the root end, then peel it. Place one of the halves flat side down. Make a series of horizontal slices as thick as you want the final dice to be, up to but not through the root end. (The root will help hold the onion layers together while you cut.) Now make a series of vertical slices, again not cutting through the root end. Last, make a series of crossways slices to dice the onion.

Preparing garlic

To loosen cloves from a head of garlic, place the head, root end up, on a chopping board and press down on it firmly with the heel of your palm. To loosen the skin from a single clove for peeling, place the clove under the flat side of a chef's knife and press firmly with the heel of your palm. Slice the garlic in half lengthways and remove any green sprout. (This sprout tastes bitter and means the garlic is past its prime.) Finely chop as described above.

Preparing chillies

Use a little caution when cutting hot chillies. Slice them in half lengthways to expose the seeds and white membranes, which is where the heat resides. Cut out the membranes and seeds, reserving them if you want to be able to adjust the heat of a dish. Be careful not to

touch your face as you work; the chilli's oils can burn your eyes or lips. Wash your hands, knife, and chopping board with hot soapy water when you're finished. If working with very hot chillies, you can wear rubber gloves for more protection.

Preparing peppers

To slice or dice a pepper, cut off the stalk end, then make a lengthways cut and open up the pepper into a flat rectangle. Cut out the white membranes and seeds. These are not hot as in a chilli, but they're not desirable in a dish, either. Slice or dice the pepper.

To peel a pepper, place it under a hot grill and turn occasionally until charred black on all sides. (You can also char it over a gas flame, holding it with long-handled tongs.) Seal the pepper in a plastic bag and leave to steam until cool enough to handle. Peel off the charred skin, then cut open the pepper and remove the membranes and seeds.

Grating

Grating is the process of reducing a food to fine particles or shreds. Lemon zest and Parmesan cheese are grated into tiny particles using the finest rasps of a box grater. Cheddar cheese and carrots are grated into shreds using the large holes. You can also grate foods using a mandolin or a food processor fitted with the right disc.

Segmenting citrus fruits

Citrus can be peeled and segmented with a knife to remove all of the tough membrane and bitter white pith. First remove a slice from the top and bottom of the fruit, cutting deep enough to expose the colourful flesh. Standing the fruit on a cut side, follow the curve of the fruit with the knife to remove all the peel and white pith. Holding the fruit over a bowl to catch the juices, cut on either side of each segment to free it from the membrane and let it fall into the bowl.

Separating eggs

Separating the yolks from the whites is easier to do when eggs are cold. Carefully break an egg and, holding it over a bowl, pass the yolk back and forth between the shell halves, letting the white fall into the bowl. Be careful not to pierce the yolk with a jagged edge of eggshell. Drop the yolk into a separate bowl. Transfer the white to a third bowl so that you are separating each new egg over an empty bowl.

Skinning and seeding tomatoes

Tomato skins tend to come off and curl up during cooking and can impart an annoying texture in some dishes. The following trick for peeling tomatoes also works for peaches and other thin-skinned fruit. Bring a pan of water to the boil. Using a sharp knife, cut a shallow X in the bottom end of each tomato. Have ready a bowl of iced water. Immerse the tomatoes in the boiling water (in batches if needed to avoid crowding) and blanch them for 15 seconds to loosen the skins. Then, using a slotted spoon, transfer them to the iced water to stop the cooking. Peel the tomatoes with your fingers or a small knife. To remove seeds, slice the tomatoes in half crossways (lengthways for plum tomatoes) and lightly squeeze and shake, using your finger if needed to help dislodge the seeds and pulp.

Dredging and coating

Dredging, or completely coating pieces of fish, meat, or poultry in seasoned flour or breadcrumbs, slows the escape of moisture during sautéing or frying and helps create an appealing golden crust. One of the most common ways to dredge a fillet is to drag both sides through the dry ingredient in a shallow bowl. Shaking the foods with flour in a large re-sealable plastic bag is a quick, tidy way to dredge. Always dredge just before cooking; if left to sit, the coating will soak up moisture and become gummy. Shake off the excess flour before you put the food in the pan.

Whisking egg whites

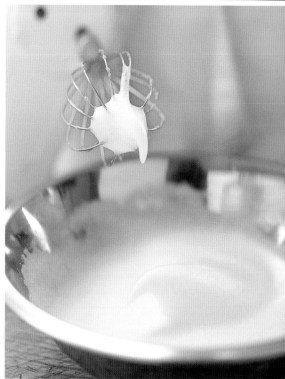

For billowing clouds, use egg whites at room temperature; more air can be incorporated during whisking than with cold ones. A copper bowl also increases volume through a chemical reaction with the egg white; cream of tartar in a stainless steel bowl can be used for the same effect. Whisk the whites vigorously with a balloon whisk or with an electric mixer on high speed. The egg whites will become foamy, increase in volume, and go from translucent to opaque. As the volume increases, stop from time to time and turn the whisk or beaters upright to see whether the egg whites are forming peaks. Gentle peaks that slump to one side are "soft" peaks, while shiny peaks that hold a pointy shape are called "stiff" or "hard" peaks. Don't whisk egg whites past the stiff peak stage; overwhisked whites become lumpy and lose their sheen, and they don't fold into mixtures as well.

Sifting flour

Sifting aerates flour to make light, evenly textured cakes. It is also used to combine flour with other dry ingredients so that a raising agent, such as baking powder, or ground spices are distributed evenly in the flour. If you don't have a special flour sifter, simply pass the ingredients through a fine-mesh sieve into a bowl. (For smaller amounts, you only need to stir the ingredients with a whisk.)

Folding

Folding is a way of combining a delicate mixture, such as whisked egg whites, with a heavier one, such as a rich cheese sauce for a soufflé, without deflating the delicate mixture. The folding should be done in a large bowl and the lighter mixture should be spooned on top of the heavier one. Using a wide, flat spoon or rubber spatula, cut down through both of the mixtures to the bottom of the bowl. Using a sweeping motion, bring the spatula up along the side of the bowl that is furthest from you, lifting up some of the mixture from the bottom of the bowl and "folding" it over the top one. Give the bowl a quarter turn and repeat the cutting, lifting, and folding action. Continue the folding until the two mixtures are just blended, which usually takes 6 or 7 actions. A few streaks can remain in the mixture. Be careful not to overdo the folding, because this can deflate a mixture and affect the final results of the soufflé or other dish.

Zesting and juicing citrus fruits

Citrus zest, the coloured portion of the peel, is rich in aromatic and flavourful oils. Choose organic fruit for zesting and scrub the fruit well to remove any wax or residue. Use only the thin outer layer of the peel, taking care not to include the bitter white pith. You can remove zest with a zester, a tool designed to take it in thin strips. A vegetable peeler or a paring knife can also be used, but will produce pieces that are short, wide, and irregular. Or, you can remove zest with the fine rasps of a box grater. Thin-skinned fruits that are heavy for their size yield the most juice. Before juicing, roll the fruit firmly against a hard surface to loosen up and break the membranes inside. Halve the fruit crossways and then extract the juice with a hand-held reamer or lemon juicer. You can also use a countertop citrus press or an electric juicer. Before juicing citrus fruits, remove any seeds from the fruit with the tip of a sharp knife, or set a sieve over a bowl to catch the seeds.

Entertaining basics

Now that you're married, you may find yourselves increasingly interested in entertaining. As you and your friends grow older and settle down, socializing by spending an evening out on the town may give way to having friends over for dinner. You may also begin to invite family for Sunday lunch. In some people's hands, a lunch or dinner party can seem effortless. But the truth is, it always requires advance planning.

The goal of planning is to make the event a pleasure both for your guests and for yourselves. If you're not in the habit of entertaining, start off slowly, inviting two or four friends over for dinner. The more people you invite, the simpler the food should be. When choosing a date and time for your party, make sure you allow yourself time to prepare: if you work all week, Saturday night is a better choice than Friday night, since you will have all of Saturday to get ready (and Sunday to recover!). Give yourself at least a week between inviting and hosting – or longer for a more elaborate party.

Consider how you'd like to serve dinner, based on the occasion or style you want to set for the party and on the limitations of your space. Be creative: if you have a small dining table, you can serve food buffet style and let guests sit on the sofa and chairs to eat, or outside on a patio. If this is the plan, you'll need to choose dishes that won't need to be cut with a knife, which is difficult when a dinner plate is balanced precariously on your lap. If you decide on a sit-down dinner, you can serve a few dishes at the same time, family style, and let guests help themselves, or you can serve dinner restaurant style: one course at a time, plated, for a more formal feel – or to work with a small table that won't accommodate several serving dishes. This decision of serving style will help determine which recipes you choose.

Planning a menu

You'll often hear it said that you should not try out a dish for the first time on guests. This is wise advice. Practise first on yourself, to make sure that you're familiar with the recipe and that it turns

JUGGLING DISHES

Once you choose a main dish for your menu, review how it's prepared to help you choose the other dishes and create a timeline for preparing them all.

Can the main course be prepared partly or completely in advance? (Hearty cold-weather braises and stews are excellent candidates for this.) If so, you'll have more time and attention available to devote to starters and side dishes. With a make-ahead main dish, these other courses can be more elaborate.

Does the main dish need any last-minute attention, just before serving? If so, it makes sense to choose accompaniments that can be prepared ahead of time, or you could assign responsibility for different dishes to you and your spouse. Read through the methods of recipes in order to find a complementary selection that the two of you can cope with easily.

out the way you expect in the amount of time you expect. You can choose from the outset to serve dishes you are already comfortable making, or plan a test run in advance of the party.

For a novice cook, coming up with a menu may seem daunting, but you'll soon discover that one decision will lead into the next. We've created several menus for special occasions using the recipes in this book: turn to pages 240–43 for ideas. To come up with your own menu, consider the ambience you would like to create at your party: very casual and festive, or more calm and formal. Luckily, most recipes can be dressed up or down, served on more casual earthenware or on your best china. Think in general about the combination of flavours, colours, textures, and ingredients that feels appropriate to the mood and occasion you want to create. The seasonality of ingredients is also important: check with the greengrocer or at a farmers' market for guidance so you don't get your heart set on serving a tomato salad when tomatoes are out of season, bland, and mealy. If you are not sure where to begin, start with the main dish and work from there to select a starter, accompaniment, and dessert.

Elements of the table

Whether your party is casual or formal, you do not need to be an interior designer to create an attractive, inviting table. When in doubt, err on the side of simplicity: start with white and then add a few accents of colour. Avoid overdecorating, and you will find that the cutlery and glasses will add plenty of sparkle to the scene.

A casual table setting reflects the easygoing style of the meal to come. Select a plain tablecloth or place mats, with napkins that match or are in complementary colours. Everyday cutlery, dishes, and glasses are appropriate, and can be augmented with a few special pieces.

Following traditional table-setting guidelines might seem at odds with the spirit of a casual dinner. But these conventions, far from being arbitrary rules of style, are intended to make the meal a more comfortable and enjoyable experience for your guests.

For each guest, put a napkin on top of or to the left of the plate, folded side facing the plate (or rolled in a napkin ring), allowing space to its right for the forks. Arrange all cutlery in the order in which it will be used, starting from the outermost item. On the left side of the plate, place a salad fork if you are serving a starter, with a larger, main-course fork beside it, next to the plate. The knife or knives should be placed to the right of the plate, the blade facing inwards. (Imagine yourself picking up the utensils and eating, with fork in your left hand and knife in right, and you'll see how these positions make sense.) If you are serving soup, set the soup spoon to the right of the knife.

Next, set a water glass directly above the knife. Place a white wineglass to the right of the water glass, and a red wineglass to the right of the white wineglass. Bread plates, butter knives, dessert spoons and forks, or teaspoons may make an appearance at more formal meals. Without bread plates, guests can put bread directly on their dinner plates or on the table or tablecloth. Forks and/or spoons for dessert can be placed crossways at the top of the plate or brought out along with the dessert. Teaspoons can come out with the coffee.

Staying organised

As the main elements of your dinner party begin to take shape, it is important to keep track of all the little organisational details and special touches that will bring everything together. Make two lists, Shopping and Tasks. Organise the shopping list into categories. Try to arrange the tasks list in chronological order so you do not forget last-minute items. It is also helpful to work out a basic cooking and serving timetable to keep everything on track. Recruiting help is a good idea for dinner parties of eight or more (including yourselves), and will give you more time with your guests.

Putting it all together

Your most important task is to make your guests feel at ease. When the doorbell starts ringing, make sure you get out of the kitchen to greet your friends warmly, take coats and offer drinks, and introduce guests to one another if they are not already acquainted. Ideally you should plan not to be cooking right when guests are due to arrive, but if one of you needs to attend to last-minute details, the other can devote him- or herself to your friends or family.

With a good plan in hand, you can use the recipes in this book to create a delightful evening for friends or a cheery holiday feast for family. Put all the elements together and you can't go wrong, so have fun and enjoy your party.

SET THE MOOD

● Lighting, music, and flowers help create a mood and ambience for a gathering, and should be planned ahead of time.

● For evening parties, use a combination of electric lights and candlelight to flatter everyone's appearance and create an inviting ambience. Scent-free, dripless regular or votive candles, such as beeswax candles, are good choices. The aroma of scented candles can come into conflict with the food, especially if you want to place the candles on the dining table.

● Music should complement the occasion or theme. Select it in advance, so it is easy to manage during the party. Set the volume low at first, to keep the music from competing with conversation. You can always raise the volume as the party gets livelier.

● If you plan to decorate the table with flowers, keep in mind that tall bouquets block guests' views across the table. Try smaller bouquets, or flowers floating in shallow bowls of water.

EXPECT THE UNEXPECTED

● Even at the most well-organized dinner party, accidents and unanticipated problems are bound to occur. The key is to stay calm and let the evening flow naturally while you deal with the situation discreetly.

● The most important thing to remember is that a party is all about enjoyment, and guests take their cue from the host. If your dinner plan is not unfolding the way you expected, have a sense of humour about it. If a side dish burns, simply omit it from the meal. If something doesn't turn out perfectly, just smile and pretend it's all come out just the way you planned. Don't apologize, and don't make a fuss, and it's likely no one will notice anything amiss.

A Valentine's Day Menu

MENU

Rib-eye Steak with Pan Jus • 94

Tossed Green Salad • 82

Ginger Carrot Salad • 155

Blueberry Fool • 196

SERVES 2

Wine pairing: Côtes du Rhône

TIMELINE

UP TO 4 HOURS BEFORE SERVING
Make Blueberry Fool and put into fridge.

UP TO 2 HOURS BEFORE SERVING
Make Ginger Carrot Salad and keep at room temperature.

30 MINUTES BEFORE SERVING
Make Tossed Green Salad.
Make Rib-eye Steak with Pan Jus.

Note: To serve two, cut the recipes for Tossed Green Salad and Blueberry Fool in half, and the recipe for Ginger Carrot Salad to one-third.

First Anniversary

MENU

Gazpacho • 72

Crab Cakes • 69

Tomato, Mozzarella, and Basil Salad • 84

Raspberry and Lemon Tart • 205

SERVES 2

Wine pairing: Australian Sauvignon Blanc or a French Sancerre (white or rosé)

TIMELINE

UP TO 2 DAYS BEFORE SERVING
Make Gazpacho and keep in fridge.
Make tart case for Raspberry and Lemon Tart.

UP TO 4 HOURS BEFORE SERVING
Make lemon curd for Raspberry and Lemon Tart.
Shape Crab Cakes and put into fridge.

30 MINUTES BEFORE SERVING
Assemble tart and put into fridge.
Make Tomato, Basil, and Mozzarella Salad and keep at room temperature.

JUST BEFORE SERVING
Sauté Crab Cakes.

Note: To serve two, cut the recipes for Gazpacho and Tomato, Mozzarella, and Basil Salad in half, and plan for leftover Raspberry and Lemon Tart.

Drinks Party

MENU

Spicy Almonds • 58

Warm Marinated Olives • 58

Gazpacho • 72

Roast Radicchio with Pancetta • 170

Prawns with Parsley-Garlic Butter • 67

mandarins or satsumas

SERVES 12

Wine pairing: chilled rosé

TIMELINE

UP TO 1 WEEK BEFORE SERVING
Make Spicy Almonds and keep in fridge.

UP TO 2 DAYS BEFORE SERVING
Make Gazpacho and keep in fridge.

30 MINUTES BEFORE SERVING
Marinate Warm Marinated Olives.
Take Spicy Almonds out of fridge.
Put Radicchio in oven.

JUST BEFORE SERVING
Sauté Warm Marinated Olives.
Slide Prawns with Parsley-Garlic Butter under grill to cook.

Dinner Party

MENU

Marinated Goat's Cheese • 61

Sea Bass with Fennel and Bacon • 123

boiled new potatoes

Blueberry Fool • 196

SERVES 6

Wine pairing: Viognier

TIMELINE

UP TO 2 DAYS BEFORE SERVING
Make Marinated Goat's Cheese.

UP TO 4 HOURS BEFORE SERVING
Make 2 recipes Blueberry Fool and put in fridge.

1 HOUR BEFORE SERVING
Prepare Sea Bass up to roasting step.

30 MINUTES BEFORE SERVING
Put Sea Bass in oven.
Put potatoes on to boil.

New Year's Eve Dinner

MENU

Gougères • 61

Winter Chicory Salad • 83

Rack of Lamb • 103

Roasted Onion Squash Crescents • 164

Crisp Rosemary Potatoes • 177

Chocolate Pots de Crème • 211

SERVES 6

*Wine pairing: Champagne or sparkling wine
with Gougères; Pinot Noir with Rack of Lamb*

TIMELINE

UP TO 1 DAY BEFORE SERVING
Make Gougères and keep wrapped at room temperature.
Make Pots de Crème and put into fridge.

1 HOUR BEFORE SERVING
Sear rack of lamb and apply coating; parboil potatoes.

50 MINUTES BEFORE SERVING
Roast squash and keep warm.
Turn up oven temperature for lamb.

30 MINUTES BEFORE SERVING
Make 2 recipes Winter Chicory Salad and keep at room temperature.
Put rack of lamb in oven.
Sauté 2 recipes Crisp Rosemary Potatoes and keep warm.

Sunday Brunch

MENU

Courgette and Basil Frittata • 51

Asparagus Mimosa • 152

Roast Beetroot and Feta Salad • 90

Strawberry Shortcakes • 201

SERVES 4

Wine pairing: Pouilly Fumé

TIMELINE

UP TO 1 DAY BEFORE SERVING
Make shortcakes for Strawberry Shortcakes and keep wrapped at room temperature.
Roast beetroot.

UP TO 2 HOURS BEFORE SERVING
Prepare strawberries for Strawberry Shortcakes.

1 HOUR BEFORE SERVING
Make Asparagus Mimosa and keep at room temperature.
Prepare Roast Beetroot and Feta Salad up to tossing step.

30 MINUTES BEFORE SERVING
Make 2 Courgette and Basil Frittatas and keep at room temperature.

JUST BEFORE SERVING
Whip cream for Strawberry Shortcakes.
Toss Roast Beetroot and Feta Salad.

Christmas Lunch

MENU

Butternut Squash Soup • 77

Spiced Roast Turkey • 116

Almond and Currant Stuffing • 185

Caramelized Brussels Sprouts • 164

Best Mashed Potatoes • 178

Christmas pudding *(shop-bought)*

SERVES 10

Wine pairing: choice of Chardonnay or Beaujolais

TIMELINE

UP TO 2 DAYS AHEAD OF SERVING
Make 2 recipes Butternut Squash Soup up to step of adding cream, and keep in fridge.

1 DAY AHEAD
Season turkey and keep in fridge.

4 HOURS AHEAD OF SERVING
Take turkey out of fridge.

3 HOURS BEFORE SERVING
Make 2 recipes Almond and Currant Stuffing.

2½ HOURS BEFORE SERVING
Put turkey in oven.

1 HOUR BEFORE SERVING
Put 2–3 recipes' worth of potatoes on to boil.
Separate 5 recipes' worth of Brussels sprouts into leaves.

30 MINUTES BEFORE SERVING
Take turkey out of oven; make gravy and keep warm.

JUST BEFORE SERVING
Heat up Butternut Squash Soup and add cream.
Sauté Brussels sprouts.
Mash potatoes.

Sunday Lunch

MENU

French Onion Soup • 81

Roast Beef with Yorkshire Pudding • 98

Ginger Carrot Salad • 155

Celeriac Purée • 169

Ginger Cake with Rum Butter • 202

SERVES 8

Wine pairing: Cabernet Sauvignon

TIMELINE

UP TO 2 DAYS AHEAD
Make French Onion Soup up to grilling step and keep in fridge.
Make Ginger Cake and keep wrapped at room temperature.
Make Rum Butter and keep in fridge.

1 DAY AHEAD
Season beef joint and keep in fridge.

4 HOURS BEFORE SERVING
Take beef out of fridge.

2 HOURS BEFORE SERVING
Put beef in oven.
Make 2 recipes Ginger Carrot Salad.

30 MINUTES BEFORE SERVING
Take Roast Beef out of oven.
Make Yorkshire Pudding.
Put 2 recipes' worth of celeriac on to boil.

JUST BEFORE SERVING
Grill topping of French Onion Soup.
Purée celeriac.

Glossary

Artichoke hearts: The heart is the most delicious and meaty part of a globe artichoke, and trimming artichokes is a labour of love. Keep jars of artichoke hearts packed in oil in the storecupboard to include in antipasto, to top a pizza, or to add to a pasta sauce.

Bain marie pan: A bain marie pan consists of two pans, one nested atop the other, with room for water to simmer in the bottom pan. Delicate foods such as chocolate and custards are placed in the top pan to heat them gently, or to melt them in the case of chocolate. The top pan should not touch the water beneath it, and the water should not be allowed to boil. A tight fit between the pans ensures that no water or steam can escape and mix with the ingredients in the top, which can cause melting chocolate to seize or stiffen. You can create your own bain marie pan by placing a heatproof mixing bowl or a slightly smaller saucepan over a larger one, although it may not be as steady or the fit as tight.

Baking dish: Made of porcelain, ovenproof glass, stoneware, or glazed earthenware, baking dishes come in many shapes and sizes. They are very versatile, being suitable for both oven cooking and serving. Most can be put under the grill too, for gratins and browning surfaces of food, but are not flameproof so cannot be used on the hob.

Baking parchment: Also called silicone paper, baking parchment is ideal for lining cake tins and baking trays. Unlike greaseproof paper, it doesn't need to be greased before use.

Baking sheet/tray: Both baking sheets and trays are flat, rectangular, and metal. A baking sheet is either rimless or has one raised edge for easy handling, whereas a baking tray has shallow raised edges on all sides. Choose sturdy stainless steel baking sheets and trays that will last for years. Non-stick sheets and trays are easy to clean.

Blender: When shopping for a blender, which is also called a liquidizer, features to look for are sturdiness, a toughened glass or heavy-weight plastic container, and a tight-fitting lid with a "trap door" that allows you to add ingredients as you blend. Blenders create a smoother purée and incorporate less air than food processors, so are the first choice for smooth soups and for baby food.

Hand-held or stick blenders are immersed in a food or mixture to blend or purée it. They are great for puréeing food in the container in which it is mixed or cooked (e.g. bowls and saucepans). This means that they can blend larger amounts of food than will fit at one time in the container of a stand blender. Hand-held blenders also tend to incorporate more air into a liquid and as a result can be used for frothy foam finishes and to whip cream. These blenders usually have only one or two speeds, and the blade must be completely immersed in the food to prevent spattering. Many are designed to hang in a wall mount for easy storage. Some have whisk attachments or small containers for blending small amounts.

Blowtorch: A small, gas-powered kitchen blowtorch is much better than a hot grill at quickly and evenly browning the top of a gratin or melting and caramelizing the sugar layer on a crème brûlée. With a blowtorch you can direct the flame at a specific area, and avoid any scorching.

Boning knife: This knife features a thin, flexible blade whose shape is designed to follow along the curve of a bone as you cut away the meat.

Box grater: This useful tool offers four different sizes of rasps or holes, allowing you to grate hard cheeses into fine powder for quick melting, or grate raw vegetables or semifirm cheeses such as Cheddar into shreds on the largest holes.

Brandy: This spirit is distilled from wine or fermented fruit juice. It's used in both sweet and savoury dishes, often flambéed to burn off some of its alcohol content while leaving behind its delicious flavour. The finest type of brandy is Cognac, which is made around the town of Cognac in western France.

Brushes: When choosing brushes for the kitchen, look for natural bristles that are firmly attached to a handle. Keep one brush for savoury uses and another for sweet, and if you like to barbecue, look for a long-handled brush for basting meat.

Bulghur wheat: Nutty-tasting bulghur wheat, also known as burghul, is made by steaming whole wheat grains, partly removing the bran, and then drying and cracking the grains. It is commonly used in Middle Eastern and Balkan cooking as the basis for pilafs, salads, and stuffings. It has a mild flavour and firm texture that make it a good vehicle for the stronger flavours of other ingredients.

Cake comb: Also called a decorating comb or icing comb, this triangular tool has jagged teeth of varying size on each edge to make decorative patterns in cake icing.

Cake tin: Round tins, generally 5 cm (2 inches) deep and either 20 or 23 cm (8 or 9 inches) in diameter, are used for baking sponge cakes. You will want to have at least two. Deeper cake tins, which may be round or square, are used for rich fruit cakes.

Can opener: Because you will use this so often, buy a good one, whether manual or electric. Newer manual can openers are ergonomically designed to save your hand from cramping as you work to open a can.

Chef's/cook's knife: This is the most useful all-purpose knife: a large, evenly proportioned, tapered blade that is generally 15–23 cm (6–9 inches) long. You will use this knife to prepare nearly every dish, for slicing, dicing, chopping, and julienning ingredients.

Chicory: This torpedo-shaped vegetable has tightly packed leaves that are normally white with yellow tips, crunchy, and slightly bitter. Radicchio is a red-leaved relative. Chicory is at its best in autumn and winter, when cool weather brings out its sweetness.

Chilli powder: Pure chilli powder – finely ground dried chillies – should not be mistaken for the commercial spice blend known as chilli powder, which usually combines ground dried chillies, ground cumin, garlic powder, oregano, and other seasonings.

Chimney starter: See page 228.

Chinese five-spice powder: This seasoning blend is common in the kitchens of southern China and of Vietnam, where it is often used to flavour poultry for roasting. It is readily available in supermarkets.

Chinese skimmer: This mesh tool is useful for scooping food from hot oil when deep-frying or hot water when blanching.

Chocolate: The chocolate-making process begins with cocoa beans. The beans are fermented, roasted, shelled, and crushed into bits that are then ground and compressed to become chocolate liquor. The liquor contains cocoa butter, referred to as cocoa solids on chocolate labelling, and the more cocoa solids in chocolate the better, and more expensive, it will be. Dark chocolate with 60–70% cocoa solids is most often used for cooking as it has a rich, delicious flavour. With a higher content of cocoa solids than this, chocolate will be more bitter; less cocoa solids and it will be sweeter. Milk chocolate, which has about 30–40% cocoa solids, is lighter than dark chocolate in both colour and flavour.

Chopping boards: The best boards are made of wood or polyethylene. Keep separate boards for raw meat and poultry and other foods, and wash them in hot, soapy water after use. An oniony board can be freshened by rubbing it with the cut side of a lemon.

Cime di rapa: Related to turnips, this leafy green vegetable has slender stalks topped with flowerheads that resemble tiny broccoli florets. Cime di rapa has a nutty, pleasantly bittersweet taste.

Citrus reamer: A tool designed to squeeze the juice from lemons, usually by means of a mound-shaped ridged surface pressed and twisted against and into a lemon half.

Coffee machine: Modern electric versions of the classic filter coffee machine can grind the coffee, brew it, and keep it warm. Others can make filter coffee on one side and espresso or cappuccino on the other.

Colander: A large and sturdy sieve, this tool is indispensable for draining boiled foods such as potatoes or pasta and for rinsing large quantities of fruits or vegetables. A colander lined with damp muslin can also be used for straining stock.

Cooling racks: Baked goods just out of the oven are usually cooled on wire racks, which allow air to circulate on all sides. The racks, which come in various shapes and stand on short legs, should be made of sturdy metal. You'll want to have enough racks to handle two baking sheets of biscuits.

Cream of tartar: This white powder is potassium tartrate, a by-product of wine making. It is used to stabilize egg whites so that they whisk up more easily.

Crêpe/pancake pan: The most useful size for this shallow pan is 20–23 cm (8–9 inches). Its flat base and long handle make it easy to spread batter evenly by rotating the pan, and its low slanting sides allow you to lift an edge of the crêpe with ease for flipping.

Cutters: Stainless steel cutters with one sharp edge come in a wide variety of shapes and sizes, plain and fluted. Apart from cutting out biscuits and pastry shapes, they can be used to cut neat shapes from potatoes and other vegetables and bread slices.

Dariole moulds: These small metal moulds shaped somewhat like pudding basins are used for individual desserts that are turned out for serving, such as crème caramel and baked or steamed sponge puddings.

Decorating turntable: Anyone who does a lot of cake decorating appreciates a turntable. Icing and piping are much easier if the cake is raised above the work surface and if you can turn the cake with a slight push.

Egg poacher: Eggs can be poached in a specially designed egg poacher, which is a shallow dish with three or six indentations, each one the right size to hold one egg, that sits over a wide pan of simmering water.

Electric mixer: Hand-held mixers are small, light, portable machines. Lacking the power and special attachments of stand mixers, these appliances are adequate for most batters and soft doughs but do not work well for stiff doughs. For long mixing tasks, such as making buttercream or beating volumes of egg whites, these mixers can become tedious to hold. They can be used with nearly any bowl or pan, however, even those set over a pan of simmering water on the hob.

Stand mixers are heavy-duty, stationary machines with large, removable bowls, a range of speeds, and a variety of attachments. The basic set usually includes a wire whisk for whisking egg whites or whipping cream, a paddle for creaming together butter and sugar and mixing batters, and a dough hook for kneading bread. Some are equipped with mincers or other special attachments. Stand mixers work better for large amounts and heavy mixtures and free up your hands, which can be helpful when adding ingredients.

Epazote: This pungent herb (also called wormseed) is looked on as a culinary treasure by Mexican cooks.

Fennel: Similar in appearance and texture to celery, fennel has stalks that overlap at the base to form a somewhat flat bulb with white to pale green ribbed layers. The leaves are light and feathery. Fennel leaves, seeds, and bulbs have a sweet, faint aniselike flavour. Select creamy-coloured bulbs topped by fresh-looking feathery green tops.

Fermented black beans: Also called salted or preserved black beans, fermented black beans are soya beans that have been dried, salted, and allowed to ferment until they turn black. Used mainly in Chinese cooking, they are distinctly pungent and have an almost smoky character.

Flameproof casserole: This large, heavy round or oval pot with a tight-fitting lid is used for slow cooking on the hob or in the oven.

Most casseroles are made of enamelled cast iron, which will not react with acidic foods the way uncoated cast iron does.

Food mill: Used to purée cooked or soft foods, this tool, which is also called a mouli-légumes, looks like a slope-sided saucepan with a perforated bottom and an interior crank. A paddle-shaped blade at the base rotates against a disc perforated with small holes. As the handle is turned, the blade forces the food through the holes, leaving behind all skins, fibres, pips, and fine bones.

Food processor: The all-purpose, spiral-shaped metal blade chops, blends, mixes, and purées. Other attachments include discs for shredding or grating and slicing, a plastic blade for kneading dough, and a paddle for beating batters. A feed tube allows you to add ingredients while the food processor is running. Despite their popularity, food processors are not capable of performing every kitchen task. For example, they are not recommended for mashing potatoes, nor can they normally be used for whisking egg whites or whipping cream. If you plan to mix very dense dough, make sure your processor motor is powerful enough, or the motor may dangerously overheat.

Frying pan: This broad pan is similar to a sauté pan, but differs in that its flared sides make it useful for cooking foods that must be stirred or turned out of the pan. Stainless steel, titanium, and enamelled cast iron are good materials for frying pans. An ovenproof cast-iron frying pan is very useful for dishes that start off cooking on the hob and then need to finish cooking in the oven.

Ginger: This knobbly rhizome, or underground stem, enlivens many sauces, salads, and marinades. Look for firm fresh ginger with no discoloration. Peel ginger and slice, chop, or grate it before using in a recipe. You can store an entire piece of ginger in the freezer and grate it, still frozen, as needed.

Grappa: This rustic Italian spirit is made from the remnants of grape pressings – stalks, seeds, and skins – after the juice has been extracted to make wine.

Gravy strainer: A porcelain, glass, or plastic jug that has a spout at the bottom, or sometimes 2 spouts, one on either side, this is used as a fat separator. Drippings from the roasting tin are poured into the jug. After the fat has risen to the top, the non-fatty gravy or meat juices at the bottom can be poured out.

Griddle: A flat rectangle or round of cast iron or cast aluminium, often with a non-stick finish, a griddle sits flat on the hob. Griddles are ideal for cooking drop scones, muffins, eggs, bacon, thin steaks, and much more. Most have depressed rims to catch grease.

Ice cream maker: Most ice cream and sorbet recipes require the use of an ice cream maker that comprises a container and a churn. The old-fashioned kind requires the use of ice and rock salt, not to mention elbow grease, but most contemporary ice cream makers use a frozen or refrigerated container and usually an electric motor.

Ice cream scoop: Two styles of scoop are popular: the dipper scoop and the half-sphere scoop. The dipper has a thick handle and a rounded, shallow bowl. The handle is hollow and transmits heat from your hand to the dipper. The half-sphere scoop has a full, deep bowl and a trigger-released metal wire that pushes the ice cream from the scoop.

Icing spatula: This long, flat metal utensil with its slender, flexible blade resembles a palette knife. It makes it easy to achieve a smooth icing finish on cakes.

Kitchen scale: Choose a kitchen scale capable of weighing small amounts precisely, in 5 g (¼ oz) increments. Electronic, digital scales are the best for this. Other essentials are that the scales can be used for both metric and imperial weights and that you can return to zero when weighing more than one ingredient in the bowl at a time. Ideally, for convenience, kitchen scales should allow you to weigh ingredients in any bowl or container.

Kitchen scissors/shears: Every kitchen should have a pair of scissors in the drawer to cut baking parchment and greaseproof paper, kitchen string, and muslin, snip fresh herbs, top and tail green beans, etc. Basic kitchen scissors have stainless-steel blades and one serrated edge. Heavier and longer poultry shears are useful for jointing or spatchcocking chicken and trimming fat and skin.

Kitchen string: Kitchen string, also called kitchen twine, is used for trussing chicken and tying joints, as well as numerous other tasks. The linen string should be soft, pliable, and natural (not dyed).

Kitchen timer: This invaluable little gadget is your best friend if you are cooking several dishes at once, entertaining, or doing other tasks at the same time as cooking. Timers range in complexity from the simple spring-activated ones to digital timers that can time three dishes at once. Most ovens have built-in timers. A clip-on timer that attaches to your apron is helpful when you need to leave the kitchen and move around the house.

Ladle: At least one ladle is essential in every kitchen. The bowl should be made of stainless steel or rigid, heat-resistant plastic and large enough to scoop up a good measure of soup or stew. The handle should be heat-resistant and long enough for easy use.

Lamb's lettuce: Also called mâche or corn salad, this very delicate and mild salad green has long, oval leaves that grow in small, loose bunches or clusters.

Loaf tin: Loaf tins give form to breads that are too moist to hold their own shape. They vary in size and shape, but the standard sizes are 500 g (1 lb) and 1 kg (2 lb). Be careful when trying to substitute a tin of a different size for the one specified in a recipe. The mixture or dough should fill the tin about two-thirds full. With less dough, you will have a flat loaf. With too much, you will have a top-heavy loaf that looks awkward and is difficult to slice.

Mandolin: This narrow, rectangular tool, usually made of stainless steel, is used for slicing and julienning. It sits at an angle on the work surface, and the food to be cut is moved over a mounted blade (with a strumming motion, which gives the tool its name). This handy tool simplifies the task of creating very thin, uniform slices.

Mascarpone: Thick enough to spread when chilled, but sufficiently fluid to be spooned at room temperature, mascarpone is noted for its rich flavour and slightly acidic tang. Although it is considered to be a cheese, it is really a thickened high-fat cream.

Meat mallet: Also called a cutlet beater or bat, a smooth, heavy meat mallet is useful for pounding boneless meat and poultry pieces until thin for quick and even cooking. A meat pounder or tenderizer is a mallet that has blunt teeth or a grid that help to break down fibres in the meat, tenderizing it.

Melon baller: Also known as a vegetable scoop, potato baller, or melon-ball scoop, this hand tool has a small bowl at one end, about 2.5 cm (1 inch) in diameter, used for making decorative balls from melon or other semifirm foods. It is useful for seeding or coring foods such as cucumbers and pears, or preparing them for stuffing.

Molasses/black treacle: A thick, intensely flavoured syrup, molasses is a by-product of cane sugar refining. The darker the syrup, the stronger and less sweet it is. Molasses gives a distinctive flavour to many sweet and savoury foods, from gingerbread, sponge puddings, and rich fruit cakes to Boston baked beans.

Mortar and pestle: These ancient tools are effective for pulverizing spices and making pastes. Mortars are bowl shaped, made of stone, wood, or pottery, with a smooth or coarse-textured interior. A pouring spout is useful. The pestle is the grinding tool. To grind ingredients, place them in the mortar, then grasp the pestle firmly and rotate and press down on the ingredients to crush them with the pestle's blunt tip.

Mozzarella: This soft and springy Italian cheese was traditionally made from the milk of water buffaloes (*mozzarella di bufala*), but now it is often made from cow's milk. It is commonly rolled by hand into small or medium balls and packed in water to keep it fresh.

Muffin/bun sheet: Also called muffin moulds or tins, these sheets may have 6, 12, or 24 cups, and can be used for American-style muffins, cupcakes, mince pies, Yorkshire puddings, and much more. The cups can be lined with paper cases (although the crust is likely to come off with the paper) or greased before being filled; however, sheets with non-stick surfaces are preferable. Sheets made of flexible silicone rubber are available.

Mushrooms: Cultivated white mushrooms may be button, when they have closed caps; open cup, when the cap is starting to open and the pinkish gills can be seen; and flat or open, when the gills, now brown, are completely visible. The latter have the most developed flavour. Chestnut mushrooms, also called portabellini or crimini, have brown caps, a meatier texture, and more flavour. Large, fully mature chestnut mushrooms are known as portabello mushrooms. To clean all varieties of mushrooms, wipe them with a clean, damp cloth or mushroom brush, or swish them very briefly in water, then drain on kitchen paper.

Non-stick cooking liner: These will prevent biscuits and other baked or roasted foods from sticking to a baking sheet or tray and wipe clean easily.

Nutmeg: The large, oval, brown seed of a soft fruit, nutmeg has a warm, sweet, spicy flavour. Whole nutmeg keeps its flavour much longer than grated nutmeg, so always grate nutmeg just before using. Use the finest rasps on a box grater, or a special nutmeg grater.

Olives: Olives pass through stages of ripeness, producing many shades of colours from green to pale beige to chocolate brown to deep purple and all the way to shiny black. Richly flavoured, dark ripe olive varieties include the little French Niçoise, Greek Kalamatas, Italian Gaetas, and the very mild, very large black Cerignola olives from southern Italy.

Olive oil: A staple of Mediterranean cooking, olive oil is both delicious and healthful. Southern France, Spain, Italy, Greece, Tunisia, Israel, California, and Australia all produce high-quality olive oils. Extra virgin oils are pressed without the use of heat or chemical solvents. Depending on the location and type of olive, the colour of the oil can range from a rich gold to a murky deep green. Oils made from mature olives, like those from southern Italy, are more golden and buttery. Oils made from younger olives, characteristic of Tuscany, have a clear, greenish hue and a flavour that is fruity and sometimes peppery. Show off the rich flavour of a special extra virgin olive oil by drizzling it over food as a seasoning or serving it as a dip for bread. Other extra virgin olive oils can be used in vinaigrettes and for general cooking, with the exception of deep-frying. Oils with a less distinctive olive flavour, labelled simply "olive oil", are also good for frying and sautéing, including high-temperature frying. Olive oil will deteriorate if it is kept in bright light, or if it gets too hot, so store it in a cool dark place (not the fridge).

Oven mitts/gloves: Essential for taking pans from the hob and tins from the oven, oven mitts and gloves should be thickly padded and large enough to perform their designated tasks with safety. Insulated gloves designed to reach nearly to the elbow are especially useful when you are working over a hot barbecue.

Oyster knife and glove: Oyster knives have thick handles for easy gripping and turning. Their wide, dull blades are strong enough to lever open the shell by inserting and twisting near the hinge. (Although similar, oyster knives are stubbier than clam knives.) Stainless-steel oyster knives will not transfer any metallic flavour to the oyster. An oyster glove is a metal mesh glove that protects the hand holding the oyster from a slip of the knife.

Pancetta: A flavourful Italian bacon, pancetta is made from pork belly, as is streaky bacon, but it is salt-cured and has a subtler, sweeter taste and silky texture. Pancetta is sold as straight or round rashers or diced.

Paring knife: A small, evenly proportioned blade usually 7.5–10 cm (3–4 inches) long. Used for peeling fruits and vegetables and for slicing or chopping small quantities.

Parmesan cheese: A firm, aged, salty cheese made from cow's milk. Parmigiano-Reggiano is true Parmesan, produced in the Emilia-Romagna region of Italy. Look for the name stamped in a pattern on the rind. To ensure freshness, buy the cheese in wedges and grate or shave it only as needed for use in a recipe. Store the cheese wrapped in foil in the fridge for up to 3 weeks.

Parsley: Flat-leaf parsley, often referred to as Italian parsley, has a more complex and refreshing flavour than curly parsley.

Pastry board/slab: Rolling out pastry calls for a smooth, hard, preferably cool surface. A pastry board may be made of hardwood or marble. Do not use it as a chopping board, or the surface will become rough (and marble will dull your knives). Marble slabs stay cool, which is important for puff pastry. They can even be chilled in the refrigerator.

Pecorino: This sharp, firm Italian grating cheese is made from sheep's milk. There are many varieties, often named according to where they are made, for example, pecorino romano, which is the original variety made around Rome and considered to be the best.

Pepper mill: Pepper mills are available in a wide range of materials and shapes. When choosing a pepper mill, keep in mind that you may want pepper ground coarse or fine for different uses, so look for a mill that can be adjusted for the grind you need. If you use coarse or flaked sea salt, you'll also want to have a matching salt mill.

Pernod: This liqueur is an absinthe substitute made by Pernod et Fils in France, a company that produced true absinthe before it was banned in 1914. Although far sweeter than absinthe, Pernod shares its anise flavour. Pernod is yellowish in colour but, like other anise-flavoured liqueurs, turns cloudy when mixed with water.

Pie tin: Buy metal pie tins. Glass pie plates let you see how the base of the pastry case is browning, but they are sometimes overzealous heat conductors that lead to a browned pastry with an undercooked middle. The rim of the tin should be wide to hold up the fluted edge of the pastry case or lid.

Piping bag: Different pastry nozzles or tubes can be inserted into the narrow end of this conical bag, which is then filled with icing, whipped cream, or a similar mixture that is piped out through the nozzle. Piping bags should be washed in warm, soapy water and turned inside out for drying. If you don't have a piping bag, you can fashion one out of a heavy-duty plastic bag – snip off one of the bottom corners to make a piping hole.

Pizza cutter: Although pizzas can be cut with a serrated knife, using a rotating pizza wheel, or pizza cutter, is more efficient. The sharp-edged wheels are 5–10 cm (2–4 inches) in diameter; the handles are short and should be fitted with a protective thumb guard. Buy a sturdy pizza wheel, making sure it has a strong handle and a large thumb guard.

Pizza peel: Using this large wooden paddle, pizzas can be transferred to the oven safely and with ease, by sliding onto a pizza stone or the oven rack for baking. Peels measure 60 cm (2 feet) or more in diameter and have a thin edge and long handle. A baking sheet can be used for the same purpose.

Pizza stone: Also called a baking stone or baking tile, this square, rectangular, or round slab of unglazed stoneware creates the effect of a hot brick oven in a domestic oven. The stone should be preheated in the oven for at least 45 minutes before baking. The pizza is slid onto the hot stone from a pizza peel. Other breads can be baked on a pizza stone.

Polenta: Polenta is cornmeal (coarse or fine ground dried maize) that is cooked in either water, stock, or a mixture of milk and stock until it thickens and the grains become tender. It may be the consistency of sloppy mashed potatoes or firm enough to slice and fry. The

quickest way to make it is with instant polenta flour, which has been precooked. Cooking regular polenta takes about 30 minutes and it has to be stirred very frequently (some say constantly). Traditionally, freshly cooked polenta was poured out onto the middle of a wooden table or onto a wooden board, cooled, and then cut with a string for serving.

Potatoes: Starchy or floury potatoes, such as King Edward and Marfona, have a fluffy, dry texture after cooking, so are perfect for baking and mashing, whereas waxy potatoes, such as Charlotte, Nicola, and Pink Fir Apple, thin-skinned and with a low starch content, are the ones to use for potato salads as they hold their shape after cooking. Potatoes such as Maris Piper, Desirée, and Wilja are good for most purposes.

Potato masher: A hand-held masher yields mashed potatoes with a coarse texture. Unlike a food processor, it will not overwork the potatoes, which can result in a gluey texture. Look for a masher with a sturdy handle and a mashing grid with some flat portions to help mash the lumps more efficiently.

Potato ricer: Ideal for preparing fluffy mashed potatoes and other purées, this utensil has a perforated container to hold cooked vegetables and fruits. When the ricer's handles are pressed together, the food is forced through the perforations, and any fibres or peels are left behind in the container.

Puff pastry: One of the glories of French cuisine, puff pastry is made by adding layers of butter to a basic dough through repeated rollings and foldings, producing a rich, flaky pastry used in both savoury and sweet dishes. Frozen puff pastry is a fine substitute for labour-intensive home-made pastry. Look for puff pastry made with butter if you intend to use it in a sweet recipe.

Quince paste: Quince paste or cheese, also known by its Spanish name, *membrillo,* or as *cotignac* in southwestern France, is made by cooking the pulp of this fruit with a high proportion of sugar, then sieving and moulding into a sliceable loaf. Quince paste is popular in Spain served with cheese.

Ramekins: A ramekin is a small, usually round ceramic baking dish with straight sides. It comes in many sizes, the most useful of which is 150 ml (5 fl oz), and is intended to be an individual serving. Ramekins are used when making baked eggs, custards, puddings, mousses, and soufflés.

Rice: Long-grain rice has elongated, slender grains that are much longer than they are wide. When cooked, the grains remain fluffy and separate, making them popular for pilafs and soups. Short-grain rice varieties tend to clump up and stick together when cooked, and are preferred for oriental and Caribbean cooking. Arborio and Carnaroli are Italian rices whose high starch content make them perfect for risotto. Jasmine or Thai fragrant rice is a perfumed rice popular in Thailand, while basmati is an aromatic, nutty rice, used in Indian biryanis and other dishes.

Rice cooker: Also called a rice steamer, this electric appliance takes the guesswork and worry out of cooking rice. The cooker sits on the work surface and is fitted with an insert for steaming rice. Some models have additional inserts for steaming other foods.

Ricotta: Made from the whey left over from making other cheese (usually pecorino), rather than from whole milk, ricotta has a mild taste and a texture similar to curd cheese. Ricotta salata is aged ricotta cheese with a soft but crumbly texture and a salty tang.

Ridged grill pan: Also called a griddle pan or char-grill pan, this is a heavy frying pan usually made of cast iron, although non-stick pans are also available. The ridges on the bottom of the pan raise the food above any fat and also make attractive charred lines on the food, so it looks as if it has been barbecued.

Roasting tin: A roasting tin has low sides in order to allow the oven heat to reach as much of the surface of the food as possible, while preventing any juices from the roasting food to escape. For joints of meat and poultry,

choose a heavy roasting tin so that the base of the food and the pan juices do not burn. Although a tin with a non-stick surface makes cleaning easy, a regular surface allows more browned bits to stick to it during roasting, which means better gravy.

Rocket: The leaves of this dark green plant resemble deeply notched, elongated oak leaves. They have a nutty, tangy, and slightly peppery flavour. Larger leaves have a coarser texture and more pungent flavour.

Rolling pin: Chief among the essential tools for pie and tart makers, rolling pins come in various styles. A heavy, smooth hardwood or marble pin at least 38 cm (15 inches) long is best. Some bakers prefer a rolling pin without handles, either a straight dowel or a dowel with tapered ends, while others prefer pins with handles. If you choose the latter, look for one with handles that move on ball bearings for the smoothest roll.

Roux: A mixture of flour and a fat such as butter or oil, a roux is a common thickening agent in sauces and in gravies. A roux is made by stirring flour into hot oil or butter and stirring the mixture over the heat for a minute or two, or sometimes longer.

Saffron: The stigmas of a type of crocus, saffron is used to add a subtle flavour and appealing yellow colour to many dishes, including rice dishes such as risotto, soups, and stews. For the best flavour, buy saffron in whole "threads", or stigmas, and check the date on the packet to make sure the saffron has not been on the shelf too long.

Salad spinner: Consisting of a lidded container with an inner colander-like basket, a salad spinner makes short work of drying lettuce and other greens, which thus prevents the vinaigrette from becoming too watery.

Santoku knife: A multipurpose knife, the Santoku ("three benefits" in Japanese) is used for fine chopping, dicing, and slicing.

Saucepan: A simple round pan with straight or sloping sides, a long handle, and a tight-

fitting lid. Saucepans range widely in size. The minimum you need is three – a small saucepan that will hold 1.5 litres (2½ pints), a medium saucepan that will hold 2 litres (3½ pints), and a large saucepan that will hold 3 litres (5 pints). The best materials for saucepans are anodised aluminium or aluminised steel.

Sauté pan: A straight-sided pan with a high, angled handle, designed to enable you to flip foods easily without fear of spilling, and usually a lid. Sauté pans are also useful for braised dishes or any recipe that calls for a lot of liquid and cooking on the hob.

Savory: Winter savory is a shrub-like Mediterranean evergreen herb with a strong, spicy flavour. It goes well with dried beans and lentils, meats, poultry, tomatoes, and other vegetables. More delicate than its cousin, summer savory has a scent reminiscent of thyme and a faintly bitter, almost minty flavour that works well with broad beans and peas.

Serrated bread knife: Its long, straight blade at least 20 cm (8 inches) long has a serrated edge that is designed to cut easily through the tough crusts of breads.

Serrated small knife: Looking rather like a miniature bread knife, with a sharply pointed blade 15–20 cm (6–8 inches) long, this is used for peeling and slicing, or to cut through the delicate skins of ripe tomatoes that might otherwise be crushed by an ordinary knife.

Sesame oil: A dark amber-coloured oil pressed from toasted white sesame seeds, toasted sesame oil has a rich, distinctive nutty aroma and taste. Like a good extra virgin olive oil, sesame oil does not heat well. It's best used in small amounts as a flavouring agent for marinades and dressings, or for soups and braised or stir-fried dishes during the final minutes of cooking. Don't confuse toasted sesame oil with the clear-pressed sesame seed oil sold in healthfood shops, which is made from raw white sesame seeds.

Sharpening steel: Before you put a knife away after use, it's a good idea to hone it. The best – and most classic – home tool to use is a sharpening steel, available wherever good-quality knives are sold. Swipe each side of the blade's cutting edge a few times across and along the length of the steel, alternating sides and holding the knife blade at about a 15-degree angle to the long metal rod.

Sieve, fine-mesh: A sieve is used for rinsing, draining, and straining, to sift dry ingredients such as icing sugar, and to purée soft foods such as raspberries, which are pushed through the sieve with the back of a large spoon. This sieving also removes any skin and pips. Wire-mesh sieves come in a variety of sizes, from very small to large, with either fine or coarse mesh. Some sieves have a long handle plus a metal hook that allows them to fit onto a bowl. Sieves are used in blanching to move food quickly from boiling water into an ice bath. When fine-mesh sieves are used to strain delicate foods such as custards, to make the sieve even more efficient, line it with a double thickness of muslin.

Sifter: Shaped like a canister, and activated by a handle that is turned or squeezed, a flour sifter forces flour, icing sugar, or other dry ingredients through a layer (or two or three) of wire mesh. A fine-mesh sieve can be used instead by simply tapping its rim to pass the flour or sugar through.

Skimmer, perforated metal: With a long handle and a large flat strainer or shallow bowl of wire mesh or perforated metal, a skimmer is designed to remove the scum or foam from the top of simmering stocks. It is also perfect for scooping small pieces of food from boiling water or hot oil.

Soufflé dish: Soufflé dishes, made of ceramic to help hold in the heat, have tall, straight sides that are usually greased and then dusted with caster sugar (or, for savoury soufflés, with breadcrumbs or finely grated cheese) to give a crisp exterior to the soufflé.

Spatulas: Cooks regularly use both metal and rubber spatulas. The angled or cranked spatula has a thin, flexible blade, usually of stainless steel, that rises in an angle off of the handle.

These spatulas are ideal for removing delicate items like meringues from baking sheets. Wide, flat, thin metal spatulas, also known as turners or fish slices, are great for fried eggs or fish. Flexible rubber spatulas, available in varying sizes, are excellent for stirring or folding in ingredients and for scraping down the sides of mixing bowls or a food processor. The most versatile ones have blades made of silicone rubber, which won't melt or stick when used in a hot pan. Have a few different sizes on hand for different tasks. Spoonulas, which are curved rubber spatulas, are dual purpose, able to both scrape and spoon.

Spoons: Stirring and spooning up food are simple tasks, but having a selection of different kinds of spoons to choose from makes them even easier. Wooden spoons are indispensable in the kitchen, as they are sturdy, do not scratch bowls or pans or add a metallic taste to foods, and their handles do not get hot. Metal spoons with big bowls are nice for stirring large quantities of thick foods, such as stews, although their primary use is the spooning of food from one container to another. The slotted spoon is not used for stirring, but rather for transferring solid foods such as braised meat out of a liquid.

Springform tin: A deep, round cake tin with removable sides secured by a clamp, this is useful for cheesecakes and other solid cakes. The sides release when the clamp is opened, making the cake easy to remove. A 23 cm (9 inch) diameter is the size most commonly used. Generally, a springform tin should be placed on a baking tray to prevent any cake mixture from leaking out and onto the bottom of the oven.

Steamer insert: Also known as vegetable or folding steamer, this is a collapsible basket made of perforated metal. The fanned sides allow them to fit into a number of different sized pans. The steamer sits on small feet so that food is kept above the boiling water, ensuring that the steam will circulate around.

Stock: A flavourful liquid created by slowly simmering chicken, meat, and fish bones

in water, along with herbs and aromatic or flavouring ingredients such as onions, carrots, and celery. Stock can be made easily at home and frozen for future use (pages 216–17). Fresh stocks in cartons are available, as are bouillon powders. Stock cubes tend to be salty, so when using these be sure to taste before seasoning a dish.

Stockpot: Also known as a soup pot, a stockpot is a high, narrow pot designed for minimal evaporation during long cooking. It is ideal for making stock or cooking large quantities of soup. Stockpots are fitted with two looped handles for easy lifting and with tight-fitting lids. They should be made of heavy-gauge metal with good heft. Anodized aluminium or enamelled steel are good choices because they absorb and transfer heat efficiently, clean up easily, and do not react with the acidity of wine or citrus juice.

Tart/flan tin: Usually round, this tin has fluted vertical sides and may be shallow or deeper. A lift-out base will allow you to remove a tart, flan, or quiche easily: place the baked tart in its tin on a large can and let the sides of the tin drop away. The tart on the tin base can then be placed on a serving plate or the tart can be slid off the base onto the plate. An alternative is a flan ring, which is placed on a baking sheet. The most useful size tart tin is 23 cm (9 inch). Smaller, individual tins are perfect for starter-size tarts and flans.

Thermometer, cooking: The best cooking thermometers (used for deep-fat frying, sugar boiling, and preserving) are fitted with a clip that attaches to the side of a pan. For an accurate reading, submerge the tip of the thermometer in the liquid, but do not let it touch the bottom of the pan.

Thermometer, instant-read: Inserted near the end of cooking, instant-read thermometers are more accurate and make smaller holes in the meat (and release fewer juices) than the dial types of meat thermometers, which are inserted at the beginning of cooking. The reading of the internal temperature will appear within seconds. When testing to check if a roasting joint of meat or bird is cooked, be sure the thermometer is inserted into the thickest part of the meat, not touching a bone. Once you have checked the temperature, do not leave the thermometer in the meat or poultry if it will continue to roast in the oven.

Thermometer, oven: An oven thermometer can determine an oven's accuracy and any variations in temperature inside the oven. Hang the thermometer from the rack in the middle of the oven, then turn on the oven. Check the temperature after 20 minutes have passed. If the temperature is off by just a few degrees, adjust for it when you set the dial to preheat the oven. It is a good idea to leave the thermometer in the oven all the time to track its accuracy. (An oven thermometer is not as successful at checking the temperature in a fan-assisted oven.)

Toaster: When selecting a toaster, consider whether you'd like to be able to toast more than two slices at a time, or if you'd like a wide slot for toasting thick slices of bread, muffins, and bagel halves. Some large toasters also have a wide slot with a removable holder for toasted sandwiches.

Tongs: No cook should be without a pair of tongs for cooking meat and poultry. Tongs allow you to turn and transfer these foods without piercing them and losing juices. An extra long pair of tongs is especially useful when you are barbecuing.

Tube tin: Any cake tin with a central tube or funnel, a feature that helps the centre of a cake to rise and bake evenly, is called a tube tin or mould, but several different styles exist. Angel cake tins have smooth, straight sides and may also have small "feet" (or an extra-tall central tube) extending above the rim, which enable the inverted tin to stand clear of the work surface while the cake is cooling, so no moisture is trapped. Fluted tube tins with flared sides are called kugelhopf tins or moulds (also kugelhupf or gugelhopf). Springform tins sometimes come with extra bases, one of which has a fluted pattern and central tube.

Vanilla extract: This is made by chopping vanilla pods and soaking them in a mixture of alcohol and water, then ageing the solution. Look for "pure" or "natural" vanilla extract, which is the real thing and which has a rich, concentrated vanilla flavour. The best is made with beans from Tahiti (more subtle flavour) or Madagascar (stronger flavour). The cheaper, synthetic vanilla essence or flavouring has a thin, chemical flavour that dissipates quickly. Always let hot foods cool for a few minutes before adding vanilla extract, otherwise the heat will evaporate the alcohol, and along with it some of the vanilla flavour.

Vegetable peeler: Sharp-edged blades and easy-to-hold handles define good vegetable peelers. Swivel-bladed peelers are more manoeuvrable, hugging the curves of vegetables and lessening your work. They will dull after several years of use and usually are replaced, not sharpened.

Vinegar: *Vinaigre*, the French word for vinegar, means "sour wine". After an initial fermentation turns the grape juice into wine, a second bacterial fermentation turns the wine's alcohol into acid, creating wine vinegar. The best vinegars are slowly fermented from good wine; lower-quality vinegars are made from poor wines that have been inoculated with yeasts for quick fermentation. Because of its high acidity, vinegar has a long shelf life and does not need to be refrigerated. Red wine vinegar is the most commonly used, although balsamic vinegar (see page 27) is gaining in popularity. For all-purpose use, look for a good aged red wine vinegar. White wine vinegar made with Champagne grapes is lighter and milder than most white wine vinegars. Sherry vinegar, another wine vinegar, is a mildly acidic vinegar with a trace of sweetness. Vinegar may also be made from other bases, such as cider vinegar and malt vinegar. Do not substitute malt vinegar for wine vinegar. Use malt vinegar when making chutneys and, of course, to sprinkle over fish and chips.

Waffle iron: Consisting of two heated plates with a raised grid pattern that are joined by a hinge, a waffle iron may be electric or used on the hob. A thick batter is poured onto the bottom plate and the other plate is closed over it. The resulting waffle accommodates luscious toppings such as fresh berries and whipped cream. Waffle irons with non-stick surfaces are easy to use and to clean.

Watercress: A member of the mustard family, watercress grows wild in cold, shallow streams. It needs clear, fast-running water to grow successfully, so commercially it is cultivated around freshwater springs. It has a refreshing peppery flavour and brilliant green leaves, which add a bright note to salads. When preparing, leave some of the stalks on as they have most of the pungent flavour.

Whisk: With a head of looped thin metal wires, a whisk is used to rapidly beat or whip ingredients. Also known as whips, whisks are made in various sizes and shapes for various uses. Elongated flat sauce whisks, or roux whisks, are used to mix ingredients thoroughly without adding excess air. Balloon whisks, which are more rounded, are used to incorporate the maximum amount of air when whisking egg whites and whipping cream.

Wok: This ingenious Chinese pan is a multi-purpose cooking vessel, ideal for stir-frying, deep-frying, and steaming. The rounded bottom heats quickly when set over a gas burner and, with the open shape, allows small pieces of food to be rapidly tossed and stirred, while the gradually sloping sides help to keep the food in the pan.

Zester, citrus: A hand-held tool with a row of small, circular holes at the end of its metal blade, specially designed to remove the zest (the outer coloured part of the peel) from citrus fruits efficiently. The zester takes the zest in very fine shreds, without any white pith.

Index

Published by

The Five Mile Press

950 Stud Road, Rowville

Victoria 3178 Australia

Email: publishing@fivemile.com.au

Website: www.fivemile.com.au

Bride & Groom Cookbook
Originally published as Williams-Sonoma Bride & Groom Cookbook

Set in Myriad MM, Perpetua, Marydale
Colour separations by Bright Arts Graphics, Hong Kong
Printed and bound in China by Midas Printing Limited

10 9 8 7 6 5 4 3 2 1

National Library of Australia Cataloguing-in-Publication Data
Pirie, Gayle.
Bride and groom cookbook.
ISBN 978 1 74178 460 2.
1. Cookery for two. I. Clark, John, 1959- II. Title.
641.5612

ACKNOWLEDGEMENTS

Photographer David Matheson
Photo Assistants Antony Nobilo, Tom Hood
Food and Prop Stylist Ben Masters
Assistant Food Stylist Ann Kidd
Copy Editor Sharron Wood
Consulting Editor Sharon Silva
Translator Norma MacMillan
Proofreaders Desne Ahlers, Carrie
Bradley, and Leslie Evans
Indexer Ken DellaPenta
Designer Marianne Mitten
Production Editor Joan Olson

Additional photography:
pages 21, 22 centre, 23 centre, 66, 80, 96, 113,
and 146 by Food Stylist George Dolese and
Associate Food Stylist Elizabet der Nederlanden;
pages 220, 232, and 234 top by Photographer
Jeff Kauck; pages 226 and 227 by Photographers
Jeff Tucker and Kevin Hossler; pages 233 top,
233 bottom, 234 bottom, 235 top, and
235 bottom by Photographer Bill Bettencourt

Ben Masters would like to thank Accoutrement in
Mosman, Essential Ingredient in Paramatta Road,
Murdoch Produce, and Broadway Butchery.